Introduction to the Book of Zohar

VOLUME TWO

THE SPIRITUAL SECRET OF KABBALAH

ORIGINAL TEXTS
OF RAV YEHUDA ASHLAG
Commentary by Rav Michael Laitman PhD

Introduction to the Book of Zohar

VOLUME TWO

LAITMAN
KABBALAH PUBLISHERS

THE SPIRITUAL SECRET OF KABBALAH

ORIGINAL TEXTS
OF RAV YEHUDA ASHLAG
Commentary by Rav Michael Laitman PhD

*We wish to extend our gratitude
to the following people who made
a major contribution
to the creation of this book:*

Executive Editor: Talib Din
Editor: Clive Borkum
Project Coordinator: Lenny Estrin
Translation: David Brushin
Drawings: Roman Ferber, Eugene Nemirovsky, Michael Gonopolsky
Production Manager: Tony Kosinec
Proofreading: Chaim Ratz
Type Setting: Baruch Khovov
Book Design: The George Partnership

Laitman Kabbalah Publishers Website:
www.kabbalah.info

Laitman Kabbalah Publishers Email:
info@kabbalah.info

INTRODUCTION TO THE BOOK OF ZOHAR
VOLUME TWO

All rights reserved.
Published by Laitman Kabbalah Publishers,
1057 Steeles Avenue West, Suite 532, Toronto, ON, M2R 3X1, Canada.

Printed in Canada.

ISBN: 0-9732315-5-6

FIRST EDITION: MARCH 2005

Introduction to the Book of Zohar

VOLUME TWO

CONTENT

Preface to the Book of Zohar 13

Introduction to the Book of Zohar 91

Our Other Books 299

About Bnei Baruch 301

How Contact Bnei Baruch 302

TO THE READER

For many centuries, the wisdom of Kabbalah was inaccessible to anyone who could not read Hebrew. Now, for the first time in the history of the Western World, readers of the English language and serious students of Kabbalah have the opportunity to learn the Wisdom of Kabbalah from the 20th Century's greatest Kabbalist, Baal HaSulam. In this text,* the student will find a systematic, graduated exposition of Kabbalah unlike any treatment found in other available texts. This text comes with a brilliant commentary by Michael Laitman, a scientist and Kabbalist who received the Tradition from that illustrious chain that includes the Ari, Baal HaSulam, and his teacher, Rabash.

"The Wisdom of Kabbalah" is an exhaustive text that the reader will certainly make a steady companion in his exploration of the Upper Worlds for many years to come. Enjoy!

Talib Din, Executive Editor
Bnei Baruch
May 16, 2004

* As Rav Laitman did not translate the Hebrew text word for word, the reader will find that the English translation does not strictly follow the Hebrew text.

FOREWORD

While working on a course of virtual lessons at the World Academy of Kabbalah that Michael Laitman teaches on the Internet, we did our best to preserve the style and spirit of his classes and discussions. This is not a literary text, nor is it a lecture on philosophy. Here you will discover secret, deep layers of information about the Upper World. In this way, through the Kabbalist, the Creator reveals the Thought of Creation and His light.

In one of his Saturday discourses, M. Laitman told us about the attitude of his Teacher, Rabash, to the manuscripts of his great father Baal HaSulam, the commentator on "The Book of Zohar". While publishing the manuscripts, Rabash never allowed himself to make even a single correction of what might seem to be a mistake. M. Laitman acted in a similar way, when he was preparing his Teacher's notes for publication. "What may now seem like a mistake will become clear when we ascend the higher spiritual level", said Rabash to his disciple Michael Laitman. We try to follow the advice of our teachers and make a point of leaving all the "mistakes" and "typos" uncorrected.

This book was not written; to its last line it was orally shared with numerous members of the virtual group, who gather in many places in the world to hear these classes.

While reading this book, you can join the community of beginning Kabbalists, provided you treat it as a very special Kabbalistic text filled with profound meaning. Succumb to your sensations, let the Upper Light lead you, correct, and prepare your soul, your spiritual vessels, for reception of the ultimate delight – merging with the Creator.

The students of
Rav Michael Laitman

PREFACE TO
THE BOOK OF ZOHAR

1. The depth of wisdom and learning contained in the Holy Book of Zohar is concealed behind a thousand locked gates.

Why is it "concealed behind a thousand locked gates"? In actual fact, no one conceals anything; everything exists within the framework of the natural laws of the creation. Unlike in this world, there is no key that can unlock the gates to enter where one may or may not be. The spiritual world is completely open; a person just advances from one spiritual level to another, and leaves one realm to enter the next in accordance with the way he changes his own properties.

In our world an object can be moved from one place to another by way of mechanical displacement, whereas in the spiritual world we need to make an inner motion in order to pass from one part of the world to another. This is what they call a locked gate; as long as the person is confined to one part, the next one remains concealed, "locked" from him.

What can be done to open it? Transform yourself in accordance with the part you wish to enter, and then you will get inside. It is pretty simple. Everything exists within man. By inwardly using his potential abilities, anyone can easily move in spiritual space, from his present state to the state of perfect infinity and merging with the Creator.

All wisdom consists in the method of advancing in spiritual space. Hence it is said that the depth of wisdom is "concealed behind a thousand locked gates". It is not concealed behind any kind of external gate.

All the locks and keys are within us. Carrying out inner actions correctly and opening the locks with our own inner keys is our method. This is the purpose of studying "The Book of Zohar" and the wisdom of Kabbalah as a whole.

> Human language, being poor and meager, can serve us neither as a suitable instrument, nor a sufficient means of expression for uncovering the full meaning of even a single sentence in "The Book of Zohar".

This means that even if we take the smallest phrase from "The Zohar", which seems quite clear to us, the interpretation of it will definitely depend on our level of attainment. By gradually developing our inner potential, by adapting ourselves to various spiritual laws and properties, we will begin to discover great depth in every word, phrase, or sentence of the book, and not the actions and phenomena that we perceive today. Depth of perception depends solely on the researcher's level of attainment.

> My explanations are only the rungs of a ladder.

The structure of the commentary to "The Book of Zohar" resembles a ladder. This does not mean that the first volume of the book is intended for beginners and the last for the most advanced students. Every sentence, every word in the text includes inner levels of attainment of all the described actions and states.

The text is composed in such a way that the reader gradually discovers an increasingly clearer picture. He should only aspire for discovering some inner information concealed in the book. That is all man can understand at this stage, but this initial tune up is quite sufficient for the book to begin affecting us in this way.

> I intended to help the student attain the heights from which he may see and investigate what the Book itself expounds. Therefore, in this preface, I find it necessary to prepare the student interested in "The

Zohar" by providing him with correct definitions, to demonstrate how to study the book and learn from it.

In other words, the goal of studying "The Zohar" is to attain the Upper World, to feel and control it, to begin living not just within the limits of this world, but to enter a greater, eternal and perfect realm.

2. At the outset, one should be aware that every concept discussed in "The Book of Zohar", whether in the language of legends or tales, concerns the Ten Sefirot: i.e., KaHaB (Keter, Hochma, and Bina), HaGaT (Hessed, Gevura, and Tifferet), NHYM (Netzah, Hod, Yesod, Malchut), and their derivatives. Just as the spoken language, consisting of the 22 letters with their various permutations, are entirely adequate for uncovering the essence of any object or learning, so too are the concepts and permutations of the Ten Sefirot sufficient to expose the entire wisdom contained in the spiritual universe.

From the study of the four phases of development of the direct light, we know that these phases (zero, one, two, three, and four) are respectively called "the tip of the letter Yud", the letters "Yud", "Hey", "Vav", and "Hey". They make up the word HaVaYaH, the Creator's ineffable name.

Partzuf Soul		Sefirot	HaVaYaH	Stages
K	K	K	— ˙ —	0
	H	H	— י —	1
	B	B	— ה —	2
	H G T N H Y	ZA	— ו —	3
M	M	M	— ה —	4
	10	5		

What does *HaVaYaH*, the Creator's name, mean? These symbols contain the information about the entire universe. The rest happens to be their various interpretations. If we describe them as *Sefirot*, they will correspond to *Keter*, *Hochma*, *Bina*, *Zeir Anpin* (ZA) and *Malchut*. We then further divide the *Sefira* ZA into six the *Sefirot Hesed*, *Gevura*, *Tifferet*, *Netzah*, *Hod*, and *Yesod*. Thus these Ten *Sefirot* are all that we have. *Keter*, the Creator's attitude to the creation, is followed by the *Sefirot*-derivatives, the last of which is *Malchut*, the creation. Accordingly, the Creator's attitude to the creation descends from *Keter* to *Malchut*, while the creation's attitude to the Creator ascends in the opposite direction, from *Malchut* to *Keter*. All that is included in the Ten *Sefirot* is called the Soul or the *Partzuf*. This is all we deal with.

We know nothing beyond that. We can only perceive what enters inside us, and call it our life.

Baal HaSulam says that the combinations of the *Sefirot* and their various, partially used sub-*Sefirot* are quite sufficient to describe all possible states, actions, and properties of everything that takes place between the Creator and the creation.

In our reality, there are three definitions.

In fact, they are not definitions, but, rather, limitations, which we need to understand properly. When we dispose ourselves to "The Book of Zohar" through these three limitations, we understand what it says, and can penetrate its deeper form.

3. First definition (limitation).

There exist four categories of knowledge called:

- *Matter,*
- *Form in matter,*
- *Abstract form, and*
- *Essence.*

If we move outside from within in our analysis, we find that the essence, abstract form, form, and matter are dressed on one another. This is how we perceive any object in our world.

For instance, here is my cup, which has the form of a vessel (Hebrew: *Kli*). The matter of which it is made is clay. When I speak of it without any reference to its shape or material it is made of, I refer to its abstract form as a *Kli*. In general, what is a glass or a cup? I speak about something abstract, unconnected with a particular, concrete object. Then the essence follows, a category, something that constitutes the notion of a cup, a *Kli* for me.

These are the four degrees of inner attainment of any definition, object, action, or property.

It is the same with regard to the Ten Sefirot. One must be aware that the Book of Zohar does not concern itself at all with such concepts as the Essence of the Sefirot or their Abstract Form. Rather, since the Form is the carrier of Matter, the book discusses either the Form of the Sefirot or the Matter they contain.

If we take essence, abstract form, form in matter and matter (in the order they descend to this world), our attainment starts from matter and rises up. Baal HaSulam says that "The Zohar" only speaks of the first two levels of attainment, matter and form in matter. So this is the first of our limitations pertaining to the study of "The Zohar".

1. Essence

2. Abstract Form

3. Form in Matter

4. Matter

The Zohar speaks only about matter and the form of matter

4. Second definition (limitation).

Everything existing in the Divine reality that is concerned with the creation of Souls and their forms of existence is conditioned by the following three states:

- *The World of Infinity,*
- *The World of Atzilut, and*
- *The Three Worlds called Beria, Yetzira and Assiya.*

The World of Infinity is absolutely divine and refers both to the state before the *Tzimtzum Aleph* and to the state of Final Correction.

The World of *Atzilut* is the World of our correction. While being corrected itself, it represents the basis, the source of our life and betterment.

The Worlds of BYA are the realm in which we exist.

Know that "The Book of Zohar" investigates only the Worlds of BYA (Beria, Yetzira and Assiya) and nothing else. It touches on the Worlds of Infinity and Atzilut only to the degree that the Worlds of BYA receive from them. Otherwise, "The Book of Zohar" does not concern itself with them at all.

The Worlds of Infinity and Atzilut by themselves are of no interest to us. What we do need to know is where we are and how these worlds can help us.

World ∞ 1. Essense

Atzilut   2. Abstract form

       3. Form in matter

BYA = (I)   4. Matter

"The Book of Zohar" always speaks about a practical application of everything that we study. It only deals with what is attained in man's Soul, which exists, acts, rules and facilitates man's correction, but never speaks of anything abstract.

Consequently, our approach to "The Zohar" should be purely practical. We should dispose ourselves so that the light it emanates can clearly indicate what we need to correct.

The essence and abstract form refer to what is above our correction. We will attain it as well, but later on, after the Final Correction; hence "The Book of Zohar" does not speak about it. Neither does it mention the Worlds of Infinity and *Atzilut*, where we ascend after the Final Correction. This is not our current task.

Our mission is to go through 6000 years (levels) of correction; therefore "The Zohar" speaks only about this process. It describes me and, through me, the World of Infinity and *Atzilut*, dealing only with what concerns me in my matter and form. Nothing at all is said of what exists without being somehow connected with me.

5. Third definition (limitation):

In each of the Worlds of BYA, there are three aspects:
- *Ten Sefirot,*
- *The Souls, and*
- *The rest of reality.*

The Ten *Sefirot* constitute the descending pure light in the form of gradually diminishing emanations. Thus, to the extent of our ability to communicate with these Ten *Sefirot*, we perceive the light.

The Souls dressed on these Ten *Sefirot* exist within the reality that surrounds them. This way, one element is inside another. There are Souls of two kinds: Upper and human. At a later stage we will understand the notion of "the Upper Souls."

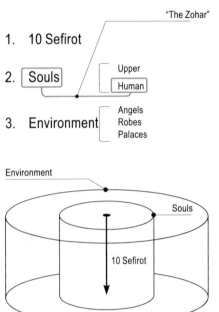

The rest of the surrounding reality is comprised of "angels," "robes," and "palaces."

These are the inferior spiritual forces that surround the human Soul. Their names indicate resemblance to our world: "angels" are similar to animals; "robes" are the forces that are external with regard to man, but very close to him; in similarity to our world, "palaces" are the forces that constitute man's more remote surroundings.

In any case, one should know that, although "The Book of Zohar" meticulously explains every minute detail of every world...

However, one should not deceive oneself thinking that everything is explained about all the worlds. "The Zohar" reveals and expounds only that, which concerns one aspect – the human Souls, and completely ignores everything that pertains to the Ten *Sefirot* or surrounds the Soul (i.e., the Upper Souls, angels, robes, and palaces).

Any other aspect that may be expounded or explained is done so only for the purpose of understanding what it is that Souls receive. "The Book of Zohar" does not utter even a single word about anything that does not relate to Souls.

These three fundamental aspects serve as our point of departure:
- *Not to pass beyond the framework of matter and form in matter;*
- *Not to pass beyond the framework of the worlds BYA;*
- *Not to pass beyond the framework of the human Souls.*

If we remain within the framework of these three limitations, we will understand correctly what "The Book of Zohar" wishes to provide us with. Thus, we will accurately receive its message through the channel that descends from it to us, and establish contact with the book.

We will neither demand something that is absent in it, nor something that we do not need. We will receive from it only what is necessary for our correction. Every single word in it speaks exactly about it. For example, if a person with a philosophical frame of mind tries to understand abstractly what is written in the book, he will definitely fail. Hence, "The Zohar" seems to be "concealed behind a thousand locked gates."

If the person wishes to reveal something about the abstract form and the essence, but has not yet achieved the necessary spiritual level, he will not be able to do that from the level of our world by way of philosophical reasoning. To this end, he will have to reach the proper level in the World of *Atzilut* or the World of Infinity, and begin his research there. In general, "The Book of Zohar" has nothing to do with these issues; it exclusively studies the process of our correction. Once we have corrected ourselves and attained the Upper Reality, we will attain all additional knowledge about the abstract form, the essence, the Worlds of *Atzilut* and Infinity, the Ten *Sefirot*, the Upper Souls, angels, robes, and palaces.

"The Zohar" cannot tell us about all this until, with its help, we correct matter and form in matter, i.e., the worlds *BYA*, in which our Souls exist. Only after the created desire is corrected will it be possible to say how it attains the higher spiritual levels. As long as this desire continues to remain egoistic, it will be unable to grasp anything above its own level.

Naturally, it will not reach the level of the abstract form or the essence in the Worlds of *Atzilut* and Infinity, because it already means to possess the property of bestowal. Neither will it be able to attain what exists beyond the human Souls, especially in the ten divine *Sefirot*, in the pure light that emanates from the Creator.

"The Book of Zohar" is written is such a way that it can adequately and positively influence the person who wishes to receive its energy in the right way, i.e., in order to be corrected. Unless the person has this intention as regards "The Zohar", then he just leafs through its pages being unaware of the great power that the book emanates.

It is so focused that its light affects us only on condition that we aspire for correction and attainment of the Upper World. The method of establishing contact with the Upper Source of correction is called Kabbalah. All that it includes is given only for attuning oneself to the Upper Light.

> 6. *You already know that the Ten Sefirot are called Hochma, Bina, Tifferet, Malchut and their root, Keter. They are ten because Tifferet consists of six Sefirot called Hesed, Gevura, Tifferet, Netzah, Hod, and Yesod. Remember always that when we mention the Ten Sefirot, we mean HuBTuM.*

That is, *Hochma, Bina, Tifferet,* and *Malchut.* As a rule, even the name *Keter* is omitted, because *Keter* represents the Creator. It is attained from the four subsequent *Sefirot: Hochma, Bina, Tifferet,* and *Malchut.*

Keter is not even designated by a letter, but by a hook-like tip of the prospective letter "*Yud*". This is similar to the descending light: the moment it begins to create something, it turns into phase one.

The light being unattainable by itself, we therefore pay no attention to it. We can speak about its property of bestowal, when we feel it inside our *Kli*. In phase two we say that it bestows delight upon us. So in the first case, we speak of what the light is in itself, and in the second – what it gives us.

7. In "The Book of Zohar" these Ten Sefirot, HuBTuM, are called by the names of four colors: white, red, green, and black.
- *White corresponds to the Sefira of Hochma,*
- *Red corresponds to the Sefira of Bina,*
- *Green corresponds to the Sefira of Tifferet, and*
- *Black corresponds to the Sefira of Malchut.*

In our world these *Sefirot* create the four basic colors.

This is similar to an optical instrument that has four lenses with colors corresponding to the ones mentioned above. In spite of the fact that the light is unified, while passing through a lens, it acquires a color and becomes one of the four lights: white, red, green, or black.

	Sefirot		HaVaYaH		Stages	
	K	—	·	—	0	↓
White	H	—	י	—	1	◡
Red	B	—	ה	—	2	◡
Green	ZA	—	ו	—	3	
Black	M	—	ה	—	4	

Thus, the light that is found in each of the Sefirot is the Creator's light, simple and unified. In actual fact, it (i.e., the Ten Sefirot) is completely colorless.

The ten (innermost) *Sefirot* of the direct light have no color, but when they pass through the worlds, they acquire different colors, dress into various shells, and thus manifest before us. That is how we perceive this world.

We can describe the same in a different way. There is only the simple, absolutely amorphous light around us. However, in our inner properties we single out in it such pictures as the still, vegetative, animal, and human levels of nature, the worlds, etc. This is achieved with the help of our inner *Kelim*. There is nothing like that in the light itself.

Thus, the light that is found in each of the Sefirot is the light of the Creator. This light is simple and unified, from the Rosh (head) of the World of Atzilut to the Sof (end) of the World of Assiya. The differentiation of this light into the Sefirot HuBTuM happens in the Kelim (vessels), also called HuBTuM. Each Kli (Sefira) is like a thin partition through which the light of the Creator passes. This is the way each Kli (partition) imparts a different color to the passing light. Thus, the Kli de Hochma of the World of Atzilut passes white light. This is because the Kli de Atzilut (vessel of Atzilut) is similar to the light itself, and the light of the Creator does not suffer any changes while passing through it.

This is the secret of the World of Atzilut about which "The Book of Zohar" says: "He, the Light, and His Essence are One". In accordance with this, the light of the World of Atzilut is defined as white light. However, concerning the Kelim of the Worlds of Beria, Yetzira, and Assiya, the light passing through them changes and darkens. Consider, for example, that the light becomes the red light of the Sefira Bina in the World of Beria, the green light of Tifferet in the

World of Yetzira and the black light of Sefira Malchut in the World of Assiya, respectively.

There are other *Kelim* already; hence, the light assumes color. This happens because the *Kelim* in the Worlds of *Beria, Yetzira,* and *Assiya* (as in *Bina, ZA,* and *Malchut*) are partially or completely uncorrected with regard to the light. If "The Zohar" speaks of colors, we can interpret them as the properties of the *Sefirot.* For instance, when we speak about the color green, it means that the property of ZA is implied, and we are at its level or receive through it.

8. In addition to what was mentioned above, the allegory of the four lights contains an additional important hint. The Upper Lights are called "Sefer" (book).

The wisdom contained in each book is not revealed to the student in the white color it contains...

The light descending to us from the Creator carries its wisdom, reveals itself. This wisdom is not attained from the clear, white color of the light of the Ten *Sefirot,* or from the essence. It is attained from matter and the form in matter, from the Worlds of BYA, through our Souls, i.e., from *Malchut's* reaction to what descends from above. Hence, we cannot grasp the colorless light of *Keter* or the simple light of *Atzilut,* but attain them through the Worlds of *Beria, Yetzira,* and *Assiya,* through black, green, and red colors.

These very colors give us an idea of what Infinity, eternity, and perfection are. Although by themselves these properties are colorless, we are totally unable to attain this achromatism. We can only grasp it after we include in ourselves all the existing colors and the immense variety of their combinations, after they intermix within our completely corrected *Kelim.*

Each of these colors takes its own place in the *Kelim*. Only from absolute attainment, as a result of absorbing the entire palette of colors, do we first come to color white, and then to absolute achromatism.

> *In other words, we do not attain the color white. We reveal everything through the Sefirot Bina, Tifferet and Malchut. These three Sefirot, which are the three Worlds of BYA, are the colors in which the Book of Heaven is written. The letters and their permutations are revealed through the three colors mentioned above. The revelation of Divine light is mediated only through them.*

> *Moreover, we must discern the following. While the white color in a book is its foundation, all the letters are "wedded" to it.*

Since the page of a book is white, the black letters stand out against its background. They seem to be stuck to it, while the white color supports them. By concealing the white color of the page, by violating its absolute whiteness, the letters pass us their wisdom.

As a result, we perceive not the color, but the *Kli*, the letters that we read. In other words, we read not the letters themselves, but the deviations we introduce into the light, i.e., black, green, and red shapes, where, as we see, the light is absent. We perceive the white color even through its absence, because we are created beings and perceive everything out of our deficiencies (*Hesronot*), desires.

All wisdom is in the World of *Atzilut* because *Atzilut* is the World of *Hochma*. *Beria*, *Yetzira*, and *Assiya* correspond to *Bina*, ZA, and *Malchut*. The World of *Adam Kadmon* (AK) is *Keter*.

The Worlds of Infinity and AK are the same with regard to us because all that is above *Tzimtzum Bet* and is not included in *Tzimtzum Aleph* is unattainable for us before the Final Correction. From this it follows that both worlds are included into the notion of the World of Infinity. We only attain the World of *Atzilut* through the Worlds of BYA because it is a form corrected by *Tzimtzum Bet*.

9. *"The Zohar" says that we attain the World of Atzilut as white and its luminescence as letters against a white background in the three Worlds of BYA. These three worlds are the colors, the letters and their permutations, as in a book. This is manifested in two ways: if the three Worlds of BYA receive the light of Atzilut in their place (under the Parsa).*

That is, the World of *Atzilut* is a mount, while all the letters, colors and their permutations are determined by our coordinates in the Worlds of *Beria, Yetzira,* and *Assiya.* As the light of Infinity passes through the World of *Atzilut* and enters the Worlds of *BYA,* we can be in and receive the light in them, or we can rise to *Atzilut* and receive the light there.

We can freely move within the Worlds of *BYA:* from *Assiya* to *Yetzira* to *Beria,* and even to *Atzilut.* Our Souls can move provided they transform their inner properties. The Soul rises to the level to which its inner properties correspond.

If the three Worlds of BYA receive luminescence from the World of Atzilut while in their place, when the light is diminished many times over while passing through the Parsa under the World of Atzilut, then it becomes merely the luminescence of the Kelim de Atzilut.

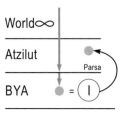

That is, the *Kelim* of the World of *Atzilut* slightly shine in the Worlds of *BYA.* The light that passes from *Atzilut* to the Worlds of *BYA* is called "*Ohr de Tolada*" (light of birth), i.e., microscopic luminescence in comparison with the light in the World of *Atzilut.*

Otherwise, the Worlds of BYA (with the Souls in them) rise above the Parsa to the place of the Sefirot Bina, Tifferet, and Malchut of Atzilut, and "clothe" the World of Atzilut, i.e., receive the light, where it shines.

27

In this case, they certainly receive the light of *Atzilut*. First, we need to enter into the Worlds of *BYA*, reach their highest point in the World of *Beria*, get as close to the *Parsa* as possible, and force all the Worlds of *BYA* to rise to *Atzilut*. Together with the Worlds of *BYA* we will ascend to the World of *Atzilut* and receive the light that is there.

> 10. *All the same, this allegory does not completely reflect the essence, because the book of wisdom of this world consists of a white background and the color of the letters in which there is no spirit (Ruach) of life.*

Actually, the allegory about the World of *Atzilut* is as a white page, and the attainment in the Worlds of *BYA*, being similar to letters, is pretty lifeless. It does not convey the vast breathtaking picture that man attains when he enters into these worlds, feels new spiritual universes, the Upper Souls, angels, palaces. He discovers a wonderful, effervescent life, reveals the forces that govern not our tiny world, but the immense universe.

Naturally, this example fails to express such sensations. Why is it so? Baal HaSulam says: *...because the book of wisdom of this world consists of a white background and the color of the letters in which there is no spirit of life. The revelation of wisdom* (in our sensations) *is not within their essence, but outside of them, i.e., in the intellect of the one studying them.*

As we ascend from the Worlds of *BYA* to the World of *Atzilut* and attain the heavenly wisdom, it exists not on paper, not outside us in some book, but turns into reality that permeates and surrounds us as a result of our inner changes.

> In accordance with this, one must be aware that the color white contained in the book is a subject of study in and of itself, and the function of the other three colors is to manifest it.

This is a very important sentence. I advise you to look at it closely.

Here I would like to remind you that we are one group that exists for the sake of achieving one Goal. There are many of us, and we wish to help each other. Only by joining our forces and desires will we be able to fulfill this great mission.

Baal HaSulam writes that when we combine our efforts and aspirations, then each of us frees himself from an existence inside a closed shell. Thus we create one common *Kli* of such enormity that, while passing through the Worlds of *BYA* to *Atzilut*, we attain not the colors of *Beria*, *Yetzira*, and *Assiya*, but the white background of *Atzilut*. In other words, we reach a state where we transcend the limits of matter and the form in matter, and begin attaining the abstract form – something that is completely inapprehensible in our world.

While reading books in this world only, we attain the wisdom contained in the letters. By reading a book in the spiritual world, we adapt the letters within ourselves and build our inner properties, configure our inner forces, and define the combinations of our *Sefirot*. While passing from letter to letter, from word to word, from phrase to phrase in the books recommended by Kabbalists, we inwardly perform spiritual actions.

By creating these letters within ourselves, we attain through them the white background, i.e., absolute wisdom, the level of *Hochma*. This is the difference between the attainment of spiritual and earthly wisdom. The earthly wisdom is concentrated in our inner *Kelim*, in our knowledge, whereas the spiritual wisdom enables us to attain the light in our sensations, to the extent of similarity of our inner *Kelim* to the properties of light.

11. It should always be borne in mind that there are four categories of knowledge, which were mentioned above, in the first limitation, namely:

- *Matter,*
- *Form in matter,*
- *Abstract form, and*
- *Essence.*

I will explain them first using actual examples from this world. For example, when we say a: "strong person", or "truthful person", or "liar" etc., we discern between the following:

- *The matter the person consists of, i.e., the body.* Matter is the fourth stage, so if we speak about a person, it means the body.
- *The form into which this matter is shaped, i.e., strong, truthful or false* (let us say a liar).
- *The abstract form, i.e., it is possible to comprehend an abstract form of falsehood irrespective of the matter of a person and study these three forms as such, without their being manifested in any matter or body. In other words, it is possible to investigate the qualities of strength, truthfulness or falsehood, to discern their merits or baseness, when they are abstracted from any matter at all*
- *The essence* (of falsehood)

12. *Know that the essence of a person, as such, is quite impossible to perceive without his material embodiment, as discussed in the first*

1. Essence	essence
2. Abstract Form	falsehood
3. Form in Matter	liar
4. Matter	body

limitation. This is because our five senses and our imagination do not offer us anything more than the revelation of the actions of the essence, but not of the essence itself.

That is, we do not perceive the essence, which is purely divine. We can more or less abstractly attain whatever derives from it, but not the essence itself.

... because our five senses and our imagination do not offer us anything more than the revelation of the actions of the essence, but not of the essence itself.

For example:
* *Our vision perceives only the waves from the essence of what we see, according to the light it reflects.*

When I am looking at an object, I do not know what it really is. I only perceive it as waves that it reflects. They return to me and create a certain form in my perception.

* *Our hearing is simply the power of influence of sound waves, transmitted through the air from some essence. This air, reflected under the influence of a sound wave, exerts pressure on the membrane of the eardrum. This is how we are able to hear that something is near us.*

The sound comes from something beyond me. That is, I know nothing about the source of the sound; I have no clue as to what it is by itself. I can only judge it by the way I perceive it.

* *Our sense of smell is the irritation of our nerve receptors reacting to smells, by the air emanating from the essence, and this is how we sense a smell.*

Everything depends on our nerve receptors and on how they transmit to us this or that smell.

• *Our sense of taste is only a derivative from a contact between some essence and our gustatory receptors.*

These four senses offer us nothing but the revelation of actions emanating from some essence. It never reveals the essence itself.

I have said on numerous occasions that the person, his "I", resembles a black box with five points of entry, our five senses. We perceive only that which enters through them from outside. Moreover, as we

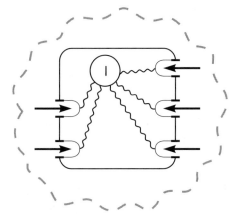

have just noted, we perceive not what enters inside, but what is detected by special membranes positioned at the entry (it is unclear how this external influence reaches us considering our inner limitations), which somehow pass the electrical signals to our brain. That is we selectively perceive the reaction of our senses to some external influence.

Naturally, if one of our senses is damaged or some of our faculties are defective, then our perception of the world will be rather distorted as compared to the normal one. Concerning the ideal picture, we have no way of knowing anything, because we cannot possibly imagine anything existing beyond us. Hence it is utterly impossible to speak about the essence.

We can imagine the abstract form, yet it is unknown whether we can do that correctly.

Even our strongest sense, the sense of touch, which is able to discern between hot and cold, firm and soft, is nothing but the revelation of actions within an essence. However, these too are only the manifestations of the essence. It is possible to cool down something hot or warm up something cold. It is possible to melt something solid into a liquid. It is possible to evaporate a liquid and bring it to a gaseous state so that it would become impossible to sense it with the help of our five senses. Nevertheless, the essence is preserved and we can again transform the gas (a totally imperceptible state of some essence) into a liquid or bring the liquid to a solid state.

It is as clear as a sunny day that our five senses will not reveal to us any essence at all, but only instances of manifestation of the essence's actions.

Baal HaSulam means that without ascending through the Worlds of *BYA* to the Worlds of *Atzilut* and Infinity in our senses, we will not attain the Creator. We will never be able to perceive something that is outside or above us. Neither our five natural senses - touch, smell, sight, hearing, and taste - nor the Ten *Sefirot* in the Worlds of *BYA* will give us anything.

If we wish to attain the Upper categories that are beyond us, we should reach the higher worlds where the white light really exists.

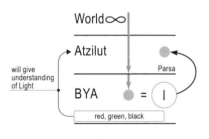

The lights in the Worlds of *Assiya*, *Yetzira*, and *Beria* are black, green and red respectively.

When all of them combined enable us to feel how they stand out against the white background of *Atzilut*, we will attain what this background really is. Here Baal HaSulam stresses that without correcting our inner sensations and rising to the Upper Worlds the person has no opportunity to attain spirituality.

Moreover, we do not even have the ability to perceive our own essence. I feel and know that I occupy a certain volume in this world, that I am solid, hot, that I think, and so on. All of these are the result of manifestations that influence my essence. However, if someone were to ask me "What is the essence from which all these manifestations emanate?" I would not know how to answer. After all, Supervision prevents us from attaining the essence. We only attain the manifestations and mode of action originating from the essence.

That is, we cannot attain ourselves, let alone the Upper Worlds, until we reach the level where the essence manifests.

13. We are fully capable of comprehending Matter, which we discussed in the first limitation, i.e., manifestations of the action of any essence.

Now he explains to what extent different levels of attainment are accessible to us. Our attainment is graduated: *Malchut, Zeir Anpin, Bina,* and *Hochma.* How correctly can we perceive each of these categories?

It is quite possible that such awareness can help me make up for the lack of knowledge. Knowing exactly what I do not know can assist me to get my bearings and avoid errors.

Matter reveals the actions of any essence, and the revelation of matter is quite sufficient for us.

The lowest level of attainment is the attainment of matter. It completely satisfies all our needs and desires. That is, when we attain, feel, and absorb the universe at this level, we have no questions left. That is the way we are created. As we begin to ascend, our needs will develop and grow, including our demands for the sensation of matter. But by and large, we are so created that we feel little necessity for it.

This explains why we do not suffer at all from the lack of any possibility to perceive the essence itself. Moreover, we do not desire it. In the same way, we do not feel the need for a sixth digit on our hand.

I am created so that five digits are absolutely sufficient for me. My brain is designed in such a way that I prefer to work with five fingers, although, if necessary, I may dispense with a smaller number, somehow compensating for the deficiency. However, I am totally unprepared to work with six or seven fingers. Nature has not provided me with any technique for such work. I cannot even imagine what I will do with an additional digit.

> *In other words, the comprehension of matter, i.e., the manifestation of the essence's actions, is sufficient for all our requirements and investigations, both in the attainment of our own essence and in the attainment of any external one.*

So we have no problem with anything that concerns matter. If we only live within its limits, we feel quite satisfied with our attainments.

But imagine a Kabbalist, who attains higher forms, feels the insignificance of lower categories, and think of his overwhelming aspiration to extend the ability of his senses ad infinitum. He wants to acquire thousands of digits-tentacles, longs for the infinite sensation of an endless diversity of colors, until all of it merges in simple, white, absolute, and all-encompassing knowledge.

We, however, seem to have no problem, and happily agree to live with our five little fingers. Larger aspirations appear under the influence of the Upper Light. It generates in us more and more new needs, while at the same time letting us understand that by having more diverse *Kelim* we could perceive a much greater world than what our five senses can pick in a rather warped way.

When something takes place outside us, we perceive it within a very limited, one-sided, and twisted range of sensations. Let us imagine that some outside influence enters into us unobstructed. Were we designed so that everything could penetrate us without any resistance from us, we would be able to perceive absolutely all outside influences. What does it mean that I perceive something which is outside me? The Creator is outside me, so I will clearly feel and perceive Him.

This will become possible if I eliminate all barriers standing in the way of all incoming information. They work as membranes letting information inside only within their limited range. If I move from the color black to green, red, and white, then I will acquire two, or perhaps, twenty new senses, in addition to my natural five. I will then be able to ascend to the World of *Atzilut*, and through these colors perceive the higher light, which will enter me unimpeded.

How is it going to happen? I will not be able to open additional apertures in my "black box". But I need not do that – the sensation of the color white will enter me through my perception of black, green, and red, followed by the Creator's achromatism. This happens because through these undistorted colors that enter into me, I will be able to feel what is inside them, i.e., the Ten *Sefirot* of the direct, pure light.

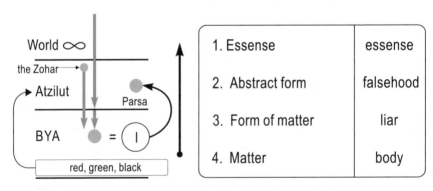

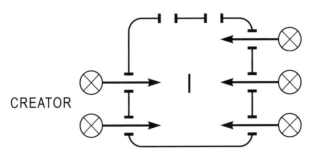

As a result, we see that even without getting out of the Kli itself, the black box, everything depends only on how it is tuned up. "The Book of Zohar" teaches us how to adapt ourselves to the Upper Radiance. The Zohar descends from the highest point of Atzilut, hence its name "radiance".

"The Book of Zohar" explains how we can perceive all spiritual information by changing our inner parameters. In other words, we attain the form in matter, the abstract form, and the essence through the matter of form.

In order to bring us to the World of *Atzilut*, "The Zohar" deals with just two kinds of attainment. After reaching the World of *Atzilut* and the state of *Gmar Tikkun*, we attain the absolute form, and, through it, the essence in the World of Infinity.

We have spoken about four kinds of attainment. When we delve into some material, both within and without us, we attain it as matter, the form that matter takes, the abstract form, and the essence.

We have also said that matter and the form in matter are entirely sufficient to safeguard us against mistakes. Another question is whether we can operate with the abstract form. Being beyond our power and clear sensations, it can be misinterpreted and misleading. It is even more so when it concerns the completely unattainable essence.

Why are we studying it? When we look for contact with the Creator, we should know exactly what we wish to achieve, what we need to hold on to in order to avoid errors on our path. We should be careful not to imagine abstract forms.

As a rule, this happens to people who seem to be very "spiritual". They will tell you about various forces they see, about images and angels, about their previous incarnations and special messages received from above. This is a totally wrong interpretation of the abstract form.

Therefore, "The Zohar" positively forbids delving into abstract forms, and calls upon the person to remain within the limits of matter and its form.

14. We also comprehend the form in matter that is described in the second restriction in an absolutely clear and satisfactory way, for we do so based on the experience of concrete actions that we derive from matter's response. Thus, we acquire all of the sublime knowledge that one can indeed rely on.

That is, matter is what our senses perceive, whereas the form in matter is something we attain as a result of penetrating matter itself.

Baal HaSulam says that we attain the form in matter absolutely, and that all the Upper knowledge we acquire at the higher levels is true and clear to us. If we advance along this path of attainment to ever higher forms of matter without abstracting the form from matter, then we unfailingly move in the right direction, towards the right goal.

If we move anywhere in this world, there always exist an "I" located at some point, some path, and some goal. While seeing the goal before me, I direct myself toward it. That is, "I" represents one of my qualities, whereas I have no idea about the quality of the goal. I do not direct myself with the help of my senses; they are of no help to me at this stage. I do not imagine how I can see this goal, how I can depict it to myself. The goal possesses a certain quality that is very different from "I". This concerns the distinction between just two levels, whereas, overall, there are 125 of them.

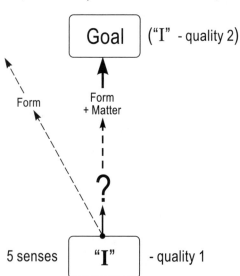

So how can I imagine it, how can I elevate myself, break through this barrier? What should my first step be and toward what goal? I cannot imagine what I want to be. In our world I may, for example, aspire to become a professor; I create this image in myself, see it, and clearly know what it is like. In Kabbalah, however, there is no way to imagine all that.

So if, instead of matter and the form it assumes, I imagine only the abstract form, I will immediately fall into delusion and my subsequent advancement will increasingly deviate from the goal.

Hence "The Zohar" instructs the person seeking spirituality to be extremely careful with forms that are detached from matter, and are unperceived by our sensations.

I cannot say that I feel something spiritual until I acquire a minimal screen. Only having done that will I be able to perceive spiritual objects and properties within it. They will be considered the acquired form of this matter because the form will be determined by the screen. The screen displays for us various properties and their combinations out of matter, which assumes a certain form.

Therefore, he says: "Thus, only from the form of this matter do we acquire all of the sublime knowledge that one can indeed rely on." In the process of studying "The Book of Zohar" we will be repeatedly emphasizing this problem.

15. The third restriction is abstract form. This means that, after the form reveals itself to us in matter, the power of our imagination allows us to detach it completely from matter.

Here Baal HaSulam does not speak about absolute abstractions that we have never seen before (e.g. angels and supernatural forces). He asserts that even when we watch something and then divert our attention from the observed object or phenomenon, we imagine it in an abstract form. We should not abstractly imagine something which previously had a form.

> One can observe abstractly or detached from any kind of matter; for example, virtues and laudable qualities that books on moral subjects speak about. When we touch upon qualities of truth, falsehood, anger, heroism, etc., we have in mind their abstract form, free from any matter whatsoever. We endow such abstract form with virtues or flaws.

Today, in particular, I was asked: "How could such a Kabbalist as Rabbi Shimon be angry?" That is, how can such a highly spiritual person have any unspiritual qualities? Where does this incomprehension emerge from? The reason lies in the separation of form (qualities, properties) from matter. If you combine one with the other, all contradictions will vanish. However, to see that, you will first have to assume those properties.

> Know that serious scientists regard the third restriction with the utmost caution, for it is impossible to rely upon it with 100% assurance. This is because it is easy to err in something that is detached from matter. For example, a non-religious idealist who praises the abstract category of truth can conclude that he would not intentionally utter an untrue word, not even for the sake of saving people's lives, if the entire world should perish.

There are many idealists who abstract some category from real life and from man, and place it above all. In other words, they detach a category from the matter in which it is clothed, i.e., from that for which sake it actually exists. Such a truth-loving person, who is ready to sacrifice the world, does not understand that in fact the abstract category of truth turns into its opposite, falsehood.

The Torah forbids it in its laws, stating that we neither have the right to accept abstract form as absolute knowledge, nor rely on it.

But this is contrary to the opinion of Torah, which says:" Nothing is above saving a Soul", even if you are compelled to lie.

Indeed, had he examined truth and falsehood when they are cast into matter, he would judge these categories according to the right, or wrong they give rise to in matter. Then, having conducted numerous experiments in the world, he would see the multitude of victims and losses that liars and their untruths cause. Moreover, he would perceive the great benefit to those that uphold the truth and those who observe the rule of speaking only the truth. He would then come to an agreement that there is no value higher than truthfulness, and nothing lowlier than falsehood.

If an idealist understood this, he would certainly agree with the opinion of Torah and accept that a falsehood, even if it delivers one human life from death, is immeasurably greater in value and importance than any abstract truth. It is because abstract categories that belong to the third restriction absolutely lack clarity. It is not worth discussing abstract forms that have not yet materialized in this world; this is but a waste of time.

There are certain periods in our life, when we define for ourselves some ideals. Later on, as we face them in real life, we see that they do not exist, and as soon as these ideals dress into matter, they acquire an unexpected, unpredictable, and in most cases, very unappealing form.

Hence, we need to accept this limitation in advance, i.e., on no account should we use any abstract notions nor set any abstract rules pertaining to the spiritual world. We have no idea what the spiritual world is like, the next level has never been clothed in any concrete form before.

We have no right to reason about the upper level from our present viewpoint; otherwise we will delude ourselves and never reach it. Thus we can only speak of matter and the form this matter assumes.

What other positive conclusion follows from this? Kabbalah pushes us toward matter, i.e., toward physical sensation of the spiritual. It warns us against engaging in abstract, imaginary actions, and at the same time it instructs us to feel the spiritual forms which our own matter will assume. That is, the screen's different forms dressed on my desires should create in me various spiritual images, and, without detaching one from the other, I would exist in them. This will be called my spiritual world.

If I now abstract one from the other, I will imagine myself in the spiritual worlds today. Most probably I will feel great while soaring in my imagination, but it will be a pure fantasy. By compelling us to remain connected with matter even though we may be studying a form, Kabbalah urges us to dress our matter (will to receive) into the proper form (will to bestow).

16. Now that we have thoroughly explained these four categories – matter, form in matter, abstract form and essence...

The author stops short of discussing the essence here because there is no point in talking about something imperceptible. We may abstractly reason about the essence without knowing what it is, but in this case all our reasoning turns into empty philosophy.

Now that we have thoroughly explained these four categories with simple examples, it is clear that:

* *In principle, we lack any possibility of grasping the fourth category, which is essence;*
* *Studying the third category can lead to fallacy;*
* *Only the first kind of knowledge – matter, as well as the second kind – form cast in matter, is there for our clear and sufficient attainment of the Upper Providence.*

If our matter, i.e., our initial egoism (will to receive) assumes the form of bestowal (altruism), intention for the sake of the Creator, this means that we enter into the Upper World's existence.

With their help, one can also grasp the reality of the spiritual levels of the Upper Worlds of ABYA. Even the smallest component will fall into these four categories. For instance, every component in the World of Beria has its red colored vessel...

The World of *Beria* is all red (*Bina*). *Hochma* is white, *Bina* is red, ZA or *Yetzira* is green, and *Malchut* or *Assiya* is black.

Baal HaSulam says that if we take any of our attainments, sensations in the World of *Beria*, *we will feel in it the Kelim of the color red, whose light translates to those existing in the World of Beria.* That is, while passing through the *Kelim* of the World of *Beria* (i.e., through my own properties, filters), the colorless light is perceived as red.

What is "red" in the spiritual? In our world the branch of this root corresponds to the color red.

The vessels of the World of Beria that have the color red represent a form that is "dressed" onto an essence. This refers to the first way of attainment. Although it is but a color, meaning a detail and manifestation of the actions of the essence, we shall never be able to grasp the essence itself, only the manifestation of its actions. We call such a manifestation "essence", "matter", a "body", or a "vessel". That is, we attain ungraspable essence as matter.

The light of the Creator "dressing" and passing through the color red represents a form that is "dressed" onto the essence. This is the second way of attainment. That is why it appears as a red light that points to it being "dressed" and emanating through the essence, that is, the body and matter of the red color.

In other words, there exists matter and there are levels that are perceived by this matter, which assumes different forms. If it is in the World of *Beria*, it assumes the color red.

However, if a person still wishes to separate the Upper Light from its essence, from its red color (i.e., to separate the color red that emerges in the World of Beria from the colorless inner light), or if he begins to study the light alone, immaterialized, this belongs to the third way of attainment, i.e., the abstract form, and it will result in fallacies.

I cannot speak of the Creator, but only about my properties that are similar to Him. I cannot say that He is kind. And what exactly is my idea of "kindness"? Is my notion of "kindness" the same as what I ascribe to Him? If I become similar to the Creator by ten per cent in the category of "kindness", then to the same extent I can testify that He is kind. I understand Him because I am similar to Him, equal with Him. Only from within my own corrected *Kelim* can I speak about similarity to the Creator. This means to remain within the limits of matter even in the expression of its form.

However, if we only speak about the abstract category of "kindness", then I will modify it in the same way as I did with the category of "truth". I will be ready to sacrifice all humankind for the sake of preserving this category. That is, it will be utterly abstracted from reality.

Why is this possible? The fact is that we consist of a huge *Kli*, some part of which is corrected. In that part I can perceive the Creator correctly, whereas in the rest of my *Kli* I will imagine Him abstractly, not clothed in my properties. So without doubt, my picture of Him would obviously be wrong because the properties in which I wish to imagine Him are still opposite to His.

Hence, on no account should the person be overly focused on abstract form. Yet it exists in us because there is a great number of uncorrected *Kelim* that are opposed to the Creator's form.

It is characteristic of man to reason about form dressed in matter, i.e., about the will and the intention to bestow that a part of his *Kelim* have acquired, about the Creator's properties that have not yet become his own. All of this exists within our Soul, which is presumably divided into two parts, corrected and uncorrected.

So what does "The Book of Zohar" speak of?

The light enters the corrected part of your Soul, which is similar to the Creator in its properties. You can characterize whatever happens in it as the form equivalent to the Creator because its properties are clothed in matter.

On the other hand, we still have many uncorrected *Kelim*, which are destined to be filled with the Creator's light. However, if we keep reasoning about the light that is still outside our *Kelim*, we will be talking about the Creator's abstract form and will always be in the wrong. This is because it is impossible to reason about the light out of the still uncorrected vessels.

Abstract forms invariably lead to erroneous conclusions; hence "The Zohar" clearly states that only after the person has achieved equivalence of form with the Creator, can he really speak about Him.

We see how Kabbalah directs the person to practical understanding and knowledge, safeguarding him against various mistakes. Unfortunately, we are constantly speaking about something that is not in us; therefore we have no way of determining our position.

Oftentimes, people tell me that they are already in the World of *Beria* or *Atzilut*, or even achieved the *Gmar Tikkun*. I understand them, of course; nothing can be proved or disproved. I can only advise him to read something, somehow show him the right direction, and try to generate more or less adequate sensations.

Each of us can see for himself how often confused thoughts visit us, and we can never be sure where we really are.

When the person enters the spiritual world, he cannot stand firmly on his feet, but continues treading on a very long path of realization, accumulation of knowledge, and studying various forms dressed in matter.

Only when the person reaches the World of *Atzilut* and begins to raise the *Kelim* of the Worlds of BYA (*Gadlut* of the Soul), can one say that he has risen above the common mistake of working with abstract forms.

Accordingly, the most stringent ban prohibits the study of the Upper Worlds, and no true Kabbalist would do it, let alone those studying Zohar. There is no use in mentioning the "essence" of even the smallest part in creation, for we are incapable of comprehending it. Since we fail to comprehend the essence of objects in our corporeal world, we will fail even more when trying to comprehend spiritual manifestations.

I can as little grasp the essence and abstract form of, say, a pencil (I cannot imagine the notion of a pencil detached from its matter). Only the form clothed in matter and mater itself constitute an absolutely reliable source of knowledge.

Thus, we have before us the four aspects from our example in the World of Beria:

• *The vessel of Beria, which represents the red color and is defined as essence or the matter of the World of Beria;*
• *The filling of the vessel of the World of Beria with the Upper Light, which is the form in matter;*

46

- *The Upper Light itself, detached from the matter of Beria;*
- *The essence.*

Thus, we have clarified the first restriction in detail: "The Book of Zohar" only speaks about the first and the second kinds of knowledge. Concerning the third and the fourth kinds, not a single word is mentioned in the entire book.

So when we study Kabbalistic books, we should never imagine anything that is not there. Otherwise we simply fail to take advantage of what is given to us, and bluntly misinterpret the author's words. We should only rely on the first two levels of knowledge, matter and form in matter.

17. The second restriction will be explained in the same way. Know that, as we explained the four kinds of knowledge in one component

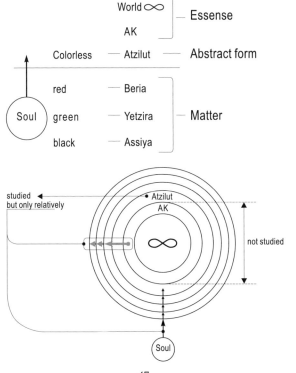

of the World of Beria, so it is in general true with respect to the four Worlds of ABYA, where the colors red, green and black in the three Worlds of BYA are matter and essence. The white of the World of Atzilut is form cast into matter, i.e., into the three worlds called BYA. The World of Infinity, as such, is essence.

Let us take a look at all the spiritual worlds (Fig. 3). The World of Infinity represents the essence (as we know, the World of Infinity includes the World of Adam Kadmon) and is followed by the Worlds of Atzilut, Beria, Yetzira, and Assiya. The World of Atzilut constitutes the abstract form; the World of Beria is matter in which this form dresses. Atzilut is colorless, Beria is red, Yetzira is green, and Assiya is black.

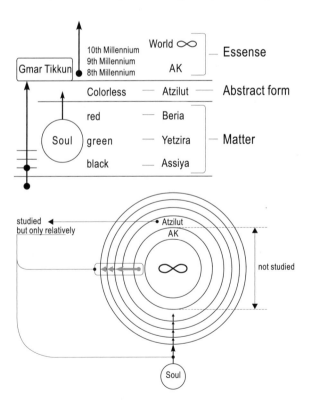

At the beginning of our research of "The Preface to the Book of Zohar" we have said that we do not study the World of *Atzilut*, but only *Beria*, *Yetzira*, and *Assiya*, since that is where the Souls are. We deal with *Atzilut* only as the Worlds of BYA rise to it, or, the other way around, as *Atzilut* shines inside the Worlds of BYA. All the more, we do not touch upon the Worlds of AK and Infinity.

As we have said in the first restriction, the essence is beyond our grasp; it is the fourth kind of knowledge that each being conceals within itself, even in the beings of our world. The white color stands alone and is not "dressed" into the three colors of the three Worlds of BYA; meaning, the light of Hochma is not "dressed in Bina, Tifferet and Malchut, but is an abstract form that we disregard.

If we attain our world from within (and we certainly will), we should always remember that we only study matter and the form cast in matter. However, the deeper, more inner properties concealed in it remain unattainable. We just imagine them because it is impossible to attain them before the Final Correction.

"The Zohar" exclusively speaks about our ascent to the World of *Atzilut* through the Worlds of BYA. (See Fig. 4) The Final Correction (*Gmar Tikkun*) takes place in the World of Atzilut. The Book of Zohar deals neither with the ascent to the World of Infinity after the Gmar Tikkun, nor with the so-called eighth, ninth, and tenth millennia.

Therefore we will always see matter and its form, whereas the abstract form and essence will remain unattainable because our correction on all the levels will only be partial. Even if some *Reshimo* emerges in us and we correct it, this correction is always limited and fragmentary.

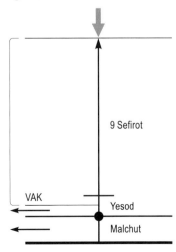

9 Sefirot

VAK

Yesod

Malchut

Let me tell you how it works. Suppose there are Ten *Sefirot*, from *Keter* to *Malchut*. We cut off *Malchut*, and stop receiving the Light that descends to us (it tries to fill *Malchut*); hence, we cannot attain the essence. Besides, when we work not from *Malchut* but from *Yesod*, we attain only the first nine *Sefirot*. We only attain them with the intention for the sake of bestowal; thus, it is said that we partially use *Yesod*. Only the part of the *Kli* called VAK is used, whereas GAR stays inactive, so another attainment (perceived as the abstract form) is severed. We attain GAR *de* VAK in *Gmar Tikkun*, and after that GAR *de* GAR.

There are four kinds of attainment, but at the moment only two of them are available to us. Therefore, we should know what we can and cannot accept as something obvious.

> *There is nothing said about it in the Zohar. It speaks only of the first kind, i.e., the three colors of BYA, considered as matter, and representing the three Sefirot: Bina, Tifferet and Malchut. The Zohar also speaks of the second kind, representing the illumination of the World of Atzilut, "dressed" in the three colors of BYA, i.e., the light or Hochma, "dressed" in Bina, Tifferet and Malchut – the form where it "dresses" itself in matter. The book of Zohar examines only these two kinds.*

> *Accordingly, if each student is not utterly conscientious that when studying Zohar his thoughts and comprehension are always within the limits of these two kinds of knowledge, he will immediately become confused on all issues, for it will strip the words of their true meaning.*

That is, if during our studies we do not clearly realize that we work with concrete forms cast in matter, we will totally miss what "The Zohar" tries to explain. Baal HaSulam warns us not to fall into that trap.

A question arises, whether it is realistic to accomplish what he describes. Can I really control myself; see myself as someone who clearly understands all of these questions during the studies, someone who can precisely distinguish these properties in himself? Is this possible at all?

Although he tells us that it is impossible, correct perception occurs subconsciously through our right attitude to reality, i.e., by focusing on the Creator through the group.

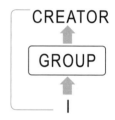

For what is a group? It is an indicator of my altruistic direction. If I correctly direct myself at the Creator through the group (I, the group, and the Creator), then I am really focused on Him. This happens because I cannot relate to the group in my desire to attain Him, unless my intentions become altruistic.

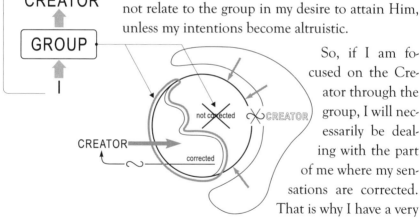

So, if I am focused on the Creator through the group, I will necessarily be dealing with the part of me where my sensations are corrected. That is why I have a very simple indicator of what I should be doing at the moment. It is my study with the group, and my aspiration to the Creator through the group.

Thus, the group helps me to stay within the correct framework and study only what I really need, at the same time avoiding the areas where I can err.

Therefore, we do not really need any special analytical and extrasensory abilities. We are provided with everything necessary for our spiritual growth.

There are a great number of people in our virtual group. All of us study, think of one another, and know that without each other's help we will not be able to attain anything spiritual. Gradually we will achieve unity, interaction, interdependence, and love; we will clearly see and feel how interconnected we are.

This grows out of purely egoistic sentiments. Quite naturally, without any mental effort, I will treat matter and the form in matter correctly, directing myself at the Creator, becoming similar to Him. I will not transcend the limits of my uncorrected, unregulated desires, in which I can imagine abstract categories and assert that their truth is above all, while totally disregarding the likes or dislikes of people. That is, the laws of the Torah testify to my correct, true state, which I can only achieve with the help of the light.

18. What we explained about the four Worlds of ABYA is in general true with regard to each one of the worlds. As it is in relation to every small component of each of them, such as in the Rosh of the World of Atzilut, so it is in the Sof of the World of Assiya. This is because every part (state) on the ladder of worlds Assiya, Yetzira, Beria, and Atzilut consists of Ten Sefirot.

We do not mention *Keter* because it is the source of pure light. Each level, each attainment consists of Ten *Sefirot: Keter, Hochma, Bina, ZA,* and *Malchut.*

The Sefira Hochma exists as the form and Bina, Tifferet and Malchut as the matter in which the form has materialized. It also has the first and the second definition, whose objects "The Zohar" examines, as well as the Sefira Hochma, when it is vacant of Bina, Tifferet, and Malchut, which is the form that is free of matter...

That is, if we speak of how the *Ohr Hochma* manifests in *Bina, Tifferet,* and *Malchut,* in the same manner that form manifests in matter. If we only speak about the worlds *Beria, Yetzira,* and *Assiya* or about the

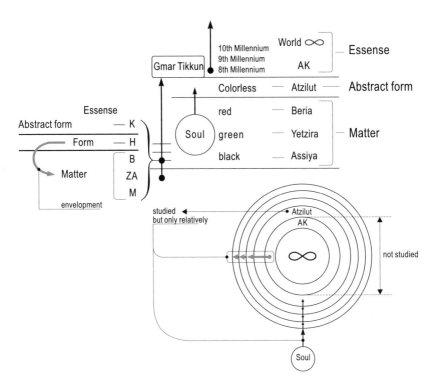

Sefirot Bina, Tifferet, and *Malchut* regardless of where they may be, then we imply matter. It is possible to talk about it as well as about the light that fills the corrected *Kelim* (because it is the form assumed by matter) or about the *Kelim* themselves in their corrected or uncorrected form. However, it is utterly impossible to speak about the light which is outside the *Kelim*, let alone imagine the essence which is even higher. There is no way we can say anything about the Creator Himself, the source of the light.

Baal HaSulam writes: "Do not think that you encounter these problems only when you reach higher levels of attainment. It occurs even at the relatively low level of the World of *Assiya*..." He says that each small level consists of its own *Sefirot Keter, Hochma, Bina, ZA,* and

Malchut, where *Bina*, *ZA*, and *Malchut* constitute matter, *Hochma* is the form, *Keter* is the abstract form, and the essence is above it.

So, we do not speak about what happens in *Keter*, for it is above the level of the Creator's thoughts. This is something we attain after the *Gmar Tikkun*. We never speak of the form that is detached from matter. We either discuss *Beria*, *Yetzira*, and *Assiya* (*Bina*, *ZA*, and *Malchut*), or the form (the light) which dresses this matter. In other words, we either speak of our *Kelim*, our desires (*Bina*, *ZA*, and *Malchut*) or, provided they are already corrected, of the light that enters into them.

We see how practical "The Zohar" is. Baal HaSulam devotes many pages of his works to this issue, and we will be discussing it while reading the book, because the correct direction to the Goal is dependent on it.

> *19. We shall now explain the third restriction. Although "The Zohar" examines each world only from the point of Sefirot, which are the illuminations of the Upper Light in these worlds, and each component on the still, vegetative, animate and speaking levels – the creations of the respective worlds, the main object of the examination is, nonetheless, the speaking level in each of the worlds.*

Baal HaSulam says that "The Zohar" studies everything that is found in the spiritual worlds. But whatever the book may deal with (be that the light inside the *Kli* or the *Kli* itself), it never speaks separately about the still, vegetative, and animate levels of existence simply because it is not its task.

All that is written in "The Book of Zohar" only concerns man, i.e., the human Souls; the way these Souls are served or how they serve other spiritual entities in the creation.

You may object by saying that millions or billions of various creatures, forces, purposes and ideas may exist in the universe. You are quite right, but "The Zohar" does not deal with it. This is because in order to research such things one needs to rise to the level that is above "The Book of Zohar", i.e., reach higher that the book's purpose.

"The Zohar's" purpose is very concrete; it must lead us to the Final Correction. Our path completely changes after that. We will continue researching the universe in our corrected properties. This research is impossible to describe in books because no spoken or written word can express it.

Therefore, "The Zohar" exclusively speaks of things pertaining to our Souls, i.e., what should be corrected at the present moment. The rest is none of its concern.

We find that a man in this world must receive nourishment from all the four levels (the still, vegetative, animate and speaking) of this world, in order to grow. Even in man's food there are four ingredients from all the four degrees that are a consequence of his body having four degrees (still, vegetative, animate and speaking). These are:

- *The will to receive in order to sustain oneself;*
- *The will to receive in excess of the need to sustain oneself, looks for excesses, but is capable of restraining only the beastly desires;*
- *The yearning for pleasures that society provides, such as universal respect and posts in government;*
- *The aspiration to the sciences.*

We usually say that man consists of four levels of desire: for bodily pleasures, wealth, power, fame, and knowledge.

- The will to receive in order to sustain oneself, which corresponds to the still level of desire;

- The will to receive beastly desires is the vegetative level of desire; the will to receive that is given in order to increase and fill one with pleasure in his vessel – flesh (*Basar*) of the body;

• The will for human pleasures, which corresponds to the animate level of desire;

 • The aspiration to the sciences is the speaking level of desire.

20. We therefore find that a reception from the first level, the measure of the need to sustain oneself, and from the second level – the degree of animate desires that exceed the need to sustain oneself, are for him reception and nourishment from the still, vegetative and animate levels, all of which are lower than his.

If I desire food or sexual pleasures (these are the two basic kinds of pleasure that my body demands), then I receive nourishment from objects that are lower than my own level: from the still, vegetative and animate levels. If I seek wealth, I too depend on the still level (money). If I am after power and fame, I already need people like myself, i.e., the human level. If I am thirsty for knowledge, I receive pleasure from a higher level that is novel to me as well as to many people. My aspirations are then considered spiritual in this world.

21. Similarly, you will learn the categories of the Upper spiritual world. Since all the worlds are imprints of one another from upper to lower, and all that is on the still, vegetative, animate and speaking levels in the World of Beria, is impressed upon the still, vegetative, animate and speaking levels of the World of Yetzira. Moreover, all that is on the still, vegetative, animate and speaking in the World of Yetzira is impressed upon the degrees still, vegetative, animate and speaking levels of the World of Assiya. Again, the still, vegetative, animate and speaking levels in the World of Assiya are impressed upon the still, vegetative, animate and speaking levels of this world.

All of these levels in each world: the still, vegetative, animate and human copy one another, each world being on its own different level of organized matter.

- *The still degree in the spiritual world is called "palaces"*
- *The vegetative level is called "robes"*
- *The animate is called "angels"*
- *The speaking level consists of the Souls of people in their respective world*
- *The Ten Sefirot in each world – is Divinity (the Upper Light dressed in these four levels).*

The Souls of people are the center of each world and receive fulfillment from the entire spiritual reality of the corresponding world. Likewise, a person in the corporeal world receives fulfillment from all the corporeal reality of our world.

In the same way man in our world represents the "crown" of nature, and rules over all the other levels (everything else only exists for his sake), the human Soul in the spiritual world is the central point of the creation and governs all levels of matter in the Upper realm.

- *In Behina Aleph, which is the will to receive in order to sustain one's existence, he receives illumination from palaces and robes, which are there;*

- *In Behina Bet, which is the excess of the animate desires that increase his body, he receives spiritual light from angels who are there in quantities above what is needed to sustain his existence, in order to develop the spiritual vessels in which his Soul is vested;*

- *The reason is that he receives from Behina Aleph and Bet, which are lower in relation to him. These are palaces, robes and angels, and their level is lower than that of human Souls;*

- *In Behina Gimel, representing the human degree of the will to receive that develops the spirit (Ruach) of man – in this world he receives from equals. Thus, he receives from equals there also; meaning all of the Souls that find themselves in that world. With their help he magnifies the light of Ruach filling his Soul;*

• In Behina Dalet of the will to receive, that is aspiration for sciences (the attainment of Kabbalah in the spiritual world is meant), he receives from Sefirot of the respective world, receiving from them HaBaD of his Soul.

Man's Soul has to develop and perfect itself in each of the worlds using everything that is in that world. This is the third restriction that one needs to be aware of; that the entire Book of Zohar speaks about every component of the Upper Worlds that we study, whether it be Sefirot, Souls, angels, robes or palaces. And although we study them as they are, the student must always bear in mind that they are mentioned only in relation to man's Soul, which receives and is filled by them. It means that they all serve the needs of that Soul. If you follow that line in your studies, you will comprehend everything and be successful in your path.

Baal HaSulam says that by strictly observing all of these limitations one will succeed on his path. That is why he provides such a detailed explanation.

We will keep returning to the limitations pertaining to the four kinds of knowledge: matter, form in matter, abstract form, and essence. We will see them in Souls, angels, robes, palaces, and worlds. Whatever we may feel, we should always separate real attainments from imaginary ones that we can neither test, nor analyze.

We have spoken of the things which we are still unable to feel. It would have been wonderful if I could, with some object in the spiritual world, show you what its matter, form in matter, abstract form, and essence are. Hopefully, we will soon reach that level. Basically, this is what we aspire to achieve.

But even now, as we speak about it, we already subconsciously prepare ourselves. The most important thing is our unity and common desire. Together we aspire to achieve one goal, attract upon ourselves the correcting light of enormous power. Whatever we learn and understand, this light propels us forward.

I strongly advise you to review this material and write a short summary of what is written here. Baal HaSulam's language is a little archaic, and the text is rather confusing, the translation loses some of the Hebrew original's poignancy and vividness. However, I recommend you to go through these four kinds of knowledge, because we will periodically speak about them. Although they look rather "dry" and abstract now, they will gradually become our main instruments of attainment, of delving into new, unknown matter.

Basically, "The Preface to the Book of Zohar" speaks about the limitations we need to observe so as to correctly perceive the information provided by the book.

There is always a problem of communication and mutual understanding between the upper and lower spiritual entities. We see it in our world too: between adults and between children as well as between adults and children. When the matter concerns two high levels, there should always be an intermediary between them. For instance, in order to raise a baby, a mother's body has a special system for producing milk. The baby sucks milk, which is then transformed into blood. Blood is further transformed into its body matter, and so on.

So, in order for the lower level to receive from the upper one, there must be certain ways of passage and modification between them. Both the upper and lower levels should have systems of adjustment, adaptability and communication. Hence, when we come to study Kabbalah, we wish to receive power from above that will elevate and change us in such a way that we may begin to feel the Upper World, acquire an additional sense of perception, comprehension and adaptation to the true universe.

Therefore, we need to adapt ourselves to the Upper World in order to take from it what it has to give us. Unless we succeed, we will be lost in our own illusions and superstitions, failing to establish contact with the upper level.

To direct us at this contact precisely, to make it not only correct, but also ultimate in its magnitude, Baal HaSulam provided us with this Preface. It is similar to a healthy baby that receives nourishment from its mother and can completely and properly digest it.

The text instructs us how to restrict ourselves (create a "tube" through which everything will descend to me from the upper level), how to receive correctly and most efficiently rise to the higher level.

Matter is our will to receive pleasure, the only thing created by the Creator. Its form is a way of receiving pleasure: "for one's sake" or "for the sake of the Creator".

We should stay within these two categories and avoid abstract forms of reasoning about egoism and altruism without any connection with matter, or speculate about the Creator, the essence. However, this is insufficient, and from Paragraph 22 onwards, we will enter deeper into these limitations, tuning ourselves up to the wave that "The Zohar" transmits to us.

We will now discuss two limitations, or, rather, a correct combination, contact, communication between the upper level that sends me the light and me.

22. After all that has been said, we are left with describing, with the help of the Ten Sefirot, all the material images that one encounters in the Book of Zohar. Such images are upper and lower, rise and fall, diminishing and expanding, small condition and large one, separation and unification, numbers and so on – in a word, everything that the lower ones cause in the Ten Sefirot with their good and bad actions (described with earthly words in "The Zohar").

How can one pass from the words of this world to expressing the same through Ten *Sefirot*? There are no words in the spiritual world, only Sentiments. These Sentiments should be transformed, vested into some images, which we can pass to one another. We can write it down or express it in some other way. We do not need a language within ourselves; it becomes necessary only for passing information.

"The Book of Zohar" explains how to pass from such word pairs as higher-lower, expansion-contraction, falls-rises to their correct interpretation and description with the help of Ten *Sefirot*. The Ten *Sefirot* comprise the physical-mathematical language of the spiritual world.

At first sight, it seems peculiar: how is it possible that the Upper Worlds are so inspired that changes in them can be described as caused by the actions of the lower ones?

That is, if I change something within me, I change the entire universe. The worlds with all the forces and spiritual entities that are in them descend and move. Can I influence the Upper Worlds from this world?

Even if you find it necessary to declare that nothing in the Upper Light is of the sort that "dresses" itself and shines in the Ten Sefirot, that it is only in the vessels of Sefirot, which are not divine, they are nevertheless created only with the creation of Souls. This is in order to conceal or reveal the degree of attainment, to the measure and with the swiftness that are required for the Souls to reach the desired Final Correction. It is as in the example mentioned above, with an optical device that consists of the four pieces of colored glass – white, red, green and black.

What is Baal HaSulam trying to convey in this long sentence? He says the following: even though nothing happens in the Creator's light, and everything only takes place in our Souls, we express the light's influence with theses words. This influence is constant, but it generates bigger and bigger changes in us.

For example, I put a glass of water into the refrigerator. The temperature of water in the glass is 20° Centigrade, while the temperature inside the refrigerator is only 10°. This means that the refrigerator's constant influence cools the water down to its own temperature. That is, the refrigerator's influence is invariable, whereas the temperature of the water in the glass is constantly changing. The same happens with us: the Upper Light exerts on us its constant pressure, but its pressure gradually penetrates our matter, our desire to receive pleasure, and changes it in accordance with its own parameters.

Kabbalah describes all transformations that take place within us under the light's constant influence. It is said: "I, the Creator, do not change My Name". His attitude to us is absolutely good, and He is constantly pressing us in order to elevate us to the level of the Absolute Good. However, since His influence penetrates us ever more deeply, we begin to adapt ourselves to it, and begin sensing our states as imperfect and remote from Him. We begin to aspire for a more elevated state, wish the light to purify us and make us similar to it.

It turns out that by His constant kind pressure, the Creator invokes in us increasingly worse sensations pertaining to our own condition, and increasingly good Sentiments pertaining to Him. Kabbalah describes the constant changes that we go through.

Basically, Kabbalah does not do that so as to tell us what else we are going to experience under the light's constant influence, from our present state up to a complete equivalence of form with the light called the *Gmar Tikkun*. It, rather, encourages us to make our own earnest effort and by our personal and independent participation shorten this process.

At that, we go through the same transformations, but they become desired; hence, we, in anticipation of the bright future states, perceive our spiritual ascent, our life as positive and pleasant. In other words, an active participation in the process of correction elevates man to a fairly good level the moment he makes his decision.

> Even if you find it necessary to declare that nothing in the Upper Light is of the sort that "dresses" itself and shines in the Ten Sefirot, that it is only in the vessels of the Sefirot, which are not divine, they are nevertheless created only with the creation of Souls. This is in order to conceal or reveal the degree of attainment.

The light is constantly playing with us. However, in actual fact, it is not a game. Since we consist of *Reshimo de Yitlabshut* and *Reshimo de Aviut* (information about the light and the *Kli*), consequently, different informational *Kelim* are alternately activated in us. Thus, we evaluate our state either from the point of the light, or from the point of the *Kli*. Therefore, it seems to us that we go through different states. The light, however, is an act according *to the measure and with the swiftness that are required for the Souls to reach the desired correction.*

> It is similar to the case where the white color in a book and the material that forms its letters are all possible in the three Worlds of BYA, where there are vessels of the Sefirot which have been created, but not the divinity. However, it would be utterly groundless to opine that they exist in the World of Atzilut where the vessels of the Ten Sefirot as well represent the utter divinity, merged with the Upper Light that fills them.

Baal HaSulam wishes to say the following: in all there are three components: the Creator, the light that is emanated from Him, and the *Kli* that changes under the light's influence in order to reach equivalence of form with the Creator. Both the Creator and His light are invariable, whereas all changes take place in us to make us similar to Him.

All of this exists in absolute unity.

23. In order to understand the above, we must recall what was said in paragraph 17, which stated:

• *The essence that creates reality is a mystery substance, which cannot be comprehended by us, in the essences of the material world. This refers to the Worlds of Infinity and Adam Kadmon, which we call the unattainable essence.*

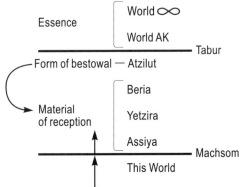

• *The World of Atzilut is the form.*

• *Three Worlds of BYA are the matter.*

• *The luminescence of Atzilut in BYA is the form dressed onto matter.*

Now let us take a look at the drawing in order to understand where we are in our research of "The Book of Zohar." There exist the Worlds of Infinity, *Adam Kadmon*, *Atzilut*, *Beria*, *Yetzira*, and *Assiya*. The Worlds of Infinity and *Adam Kadmon* represent the essence; the World of *Atzilut* is the form, while the Worlds of *Beria*, *Yetzira*, and *Assiya* constitute matter. Below them are *Machsom*, or *Sium*, and this world.

We spend our time in this world only during a preparation period before we enter the Upper World. Kabbalah tells us about a stage that begins after we cross the *Machsom* and commence our ascent. From that moment, matter (our desire) gradually emerges in us, and takes the form of the World of *Atzilut*. That is to say, the World of *Atzilut* dresses into matter and gives it its form of bestowal. Matter is reception, desire to receive. This desire begins to acquire the form of bestowal.

Now let us try to understand how we attain Infinity. What is "Infinity" for us? Is it simply a lack of comprehension? In such a case it may not be called this name. If we use a certain word to denote something, it means that we first attain, grasp, weigh and graduate it within us, and only then do we give this sensation or state a name. That is to say, if I call

64

something Infinity, it means that I have experienced that state, and after measuring it in accordance with all accepted standards and rules, give it a name. Thus, Infinity is one of precise physical categories, definitions, measures.

Baal HaSulam asks: *How can you name something that is not compre-hended?*

And gives this answer: *The name of the World of Infinity does not ex-press the essence of the One Who Creates Reality per se, but rather points out that all the worlds and Souls are included in Him. This is reflected in the intent of the creation about which it is said "the completion of the action is in its initial design" –connection of all Creation with Him until complete correction. This is what is called the World of Infinity.*

Inasmuch as there is a state in which both the first and the last thoughts merge into one, this merging is called Infinity. We cannot at-tain it our present state because we have not yet reached the final state. Thus, Infinity means confluence of the two extreme points of the cre-ation. The same is true with our world: when we cannot coordinate cause and effect, everything seems to consist of contrasting, unrelated details.

This happens because the notion of Infinity seems truly infinite to us. However, as we begin correcting our inner properties and rise to the light's level, these notions merge within us, and all contradictions disap-pear. Good and evil, light and darkness dissolve in one all-embracing notion, and the definition of Infinity vanishes. We enter into it, and it becomes real, clear and attainable.

We also call the World of Infinity the "first state of Souls" when all Souls exist in the Creator, filled with all possible delights, the full volume of which will be received at the state of Final Correction.

24. Let me give an example from our world. Let us say a person wants to build a nice house. His first thought pictures a house with all the rooms and amenities just as it will be when its construction is finished. After that, he lays out the plan of construction in all of its details to explain it to the builders, one detail at a time: wood, bricks, metal frames, etc. Only after that does he begin building the house for real and continues building it until it is done, just as he planned it initially.

You should know that in the World of Infinity, which is the mystery of initial design, all of the Creation is prepared in its complete perfection. However, this allegory does not entirely convey the meaning, because the future and the past are one for the Creator, and the initial design is being implemented in Him. He does not need any instruments for action, as we do. Therefore, the real reality is in Him.

We perceive our remoteness from the Creator as Infinity. If we try to combine within us opposite notions, so that all of them will merge into a single whole, we will enter the World of Infinity, which thus ceases to be infinite, and becomes real, where the present, past, and future merge into one.

We should do our best to pass from our usual notions of "eternity", "infinity" to more concrete, correct, spiritual definitions. All the spiritual notions exist within us, but we only understand them when they are opposed to each other: good and evil, black and white, limited and unlimited, reception and bestowal, etc. If we make a point of superposing these notions in our inner properties, Infinity will gradually become our reality.

This is exactly what happens in the Creator; hence in Him a thought and an action are the same. In the course of our advancement, we will be trying to unite all the notions with one source. We will enter a constant and absolute state when time becomes irrelevant. Little by little, we need to get used to this state. In the article "Habit Becomes a Second Nature" from his book entitled "Shamati" ("I Heard") Baal HaSulam writes that all the concealed, implicit qualities and states are within us because we exist in our present state only in our perception. From the Creator's perspective, we are in a state of perfection and infinity, in the only state that was ever created by Him. Our task is to correct our sensations, feel our true condition.

Baal HaSulam says that we can achieve this state with the help of ongoing exercise, by developing a habit, which will turn into our second nature. Any action in our world gets into the field of our vision or stays beyond it only depending on whether we can attune ourselves to that action. While learning and acquiring proper habits, we begin to perceive all kinds of events that were passing unnoticed before. It is the same with the spiritual: first, we gradually acquire special senses, and then we can perceive spiritual reality.

"The Book of Zohar" says that the category of Infinity is based on contrast, that spirituality is where the past, present, and future merge. "The Zohar" encourages us to develop rudiments of these sensations.

Baal HaSulam continues with the example of a house: *the World of Atzilut is like a thoughtful and detailed plan that will be realized.*

The purpose is to build a house (i.e., the Worlds of Infinity and Adam Kadmon). The World of Atzilut is a form, which can be clearly imagined. This is a detailed plan of the house with drawings and specifications – all that exists on paper, but has not yet materialized.

You should know that both the initial design, which is the World of Infinity, and deliberative detailed plan, which in its own time will be realized in reality, do not have anything to do with creatures, because everything is still in the design stage where nothing yet has been implemented into practice. That is to say, the worlds of, Infinity, Adam Kadmon, and Atzilut are completely detached from the Souls, from you and me.

A person does similarly: although he has thought out all the details (bricks, metal pieces, wood) that he will need during construction, he does not yet have anything save his own mental image of the house.

The main difference is that the mental plan of a person is not reality, while the Creator's design is the reality itself and is incomparably greater than the reality of creatures.

Therefore, the third state of the creation is absolutely real. In comparison with it (the Worlds of *Atzilut*, *Adam Kadmon* and *Infinity*), our state is spiritually illusory; it is perceived only within us. This resembles a sick person lying unconscious in his bed. Although he is in this world, he cannot feel it. Or, imagine a person in a dark room, unaware of the enormous world around him.

Thus, we have explained the mystery of the World of Infinity and the World of Atzilut; everything that they convey relates only to the creation of creatures as they all exist in the design, but their essence has not yet been revealed. Just as in our example with a house, there is nothing yet in humanity's construction plan: no bricks, no wood, no metal pieces.

25. The three Worlds of BYA, along with this world, are the embodiments of a planned action, just as construction material is needed before construction is complete. Correspondingly, the Upper Light shines in the Worlds of BYA to the extent that Souls must receive it in order to reach their completion. The Upper Light "dresses" itself into ten Kelim Keter, Hochma, Bina, Hesed, Gevura, Tifferet, Netzah, Hod, Yesod, and Malchut, which are the real Kelim relative to the Creator. That is, they are not related to the Creator, but, rather, newly created for the Souls' needs.

The infinite light dresses into the Ten *Sefirot* of the World of *Atzilut*; through them, it enters into our Souls, and transforms them accordingly.

26. From the example above, one should understand how the three components in the house design are related to one another by causes and consequences, where the root of everything is in the initial design.

There will be no element in the plan that is not aimed at the comple-
tion of the action taken in accordance with the initial plan; nothing
will be put into practice during construction that was not already
included in the initial plan.

Both in the Worlds of *BYA* and in our world, everything happens
only in accordance with the initial plan, which is instantly realized in the
World of Infinity. In actual fact, we cannot influence anything around
us. We gradually come to that conclusion in the course of our life... The
only area where we can apply our effort is in accelerating our entry into
the spiritual world, and in merging with the Creator. This issue is left to
us; it depends on the changes that our *Kelim* go through from our present
state up to complete equivalence of form with the World of Infinity.

However, all of our states are as fixed and predetermined as every
stage in a construction plan: first, digging a pit, building a foundation,
erecting buttresses, etc. Hence, we cannot really change anything in this
world save our own aspiration to the Purpose of creation. If we do that
of our own free will, we feel comfortable, because the difference between
our aspirations and the Creator's state disappears, and in the course of
our convergence we attain the World of Infinity. We and the Creator are
the two main opposites that include all the other contrasting pairs: good
and evil, up and down, black and white, and many other parameters and
categories. All of them begin to converge, and by merging into a single
point, they usher us into a state called the World of Infinity.

You should understand that there is not even a slightest new element
that was not originated in the World of Infinity. That is, the Souls
in their initial state are in their perfect state of Complete Correction,
which is consistent with saying "completion of action is in the initial
plan."

Everything that will be revealed in the Final Correction exists there
and initially emanates from the World of Infinity into the World of

Atzilut. This is the same as the mental plan in the example above, where the initial design is realized as the house is being built in reality. This happens with us, the Souls in the Worlds of BYA.

Therefore, there is not the smallest component in this world that did not emanate from the World of Infinity, and this defines the condition of all Souls in the initial state. The World of Atzilut emanates from the World of Infinity, which is the personal relationship toward every new component existing in our world. From the World of Atzilut, every new emanation into the three Worlds of BYA unfolds into action, into the Worlds of Yetzira, Assiya and the lowest level in our world, and is revealed as the Creator's attitude toward creation.

Let us understand that there is nothing new existing in this world that did not emanate from the common root in the Creator's World of Infinity, his personal root in the World of Atzilut, that came down into the Worlds of BYA and became the creation by unfolding into our world.

That is to say, if we observe a creature or an action in this world, we should take it as the Creator's act descending from the World of Infinity. In accordance with it, we need to check very well whether we should intervene in the process, or just change our attitude to it. We see that all of man's attempts to change the world lead to deterioration in ecology, to bigger disappointments and suffering. The reason for that lies in our conviction that everything does not descend from the World of Infinity, but depends on our actions.

If the person stops interfering in the surrounding world and only concentrates on his inner work (i.e., on his attitude to the world), he can transform it beyond recognition and elevate his own perception of the world to the state of Infinity and perfection.

By giving up his attempts to change this world mechanically outside himself, but, rather, trying to correct his attitude, his inner sensations, man truly acts. This is the most efficient means and the greatest power that is given to us in the entire universe. Whatever inner attitude we may have towards the world, our senses cannot perceive the influence of this attitude on the universe. I believe that science will clearly demonstrate it to us in the near future.

Be that as it may, "The Zohar" teaches us that everything descends from the World of Infinity and all that takes place in our world is a consequence of what happens there. By changing our attitude to it, by aspiring to it, by seeing everything as if it is already there, we can reach it.

27. *At the same time, we need to understand that all the changes that take place in the World of Atzilut have nothing to do with the Creator himself. We are speaking only about Souls, to the extent of their receiving from the World of Atzilut through the three Worlds of BYA. This world corresponds to the World of Infinity just as the mental plan correlates to the initial design. However, these two worlds (the World of Infinity and World of Atzilut) do not contain any Souls yet. As it is in the mental plan of a person, there is no real wood, nor iron pieces, nor bricks.*

Souls start opening up in the World of Beria. That is why the kelim of the Ten Sefirot, which measure the volume and pace of Souls, are undoubtedly not divine. Rather, they are newly created, because the Upper Light does not contain any changes or quantitative characteristics. That is also why we correlate the kelim of the Ten Sefirot of three Worlds of BYA with the colors red, green and black.

The Worlds of *Beria, Yetzira,* and *Assiya* are the consequences of the *Sefirot Bina, Zeir Anpin,* and *Malchut.* The colors red, green, and black correspond with them, being the results of the Worlds of *Beria, Yetzira,* and *Assiya.*

Moreover, it is impossible even to think that they are divine, because the Upper Light does not undergo any changes.

These are our inner uncorrected or partially corrected properties against the white background of *Atzilut*. Therefore, before man enters the World of *Atzilut* and reaches the property of *Bina* (complete bestowal), nothing of what he attains is considered quite true. Man is already in the spiritual world, but has not yet reached his true, ultimate state.

> *However, the light that is "dressed" in the ten Kelim in Worlds of BYA is a divine, simple unity without any disturbance. Even the light filling the lowest Kli in the World of Assiya is simple divinity without slightest change, because light has only one nature. Any change is made by the Kelim, the Sefirot that are not divine (i.e., do not refer to the Creator) and consequently have the three aforementioned colors (red, green, and black). These three colors form the basis for numerous combinations.*

We (the Souls) receive the light from the Worlds of *Beria*, *Yetzira*, and *Assiya* through three filters: red, green, and black. The color white of *Atzilut* passes through these three filters and descends to us already tinted. We perceive these colors and their numerous combinations as a complete palette of our sensations. The Hebrew letters originate in the same three *Sefirot*: *Bina*, *Zeir Anpin*, and *Malchut*. The first nine letters from *Aleph* to *Tet* correspond with *Bina*, or the World of *Beria*. The second group of letters, from *Yud* to *Tzadi*, corresponds with *Zeir Anpin*, or the World of *Yetzira*. The last four letters, from *Kuf* to *Tav* originate in *Malchut*, or the World of *Assiya*. In all, the Kabbalistic alphabet comprises twenty-two letters.

> *28. It is obvious that the Kelim of the Ten Sefirot of the Worlds of BYA receive all their parts and details from the World of Atzilut. They exist there as the mental design of all the parts which will be realized in a corresponding order when the Worlds of BYA are built. Every slightest detail or action had been completely formed in the World of Atzilut before it descended to the Worlds of BYA.*

Baal HaSulam encourages us to stop thinking that our actions can change anything. If we can adopt this truth, our attitude to life and to the world will change. We will stop wasting our energy on something we cannot change, but instead, will start looking for a point with the help of which we can transform the world.

> According to this, we discern that the Kelim of the Ten Sefirot HuB-TuM of the Worlds of BYA receive from the corresponding Kelim HuBTuM of the World of Atzilut; that is, from the mental design. Therefore, any single part, i.e., in the Worlds of BYA, receives from the corresponding Sefirot: Keter, Hochma, Bina, Zeir Anpin, and Malchut of the World of Atzilut.

> So, if we discover within ourselves the slightest spiritual detail consisting of Ten Sefirot, we can reach through it the Ten Sefirot of Atzilut because they are directly connected between them. We call the color of the Kelim de Atzilut white, which is not even a color—it is colorless. However, it is the source of all colors.

All the roots of the Ten Sefirot emanate from it, which give us the entire gamut of sensations.

> Similar to the white color of the pages of a book of wisdom (notwithstanding the fact that nothing can be comprehended through the white color), it is the carrier of everything that is in a book of wisdom. That is why it shines around every letter and inside every letter, giving them their shape and determining a special position of every combination.

We cannot see the wisdom of the white color of Atzilut; it manifests through its luminescence in the Worlds of Beria, Yetzira, and Assiya.

> Similarly, we can say that the material of the letters (red, green, and black) is absolutely unattainable. This is because the material is lifeless. We receive all our attainments and knowledge through the

material of the book, which is white. The luminescence around and inside letters gives them their shape, which reveals the wisdom of a book to us.

That is to say, on the one hand, we read the letters; while on the other hand, we read the white color around each letter. Only by superposing the two notions of Infinity, by elevating our sensations, our letters, to the level of the World of Infinity, where they merge into a single whole, and the attainment of the true wisdom takes place.

This is the essence of the Ten Sefirot de Atzilut. They are similar to the white color, and nothing can be known of them: neither quantity, nor changes. However, at the same time, the shining of white onto the Worlds of BYA, which are the three colors of letters, creates the Kelim of Ten Sefirot de Atzilut.

29. From the above, one should understand that the splitting of the World of Atzilut into three components, as described in "Corrections to Zohar", are "He, His light and His actions which are one".

If in our present state we feel the universe around us and ourselves in it, we can complement that picture with the Creator and His influence. As a result, we come up with a pretty complex picture. In reality, however, when we ascend to the spiritual world and enter the World of Atzilut, the Creator, His influence on us, the universe that we perceive, all merge into a single whole called "the Creator's merging with the creation", endless, limitless, boundless Oneness.

Such merging takes place at the level of the World of Atzilut and higher, when *"the Creator, His light, and His actions are one," hence Atzilut emanates the white color in spite of the fact that there exists only a simple unity with nothing from created beings. This is because the Creator means Divinity itself (the property of bestowal), whose essence we do not comprehend. "His actions" constitute the ten Kelim HuBTuM existing in Him, which were likened to* the color white in a book of wisdom. Even quantity is impossible to discern in the white, for nothing there would make any quantity, as it is all white.

We can characterize neither the Creator nor His actions in the World of *Atzilut*. Therefore, "The Zohar" speaks of nothing from *Atzilut* and above, but only about the Worlds of BYA, because otherwise it is impossible to convey the information to us. We will simply be unable to receive it.

> The matter of the letters begins in the Worlds of BYA. We first find them in the Kelim: Keter, Hochma, Bina, ZA, and Malchut of the World of Atzilut, but only with the help of the color white, which allows for the letter's shape, whereas there is no color in itself. When we ascend to the World of Atzilut through the Worlds of BYA, we see that the color white has a multitude of forms, although it is formless, that the Creator performs many actions, although in reality he performs none. Various contradictions begin to merge and disappear in this simple unity, in this attainment of perfection.

> The ten Kelim in the World of Atzilut reveal themselves in numerous changes according to their shining in the World of BYA, which is similar to the way a mental design is implemented in reality when a house is built.

> Thus, all the changes taking place in the Worlds of BYA occur only under the influence of the shining of the Kelim of the Ten Sefirot HuBTuM de Atzilut. Pertaining to those receiving in the Worlds of BYA, we can differentiate all the numerous changes taking place in the color white. As for the World of Atzilut itself, it is just as the color white does not acquire the colors of the letters. Indeed, there is no quantity whatsoever in it.

We do not attain the white color with the help of other letters, i.e., by means of the worlds BYA that superpose the World of *Atzilut*.

We attain nothing, for there is no quantity or action in it, only a simple, unattainable light.

Kabbalah speaks about how we should correct our perception of the surrounding world in order to feel the World of Infinity instead of it. Everything depends on our sensations and correct adaptations to the true reality in place of the illusion, which we feel in our five senses.

We have said that the notion *"the Creator, the light and His actions in the World of Atzilut are one"* does not fall into several categories the way we perceive it in our world. Our world, our actions, the Creator, His actions, - all of this - and we seem to be absolutely disunited. Nevertheless, as we correct our perception of reality, it will merge within one all-embracing Upper Force, which rules over all.

30. "His light" refers to the light inside of the white color of Atzilut that are Kelim. This light is understood by us only as it concerns the Souls receiving from the World of Atzilut. However, we do not mean the Divinity per se, which is the mystery of the word "He."

There exists two notions of light: one refers to the word "He", the other shines out of this category as the color white. It enters the colors red, green, and black of the Worlds of *BYA*, and descends to us, the Souls.

That is to say, when the three Worlds of BYA rise up to Atzilut with the Souls of people, the light that they receive there is determined as Ohr Hochma or Ohr Haya. It is also called "this white light."

Hence, we say that out of the five *Sefirot* (*Keter, Hochma, Bina, ZA,* and *Malchut*) *Keter* is colorless, *Hochma* is white (the World of *Atzilut*), while *Bina, ZA,* and *Malchut* are red, green, and black respectively. This is how the colors are distributed. In other words, *Hochma* (*Atzilut*) is white, but only with regard to us. However, if we only speak about the color itself, it has no name there at all.

*From this point of view, we call this light "His light", as it is written:
"He, the light and His actions are one." All three of these components are said to merge above the Parsa of the World of Atzilut into
one notion, the Creator. This light never descends below the Parsa de
Atzilut. Only its tiny luminescence can do so.*

We know that *Ohr Hochma* can only be present in the World of
Atzilut, but never under the *Parsa*. It only shines below the *Parsa* in order
to "tempt" the *Kelim* by its luminescence and attract them to *Atzilut*.

*That is why it is impossible to comprehend the World of Atzilut per se. We
only perceive it as the white color of a book's page, which serves a basis
for printing the letters.*

*31. The way "The Zohar" describes the Kelim HuBTuM in the
World of Atzilut, which increase or decrease as the result of people's
actions, means that in the Upper Light itself there is nothing but its
simplicity, because no changes are possible in it.*

At our lessons, we study the World of *Atzilut*, the Worlds of BYA,
how the Souls raise their desires to the world *Atzilut* through the Worlds
of BYA, and how the World of *Atzilut* begins to emanate the light and
pull us up to itself. We learn that certain actions take place in the world
Atzilut under the influence of MAN, our desires. That is, by our actions,
desires, demands, we can cause changes, developments.

Baal HaSulam says that there is another aid for the correct understanding of "The Zohar." If we disregard it, we will not receive the
spiritual information and will fail to understand what is really written in
the book. We will be as millions of other people, who kept reading "The
Zohar" one generation after another without understanding anything
and imagining all kinds of fantastic pictures.

So should what the correct tune-up to "The Zohar" be? The conclusion is that we never affect anything in the World of *Atzilut* with our
actions. And as for all the actions that take place in *Atzilut* with regard to

the Souls, it only seems to us that only they happen in *Atzilut* and only with regard to the Souls.

From what we see in this world, where all of our actions take place, we come to believe that the same actions happen in the World of *Atzilut*.

As much as we become worthy of receiving the light in our world, we receive it. When we fall and become unworthy of the light, it disappears. It seems to us that it happens above, in the World of *Atzilut*, the source of the light. In actual fact, it is constantly and unfailingly shining upon us, whereas all the changes occur within us. This is the same delusion as in trying to change the world around us. It stems from the same source: We erroneously believe that all changes take place outside, and not within us. However, everything depends on the person's inner *Kelim*, his sensations.

Therefore, let us repeat: we should perceive the World of *Atzilut* as something constant, invariable. The phenomena that we research as its changes with regard to us (rises, falls, AVI and ZON ascending and descending in the worlds, *Atik*, AA, AVI, YESHSUT, and ZON of the World of *Atzilut*, *the Partzufim* that change depending on our MAN), all of this we perceive within us.

In reality, no changes ever take place in the World of *Atzilut*. It is very important for us to develop a correct attitude to the universe and to receive the information that is contained in "The Book of Zohar." All that is written there aims at generating necessary changes in us. All our efforts should be directed inward, all the changes in our *Kelim* (from our present state up to the World of Infinity: boundless attainment) take place only within us. Such an understanding can save us many years of futile effort, search, and confusion.

32. *This is similar to a candle for which it makes no difference whether you light up tens of thousands of other candles from it or none. There will be no change in the candle itself. The same is with*

regard to Adam HaRishon. It matters not whether he will father numerous sons like himself or none at all, for there will be no changes in Adam HaRishon himself.

Similarly, there are no changes in the World of Atzilut, whether the lower ones receive immeasurable abundance from it or receive nothing. All of the growing (advancement) concerns only the lower ones, and occurs within them.

33. *However, why do those who have attained the knowledge of "The Zohar", i.e., the great sages who already live in the World of Infinity, need to describe all the changes in the World of Atzilut. Why do they entangle us this way? They have attained it; for them it is their essence, existence, reality. So why do they describe it in such a confusing form? Do they intend to purposely baffle us? Would it not have been better to describe it in relation to receiving in the Worlds of BYA, and not to pile up so many definitions in the World of Atzilut, to which we would have to look for some kind of excuses?*

Baal HaSulam asks the question that should necessarily arise in our mind: "Why is Kabbalah written in this way? It seems to be thoroughly misleading: it tells us of what happens in the Souls as if it takes place in the worlds." Here is how Baal HaSulam answers: "The same occurs in our world. It seems to us that everything happens outside, that is why we describe our reality the way we do." In actual fact, as we begin to attain the spiritual, our perception of the world changes so that we see and feel it as something invariable, static, and gradually dissolving in our spiritual vision. But until we do feel this way, the world looks quite tangible, consisting of numerous real objects, actions, forces. Why is it all so confused?

Baal HaSulam writes:

That has in it a big secret. When Kabbalists mention the word "secret", it means that they wish to reveal something to us. This is because in our imperfect state we cannot sense the true reality of the World of Infinity. What we feel is our present condition. The difference between our present state and the World of Infinity is called a "secret". This secret was expressed by the prophets, i.e., by the Kabbalists who have reached a certain level of spiritual attainment called "prophecy".

Here is what they say:

This has the manifestation of Divinity, of the Creator's special power, because these images create an impression that they exist outside, although in reality they only exist in the receiving Souls to show them as if the Creator Himself takes part in all the actions together with them. The Soul asks and the Creator responds, moves toward it, while the Soul advances toward Him. Why does the Creator fill the Souls with a sensation as though something happens beyond them? Baal HaSulam answers: *in order to maximally increase the comprehension of the Souls.*

When I feel that apart from my personal aspiration for the spiritual, the spiritual also advances toward me, I perceive the Creator's plan in addition to my own actions. By manifesting Himself to me, the Creator as it were is moving in my direction. In fact, He just reveals His plan to me, which I perceive as movement toward me. Thus, beside my own action, which elevates me to the spiritual world, I also receive an additional part of the Creator's mind. This is a very subtle point. If the person interprets it correctly, he or she begins to understand the Creator's thoughts in each sensation or action.

It is similar to the father who is hiding himself from his favorite little son in grief and in happiness, although he has in him neither grief nor happiness. We imagine the Creator as "Terrifying", "Cruel", "Kind", and "Loving", in all of His possible manifestations, as if He always changes. *He does that only to force his favorite son to widen his understanding, and to play with him. Only when he grows up and becomes wiser will he discover everything that his father did for him, and learn that there was nothing more than necessary for playing with him.*

The same is true with us. In spite of the fact that all of these images and transformations begin and end in the impressions of Souls, this manifestation of the Creator in our perception creates an imaginary picture, as though they all exist within Him. The Creator does that in order to maximally increase the comprehension of the Souls in accordance with the thought of creation, which is "to delight His created beings". In other words, man should acquire the Creator's mind and achieve His level.

34. Do not be surprised by the fact that you will find similar examples in the Creator's governance of this material world. Take our vision, for example. When we see the enormous world before us in all its magnificence, we do not see it as it really is, but only as it is perceived within us. That is, in the rear part of our brain, there is some kind of photo camera that draws everything that we see; not what really exists outside us.

Moreover, the Creator designed our brain in such a way that, like a special mirror, it creates in us an illusion that everything we see exists outside our brain. Although what we see outside of us is not reality, we should still be grateful that the Creator made this mirror in our brain that allows us to see and to comprehend everything that is outside us. By doing so, He gave us the capacity to learn, to get complete and clear knowledge, to measure every subject inside and outside. But for that, most of our knowledge would have been non-existent.

Why is this so? By studying ourselves and the outside world and thanks to the difference between these two states we have an opportunity to develop. Therefore, by feeling ourselves and the Creator Who is, as it were, playing and interacting with us, we not only evolve, but also acquire His wisdom, His thoughts.

The same is true in relation to Divine wisdom. In spite of all the changes that happen inside of the receiving Souls, they see everything in the Giver. Only in this way are they privileged to receive all knowl-

edge and all pleasures in the plan of creation. Other than that, judge by the example. Although we practically see everything in front of us, every sensible person knows precisely that everything we see is only inside our brain. The same is true with the Souls. Although they see all images in the Creator, any researcher of the Upper World knows without doubt that everything is only within them, and not in the Giver.

There is a saying in Kabbalah: "I will know You from within myself." The time has come for us to begin adjusting our perception of both inner and outer reality. We need to realize that we exist in the absolutely corrected, perfect world, and that everything that happens around us is a result of our false, inadequate perception. By correcting it, we can also correct the world in which we live, and our existence in it. If we succeed to correct our perception of the world, we will enter the sensation of the Upper Realm and the Creator, and "The Book of Zohar" will show us how we can fill our Souls correctly.

35. The *Torah* laws forbid making any images. They even prohibit depicting nature, let alone people. This is because man should be engaged in creating inner images.

The meaning of the saying is that the Sefira Malchut, which includes all worlds and Souls, and is the root of all the Kelim, creates this picture inside itself.

The picture that we perceive in *Malchut* is the Creator's picture. That is to say, what we see in the surrounding world, in ourselves, and in what we will later see in the Upper Worlds, is basically a projection of the Creator's light on *Malchut.*

The matter does not concern Malchut as it is in its own place, but, rather, the situation when Malchut descends and spreads to the created beings, becomes visible to all of them in accordance with their perception and imagination. In other words, Malchut exists only with regard to the receivers, and not by itself. This is the correct perception of the universe.

The Creator says: "In spite of the fact that I appear to you in your properties, i.e., in your perception and imagination, who are you going to compare Me with?" Indeed, before the Creator created the picture of the world and gave it a form, He was the only one that existed in the world without any form or image.

The person who attains the Creator in this world perceives Him as some image. In the Worlds of *Assiya, Yetzira,* and *Beria* we always attain His images, i.e., various forms of His manifestation in us. Afterwards, as we rise from the Worlds of *BYA* to the World of *Atzilut* and elevate the entire universe with us, we become a part of the Upper simple light.

That is why all hints that are contained in the letters, dots, or holy names are nothing but imprints of our Kelim in the Creator's simple light.

This happens because the Soul consists of 613 *Kelim,* which we have to correct. Of them, 248 comprise our properties of bestowal (*Galgalta ve Eynaim*), and 365 constitute our properties of reception (AHP). All of them can be subdivided into five parts in accordance with the Creator's ineffable Name. He projects Himself onto us in such a way that the four letters of His Name form a four-phase superposition on our 613 properties. Hence, it turns out that in whatever world or on whatever level I may be, I always expose my Malchut to the Creator's projected image. This is why man is always called "Adam", whether in the World of *Assiya, Yetzira,* or *Beria.* This is a kind of the Creator's prototype, which exists on the level where one can project His image on himself.

36. *At first glance, we might find a contradiction in what was said above. Earlier it was said that all the forms emanate only from the Sefira Malchut to the receivers; whereas here it is said that they come from Beria (Bina) and below.*

In reality, forms and images come only from Behina Dalet, which is Malchut. All the Kelim come not from the first Ten Sefirot - Keter, Hochma, Bina, and Tifferet - but from Malchut. However, the properties of mercy and restriction interacted in the World of correction. This means that Sefira Malchut (of restriction) ascended, and made its way into Sefira Bina (the property of mercy).

In accordance with that, from this moment on, the Kelim of Malchut became rooted in Sefira Bina. Thus, the Zohar says that the genuine roots of images (Kelim) are in Malchut. But after that, it says they are in the World of Beria, which means it results from the interaction made for the correction of the world.

In addition, the sages said: "Originally, the Creator created the world based on the property of judgment, but saw that the world could not exist, so He made his interaction with mercy". You should know that the Ten Sefirot KaHaBTuM have many names in the book of Zohar in accordance with their numerous functions.

When they are called "Keter-Atzilut-Beria-Yetzira-Assiya" their task is to distinguish between the Kelim "de Panim" that are called "Keter-Atzilut" (Keter- Hochma), and the Kelim "de Achoraim" called Beria-Yetzira-Assiya" (Bina-Tifferet-Malchut). Such a division results from the interaction between the properties of judgment and mercy.

Since the Zohar hints at the interaction between Malchut and Bina, the Sefira Bina is called "Beria." Before this interaction happened, Bina had neither form nor image, even in relation to receivers.

37. So it continues: "...but after He had given this form to the structure of "Adam Elion", He descended and "dressed" in it. He is called HaVaYaH, which means the Ten Sefirot KaHaBTuM because the tip of letter "Yud" is Keter, "Yud" is Hochma, "Hey" is Bina, "Vav"

is Tifferet, and last letter "Hey" is Malchut. This was done so that the Creator could be attained through His properties, Sefirot.

38. Here is an explanation of what was said above. After her interaction with the restrictive properties of Malchut, from Beria (Bina) and below, images and forms descend to the Souls. It happens not in its place, but only where the receivers are.

It is said: "He gave a form to the structure "Adam Elion", and came down and "dressed" into this man's form." Thus, man's form consists of 613 Kelim resulting from the Kelim of a Soul. Since a Soul had 613 spiritual Kelim that are called "248 organs and 365 tendons, it is subdivided into five parts in accordance with 4 letters of HaVaYaH:

- Tip of the letter "Yud", her Rosh is Keter:
- From Peh to Chazeh is Hochma;
- From Chazeh to Tabur is Bina;
- From Tabur to Sium Raglin there are two Sefirot: Tifferet and Malchut.

The Torah describes the Partzuf Adam, which represents the 248 affirmative commandments corresponding with "248 organs" and 365 negative commandments corresponding with "365 tendons." It has five parts – the five books of Torah. This is called "the image of Adam Elion", which means that Adam, in the World of Beria (Bina), where the Kelim start and continue to places where the Souls are. This is called "Adam Elion" for there are three Adamic properties in the Sefirot:

- Adam de Beria;
- Adam de Yetzira;
- Adam de Assiya.

However, Keter and Hochma do not have any image that can be related to any dotted letter or the four letters of HaVaYaH. Since the matter concerns the World of Beria, it is confirmed: "Adam Elion".

Always remember that the Zohar says there are no images in the place of Sefirot Bina and Malchut, only in the receivers' place. Since all these Sefirot give the Kelim garments for the Souls to attain the Creator with the help of light descending to them within certain limits in accordance with their 613 organs, we call givers "Adam" as well. However, they are the color white there.

39. It should not be difficult for you to understand because all four letters of HaVaYaH and the tip of the letter "Yud" are the five Kelim that are always called "letters", which refer to the five Sefirot KaHaBTuM. The tip of the letter "Yud" and the letter "Yud" in the name of HaVaYaH hint at the presence of the Kelim in Keter and Hochma.

The fact is that when it is said that "images" and "properties" representing Kelim that begin from the World of Beria and below, the matter only concerns the three Sefirot Bina, Tifferet, and Malchut, but not Keter and Hochma, from the point of essence of the Sefirot.

However, you should know that Sefirot are included in each other. There are Ten Sefirot KaHaBTuM in Keter, Hochma, Bina, Tifferet, and in Malchut. In accordance with that, we find that each of the five Sefirot KaHaBTuM has three Sefirot: Bina, Tifferet and Malchut from which Kelim originate.

From that, you need to understand that the tip of the letter "Yud" which refers to the Kelim of Keter, points to Bina and TuM that are included in Keter. The letter "Hey" of the name HaVaYaH that represents the Kli Hochma, points to Bina and TuM that are included in Hochma. Thus, both Keter and Hochma, included even in Bina and ZON, have no Kelim, while Bina and TUM, included even Keter and Hochma, have Kelim in them.

From that perspective, Adam really consists of five parts. This is because Bina and TuM perform an act of bestowal in each of the five Sefirot, which is concealed in the name "Merkava de Adam." In accordance with that:

- Adam on level Keter is called "Adam Kadmon,"
- Adam on level Hochma is called "Adam de-Atzilut,"
- Adam on level Bina is called "Adam de-Beria,"
- Adam on level Tifferet is called "Adam de-Yetzira,"
- Adam on level Malchut is called "Adam de-Assiya".

40. There are ten Names of the Creator, which are correspondingly imprinted on our ten basic properties – Sefirot.

• Sefira Keter is called Ekie;
• Sefira Hochma is called Yud-Key;
• Sefira Bina is called HaVaYaH;
• Sefira Hesed is called El;
• Sefira Gevura is called Elokim;
• Sefira Tifferet is called HaVaYaH (simple one, different from Bina);

Since Tifferet and Bina are on the middle line, they resemble one another; therefore they are designated by the same name, albeit it is spelled differently.

• Two Sefirot – Netzah and Hod are called Tzvaot;
• Sefira Yesod is called Chai;
• Sefira Malchut is called Adni.

There is no need to memorize these names; later on we will understand how they originated. We are speaking about the ten none erasable Names. They are called none erasable because if the scribe who writes the Torah scroll makes a mistake in one of them, the entire segment must be destroyed; it is forbidden to correct such mistakes.

What does that mean in our world? Man cannot perceive the world's picture correctly, unless his Ten *Sefirot* are properly attuned. As with a violin, one can play it only if its strings are properly tuned up. Thus, they form a certain interrelation with one another, each one of them being in its standard, correct state.

Similarly, if at least one of the Creator's Names resonates in us incorrectly, i.e., one of our properties will not be completely similar to His, we will not be able to perceive His manifestation. That is to say, being made up of Ten *Sefirot*, we perceive the Creator's action in ten of His emanations.

At the same time, when we attain all Ten *Sefirot* and completely fill them with the Creator's image, an amazing phenomenon occurs. All Ten *Sefirot* merge, the boundaries between them disappear, and they form the general, Infinite, white light of *Atzilut*, where we ascend upon attaining all the levels of the Worlds of *BYA*.

This is what Baal HaSulam writes in his "Preface to the Book of Zohar". This "Preface" deals with the limitations, which exist between us and our perceived reality. All that we experience within us is only perceived in our egoistic *Kelim* to the extent of their correction. If our properties coincide with those of the Creator, we will be able to understand and sense Him better and better. It is the same as when a radio receiver picks a certain outside wave only because its own wave contour is identical to the outer wave.

In other words, only our equivalence of form with the Creator will enable us to enter the true universe and exist in it. At the beginning, we need to do it in our 613 *Kelim*, subsequently felt as Ten *Sefirot*. Afterwards, they are felt as a single whole, the Creator's general manifestation regarding *Malchut*. When *Malchut* finally becomes similar to the Creator, it completely merges with the light in its nine first *Sefirot*. All images fade and disappear, whereas we become one with the Infinite, white light.

> 41. Unless the Creator's light spreads onto all created beings by way of filling these holy Sefirot, how can the creatures be honored to know Him, and to fulfill the following: "The earth will be filled with knowledge of the Creator?"
>
> An explanation is that the Creator tricks the Souls into believing that all the changes in the Sefirot happen in Him. The purpose of that was for the Souls to get to know and comprehend Him. Thus, the saying, "The earth will be filled with knowledge of the Creator" is going to be realized.
>
> 42. And woe to them who compare the Creator with any kind of measure, or say that this measure is in the Creator, even if it is a spiritual measure which appears to the Souls. This is especially so if it is a material measure that stems from mortal human nature, whose foundation is dust.
>
> Although the Souls perceive all the changes that occur in them as taking place in the Giver, it should be clear to them that there are neither changes nor measures in Him. He is Divine, and it only seems to them, as it is said: "I am similar to what prophets have said."
>
> Woe to them who err, because they will immediately lose their divine abundance, let alone the fools who see Him as an embodiment in flesh and blood, transient and flawed.

INTRODUCTION
TO THE BOOK OF ZOHAR

This Introduction is one of four explanations that Baal HaSulam wrote for the "Book of Zohar" to furnish a person with an outlook on evolution, to show where this book leads, and to what goals and heights it should elevate him. In this book, Baal HaSulam researches the deepest layers of the universe. He tries to explain the properties of our reality, to unveil its depth and the extent of our comprehension of it. He tells us how we can change it and ascend to a different, Upper Reality.

Most importantly, this Introduction speaks about our active part in this process. It is very good and commendable to be simply studying Kabbalah. Yet, can we change anything with the help of this knowledge? This is where the study should lead us. This is the only aspect of Kabbalah that should interest us.

"Introduction to the Book of Zohar" is a very deep, summarizing text. While "Introduction to the Study of the Ten *Sefirot*" speaks of the person's path and the levels he ascends on his way to the Goal, this composition is an immersion into the universe. As a submarine dives into the ocean, so does the Zohar descend with us to the unimaginable depths of reality.

As the article, "The Essence of the Wisdom of Kabbalah" says, the task of Kabbalah is to reveal the Creator to the person. The Creator created man and conceals Himself to let him rise to His level. Otherwise, we would feel no need to reach out to Him, to grow and become similar to Him. The Creator is like a loving mother who teaches her child to walk. She places him on his feet, and then moves slightly away to compel the child to make a few steps towards her. She then moves farther away to encourage him to make a few more steps and so on. This is how our children grow, and we are supposed to grow in the same way with regard to the Creator. We should always perceive His concealment as an appeal to get closer to Him.

The book of Zohar expounds the profound processes that unfold in us while we gradually reveal the Creator. This is called ascending the ladder of the spiritual worlds. Kabbalah tells the person what he sees and feels while gradually ascending this ladder of similarity to the Creator. He can only be revealed to the extent of our equivalence with Him; the more likeness there is between He and I, the better I can feel Him. Therefore, it turns out that to be similar to the Creator is the same as to feel or reveal Him.

> 1. In this introduction, my wish is to clarify issues that seem simple at first. Everyone has tried to explain these issues, and much ink has been spilled in these efforts (throughout the history of humankind). Yet to this day, we have not reached a clear enough knowledge in these matters.
>
> The questions are as follows:

Both ancient and modern philosophers and scientists have been puzzled by them.

What questions are these? They are fundamental and critical to our essence and existence.

> First question:
>
> What is our essence?

Who are we? Are we animals or are we human? Are we intelligent beings? Do we exist or only imagine that we exist? It is quite possible that we are completely different than we imagine. In fact, when we look at any other small animal, such as a dog or a kitten, our impression about it, about its nature, is completely different.

How can we objectively see ourselves as though we are looking from outside? What does it mean to see from the outside? Starting from where can we imagine ourselves? The question about our essence consists of many conditions.

Second question:

What is our part in the long chain of reality, of which we are but small links?

We can see that we have gone through some states. This world has gone through some states with or without our involvement. Alternatively, perhaps it exists by itself; or we somehow exist in it. Nevertheless, we see everything from the perspective of historic consequence, the cause and effect chain of reality.

Do we play any role? This chain exists for a reason, and so do we. Do we exist parallel to the chain or inside of it? Do we determine the development of this chain and its consequences? Can we influence reality or do anything about it? What is our role? The answer to these questions includes knowledge of all potential development, cause and effect, beginning and end, all the processes, all the intermediate levels, and knowledge about our potential impact in this process.

Third question:

When we look at ourselves, we feel that we are so spoiled and low that no one is more despicable than we are.

Baal HaSulam addresses here the particular inner attainment in which we can actually perceive ourselves. We can feel our insignificance and meanness with the help of the descending Surrounding Light, the *Ohr Makif,* in direct proportion with the descending Upper Light. If we genuinely attract it with the help of the group and serious study, the Upper Light demonstrates to us the insignificance of our essence.

> *What is the actual matter here? The matter is that, in addition to the animal essence, we have something that is above animal existence. This something is called our egoism. It is based on our aspirations to wealth, honor, fame, power, and knowledge. Animals do not have these aspirations. This is called "Kina", "Ta'avah", and "Kavod" – envy, inclination to pleasures, and aspiration to honor. These aspirations bring a person to a level above the animal. Since they are above animal qualities, these aspirations and qualities are praiseworthy. On the other hand, their common natural utilization puts us below all other levels.*

Therefore, Baal HaSulam says:

> *When we look at ourselves, we feel that we are so spoiled and low that no one is more despicable than we are.*

Animals kill other animals because it is integrated in them at the level of instinct. A lion kills only in order to fulfill his small desire to be sated. However, egoism in humans is so much higher than for its own sake; humans want to destroy everyone. Consequently, the additional egoism that elevates us above animals actually makes us lower than animals.

> *However, if we look at the One who created us, we would think that we were supposed to have become the crown of everything, higher than everything, because an excellent Creator should only perform excellent actions.*

Baal HaSulam tells us here about people who can roughly imagine what the Creator, Perfection, and a desire to bestow mean.

Yet, how did it happen that a perfect Creator created such a mean being that is so much meaner than the rest? What is He like, if He is perfect? Additionally, are we perfect or imperfect? We have observed from Universal laws that imperfection does not emanate from perfection.

Fourth question:

Our mind makes us acknowledge the Creator's absolute kindness and that He only performs kindness, so that there is nothing higher than He.

Fundamentally, our mind does not agree to that. Many believe that the world is governed by a single "evil force". Kabbalists tell us about the essence of the Creator. They are on a different level of attainment. Baal HaSulam provokes us with questions that have not yet materialized for us. Nevertheless, they have been already resolved for him.

Hence, he offsets what he conceived on the upper, perfect level to our imperfect condition. He does this from the foundation of these two points where the first point is he being at the state of the Creator and another point is we at our current state. He demonstrates a difference between these states that are called questions. All our questions come from discrepancies and oppositions to his state. So he says:

Our mind makes us acknowledge (from its perception) *the fact that the Creator is all kind and performs only kindness, so that there is nothing higher than He. However, how could He create so many forms which, from the very beginning, are destined to spend all the days of their existence in suffering and grief?* (Now he is asking at our level). *If that was not done in kindness, could it at least have been done with less evil* (He created us)?!

Why did He create us to harm? In addition, why, even now when we are just beginning to study the path we must take in order to reach the Purpose of creation, do we see that every step of the way consists of continuous falling and rising, that the lower the falling, the higher the rising?

Nothing is comprehended unless a *Kli* has been comprehended first, a suffering, and feeling of worthlessness, inferiority, depression, emptiness, opposition to the Creator. Only then, follow the revelation of the Creator and unification with Him.

Why should it all be done this way? Why were we created inferior? Why should we comprehend perfection from our inferior state?

Fifth question:

How could insignificant, temporary, and impure forms come from the Infinite, something without beginning or end (our "final state", as conceived by Baal HaSulam)?

How can this be? The fifth question appears similar to the third one. He states that, *"When we look at ourselves, we feel that we are so spoiled and low that no one is more despicable than we are. If we look at the One who created us, we would think that we were supposed to have become the crown of everything, higher than everything, because an excellent Creator should only perform excellent actions."*

Here he says something similar: *When we look at ourselves, we feel that we are so spoiled and low that no one is more despicable than we are.*

The five questions that he addresses here concern our state with regard to the Creator's. These questions can only be raised and cleared up by someone at His level as compared to ours. Baal HaSulam tells us about the discrepancies between these two levels. He wishes to explain to us why it is necessary to have this difference and how we may reach perfection. This is our challenge, to conceive where we are, where the Creator is, and how to overcome this chasm between us.

Why does he raise these questions? In this Introduction, he partially explains it, but actually, he raises these questions in order to comprehend them. During these lessons, we will discover that not only must we understand these questions while studying this Introduction, but also actualize them within ourselves and subsequently use them to climb to the level where we need to be. That is why we need to study the book of Zohar. Hence, he uses this explanation in his Introduction to this book.

2. In order to comprehensively clear all this up, in advance, we have to carry out certain studies where the subject is not a "forbidden area", meaning, the essence of the Creator. This can in no way be comprehended by our mind; hence, we have neither thought nor concept of Him. The compulsory field of research is the study of the Creator's actions.

In general, we can understand the questions: "What is the Essence?", "What is our role in a chain of reality?", and "Why are we defective, while the Creator is perfect?" and so on. So, for what do we need preliminary studies?

We need them to understand these questions accurately. In other words, we should approach them in a different way, for it is said, *"Many people (in the course of history) have attempted to disclose these questions, and much ink has been spilled"*. Yet in the end, the questions have remained unanswered.

How can we resolve these questions, find the answers, and actually become fully aware of them within ourselves? In order to look at these questions and correctly move towards their realization, it is necessary to put us in an unambiguous position with regard to them. This is what Baal HaSulam does in his studies. He says:

In order to clear all this up comprehensively, in advance, we need to make some preliminary inquiries, where the subject is not a "forbidden area", i.e., the essence of the Creator... Why is it forbidden for us to study the essence of the Creator? Further, he answers this: *...which can in no way be comprehended by our mind.*

Since we cannot comprehend the Creator's essence, we should not study it. This is unattainable for us at our current level of development. Therefore, the only thing we should do is study all that we can possibly comprehend. Moreover, perhaps, if we study what we are able to attain, we will approach the incomprehensible area, the essence of the Creator.

Here he says: ... *the Creator's essence, which can in no way be comprehended by our mind, hence we have no thought and concept about Him...and the compulsory field of research (i.e., the Creator's instruction), is the study of the Creator's actions. As we are told, "Know the Creator and serve Him".*

If I attain Him, His actions, and His instructions, I will be adapting the correction internally. I will place myself in likeness to Him and this will be called "I perceive His actions and serve Him", work "for the sake of Creator".

It is also said, *"By Your actions I will know You".*

I will attain Him by adapting my actions to His and by becoming similar to Him. If I begin my exploration of Him straightforwardly, this will be called "philosophy." I will not achieve anything this way. I can only comprehend and attain the Creator if I become similar to Him, and then all those conditions and qualities that exist in Him will be formed in me. Subsequently, I will be able to understand His intentions, something that precedes His qualities and actions. From the *Guf* (body) of the *Partzuf* I will rise to its *Rosh* (head).

If I make my body, i.e., all of my desires, similar to all of the Creator's actions, then the inner body of my soul, my desires, the body of the *Partzuf* will be formed. The *Toch* (inner part) or *Sof* (end) of the *Partzuf* will be similar to the Creator's influence on me. This is called "nine of my reversed *Sefirot* become similar to nine of His direct *Sefirot*". It allows me to reach complete balance with the Creator and to grasp His thoughts, the *Rosh* of the *Partzuf*.

Thus we can come to an understanding of the Creator. If the person specifically acts in this manner, he reveals in his study the opportunity to ascend from the level of the creation to the level of the Creator. If we are willing to do this, what kind of inquiries should we make?

First Inquiry:

How can we see creation as something newly formed, something new, something that did not exist in the Creator before it was formed. How can anyone in his right mind understand that there is nothing that was not in the Creator? Simple common sense makes us acknowledge that. One cannot give if he does not have that which he is giving.

If the Creator creates something, it has to be within Him in some form. How can it be that something suddenly appeared from nothing, out of nowhere? What does it mean "out of nowhere"? Has He thought of this? Has He made any plans? What has induced Him to this? From where has he taken the material – thoughts, feelings, and actions to make the creation? Was there a point in Him from which it all began? How can it be if there was nothing within Him, no starting point? Should not there be a beginning? If so, how is it possible to imagine that we appeared not from Him, but from nothing?

I recommend that you stop and try to remember all I say. Do not make an inner effort to adapt the material and put everything within you on the right shelves. Please do not do this!

You should take it easy or it will not enter you. There is no need to be tense; study it freely, with love. Do not attempt to memorize anything! We cannot possibly remember anything of what we learn.

Suddenly we feel that we can only understand something new if it penetrates us from within, becomes our nature. Do not imitate the philosophers who have "spilled much ink" for thousands of years. Nothing has come out of it!

We should reproduce all of these actions within ourselves. When they become our inner properties, we will know, feel, and see it all. Otherwise, our useless attempts to sort this data will fail.

While studying try to concentrate on what we wish to achieve, where we want to be. The most important thing is not to know, but to attract the light of correction, which would elevate us to these states. This is what we should be thinking about during our lessons.

By aspiring to one goal, we try to draw on ourselves the Surrounding light. To this end, we read what the author wrote while being on the high level of attainment where he is merged with the Creator. He wrote his books not to enlighten poor philosophers or us. He instructs us to "know the Creator and serve Him", to adapt His actions in ourselves and become similar to Him. The result will be as King David says, "By Your actions I will know You". This is where our focus must be. So let us stop racking our brains in vain and try activating our hearts, and most importantly the point in them.

Second Inquiry:

Can you say that, from the aspect of the Creator's almightiness, He certainly can create something from nothing, meaning something new that is not in Him?

If we say that He can do everything, then of course, He can create something from nothing, meaning something new, which is not in Him at all. Then the question arises, what kind of reality can we refer to as having no place in the Creator, but is a new formation?

Suppose that we accept our first inquiry as an axiom: yes, the Creator has created something from nothing. We are yet to come to this conclusion, but for now let us admit that we have already accomplished it. In that case, He has created something that is completely not within Him.

Then the question arises, what kind of reality can we refer to as having no place in the Creator, but is a new formation?

So what was it that the Creator decided to create, something that is not within Him and in which He felt the sudden need? Does it not follow that there is an absence of perfection in Him? That something was missing, and now this something is in demand? Alternatively, if He was perfect before and afterwards, why has He made something new? If this is so, obviously this new "creation" has nothing to do with perfection.

Third Inquiry:

The Kabbalists say that the human soul is a part of the Creator. Therefore, there is no difference between Him and the soul.

There is a person within whom there is an animal soul, a vital force that sustains alike both animals and us. Besides this, we have a tiny particle of the Creator Himself. The soul is within us, but it is a small part from Above. When it is above, it is a small particle; when it is within us, it is already a soul.

The difference is that He is the "whole" and the soul is a "part". This resembles a stone carved from a rock. There is no difference between the stone and the rock except that the rock is a "whole" and the stone is a "part". Thus, we must ask: Although a stone carved from the rock is separated from it by an axe made for that purpose, causing the separation of the "part" from the "whole", how can one imagine that the Creator separates a part from His essence to become detached from Him, meaning a soul, to the point that it can only be understood as part of His essence?

An Axe is a *Kli*, a tool, a material force that splits a "part" from the "whole".

So what is the spiritual axe that cuts a part from the whole? Why does the carved off part remain unchanged with the same properties that are in the Creator? Does the Creator suffer form this process? A piece was cut from Him! Was that part of his perfection reduced? Is it possible that He became imperfect? Does He lack anything? What is the connection between a part (a soul) separated from the Creator and the Creator Himself? Alternatively, is this part completely detached from Him?

3. Fourth Inquiry:

Since the system of impure forces and the Klipot are so far from the Creator's purity that nothing farther remote can be conceived, how can they be emanated from the Creator, much less sustained by Him?

The Kabbalists wish to make our life easier, so they tell us everything in advance. In addition to the usual questions they ask many others, which we would never think of. Here Baal HaSulam speaks about the system of impure forces (*Klipot*) that are absolutely opposite to the Creator. He gives birth to this system of impure worlds and constantly sustains it with His purity. What connection can exist between them if they are opposite?

We say that if spiritual properties are opposite, there can be no contact between them. If they ad-

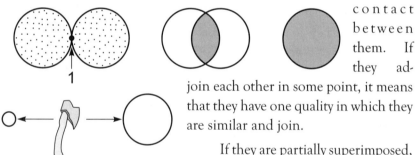

join each other in some point, it means that they have one quality in which they are similar and join.

If they are partially superimposed, it means that some of their qualities are similar to each other. If they completely overlap, they are equivalent. The creation is initially opposite to the Creator and separated from Him.

This is what happens with impure forces. There is the Creator and the *Klipot*.

Klipot are born and sustained by the Creator, whereas in fact they are completely separated from each other. How can this be? The Creator creates and sustains *Klipot* while at the same time being completely separated from them. This question demands an explanation.

Fifth Inquiry refers to the *"resurrection of the dead"*.

Baal HaSulam says there is a state called "resurrection of the dead". We should agree upon definitions: by "the soul", we mean bestowal or the intention of bestowal. By

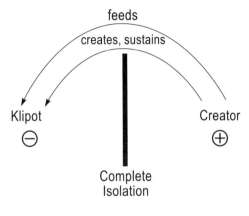

"the body", we mean the *Guf* of the *Partzuf* or desire. By "resurrection of the dead", we mean rising of the dead bodies (desires).

> *Since the body is so despicable, it is doomed to perish and to be buried.*

What does it mean, "doomed to perish" and "to be buried"? By the body, we mean desires from the moment of birth, because they have egoistical intentions. "Doomed to perish," means to be completely cut off from the light, become dead. The person considers his "desires with egoistic intentions" to be dead. He is neither able nor willing to use them, wants to bury them. After that, the desires go through corrections, i.e., the intention for one's own sake (which is the intention of the *Klipot*) is transformed into the intention for the sake of the Creator, for the sake of bestowal. This process is called a resurrection of the dead bodies.

The body (of desires) does not change. Only the intention does. The body itself is neutral. There is the egoistical intention "for one's own sake" or the screen that generates *Ohr Hozer* (Reflected light), the intention "for the sake of the Creator". The intention "for one's own sake" is called *Klipa*. The intention "for the sake of the Creator" is called *Kedusha*. We need to come to the point when the intention "for one's own sake" will be dead in us. If we achieve the intention "for the sake of the Creator", that will be the resurrection.

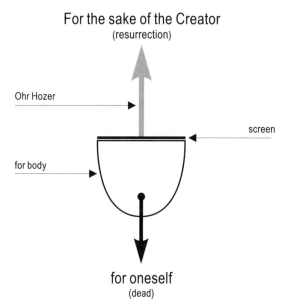

For the sake of the Creator
(resurrection)

Ohr Hozer

screen

for body

for oneself
(dead)

Let us look at what Baal HaSulam writes. While reading the text without commentaries, one may think of fairy tales about the resurrection of dead bodies that arise from the graves and wander around.

Why then does the body return and rise at the "resurrection of the dead"? Could the Creator not delight the souls without it?

Baal HaSulam's question concerns neither the body nor the soul, but rather the reason why we have to go through all these transformations. Why do we have to stay in *Klipot* until we consider them dead and bury them, until they are completely decomposed? We can use the body (desire) and start working on this desire "for the sake of the Creator" only after we free ourselves from the egoistical intention.

Let us suppose that I have a desire with initially egoistic intentions, everything for my own sake. This is my first state. My second state is when under the influence of the Higher Light that I draw upon myself by reading Kabbalistic texts, these desires begin to gradually leave me. I begin to feel my condition as evil and it slowly comes out of me. I sense that they (desires) are dying and reach the condition when I am completely free of them. On my next level, I begin to adopt the Creator's properties and aspire to Him. This is called resurrection of the body.

By "the body" we always mean the desire. It remains the same; nothing happens to it, only the intention changes. The body always consists of the same desires. I always have 620 desires in my body.

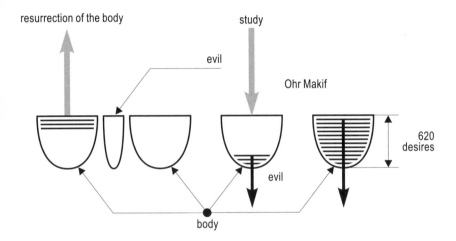

By and large, we can easily understand this. The question always arises about another matter. Why are we bound to receive bad intentions "for our own sake" to begin with? Why should we see them as bad, and then wish to be completely free of them and finally begin to acquire good intentions?

Baal HaSulam says:

Why then does the body return and rise at the "resurrection of the dead"? Could the Creator not delight the souls without it?

Why can we not receive good properties from the beginning and be one with the Creator at once? Why do we have to discover Him through bad properties?

Furthermore, the Zohar says that before the body rots entirely, the soul cannot ascend to its place in Heaven, while there are still remnants of it. That is until all intentions "for one's own sake" disappear; the soul will not be resurrected and merged with the Creator in the similarity of properties.

Even more bewildering is what our sages said of the dead bodies that are destined to rise with their flaws, so that they will not be mistaken for others.

Although we say that the bodies, desires, death, and resurrection refer to intentions, one still finds it extremely difficult to perceive it correctly.

There arises a question: Why should we go through it all? Mortification of our intentions seems clear enough. Transformation of the intention "for one's own sake" into the intention "for the sake of the Creator" is clear too. The problem is different: unless the bodies remain in their flaws, we will not be able to make them similar to the Creator.

The Creator will then cure their flaws. We ought to understand why it is important to Him that they will not be mistaken for other bodies...

Someone should know if the body is different or not; only after that will the Creator correct and revives it. When we reach the stage called "resurrection of the dead bodies" (our dead desires), we clearly understand that this is our body and nothing has changed in it except one thing: the realization that we rid ourselves from our past intentions and now we wish to obtain the intention for the sake of the Creator. As it is said, the Creator then cures their flaws.

We ought to understand why it is so important to the Creator that they will not be mistaken for other bodies that he would recreate their flaws and then cure them.

Besides the resurrection of the body, there should be a realization of flaws. When they are dead and we have none of them left in us, we should then retrieve them, have them manifest within us in order to give each of them up and correct it.

What does this process look like?

I initially have egoistical intentions, on which I perform a *Tzimtzum* (Restriction). I have no desire to be in any way connected with them. I get rid of them and remain empty. After the *Tzimtzum*, how can I correct them in me?

After I buried all of these dead intentions and they decomposed completely I now begin to resurrect them. I have gained strength and acquired a screen. While excavating each of my egoistical intentions from the ground I say: "Here is my true original property – the intention for my own sake. Now I will transform this intention "for my own sake" into the intention "for the sake of the Creator".

In other words, my egoistical intention comes back to life, and I correct it into a positive one, because I need to make a *Tzimtzum* on the way.

Previously all of my past intentions were 100% negative, so I eliminate them. I remain empty, i.e., I stop using any of my intentions, and let them "decay". I then resurrect them. In what form? I revive them in a negative form, although not the entire 100%. I correct just 1%, and gradually reach 100%.

1. **100%**   ⟶   realization of evil

2. **emptiness**   ⟶   TA + screen

3. **resurrection**   ⟶   from 1 to 100%

4. **correction**

1 – I come to the realization of evil;

2 – I remain empty, perform *Tzimtzum Aleph*.

The person must go through these stages. Resurrection of the dead should take place in him after he executed *Tzimtzum* and obtained the screen.

Let us read it again.

Fifth Inquiry refers to the "resurrection of the dead".
Since the body is so despicable, it is doomed to perish and to be buried.

This includes a complete realization of evil, of my primordial egoistical desires.

Why then does the body return and rise at the "resurrection of the dead" (after I buried it and it remained empty)? Could the Creator not delight the souls without it?

No, He cannot.

Furthermore, the Zohar says that before the body rots entirely (until all of my desires die and rot in the ground), *the soul cannot ascend to its place in Heaven, while there are still remnants of it* (I will not be able to fill myself with the light).

Even more bewildering is what our sages said of the dead bodies that are destined to rise with their flaws...

Why should I revive all of my negative desires? This seemingly returns me to my negative properties.

... so that they will not be mistaken for others. I should admit that all of them are my natural properties.

The Creator will then cure their flaws. I should realize that I would never be able to cure these flaws by myself. They can only be cured if I realize them as evil and ask the Creator for a remedy.

We ought to understand why it is so important to the Creator that they will not be mistaken for other bodies that he would recreate their flaws and then cure them (why should these desires be the same as before?).

We should comprehend the resurrection of the dead in this manner alone, and the way it should be realized.

Therefore, little by little we become accustomed to Baal HaSulam's writings and try to understand the flow of his thoughts. We just need to absorb all that we read. It does not matter how much of it we comprehend. We simply wish to be close to him. To the extent of our desire, the light will descend upon us from the level on which he explains it all.

Our will to be on that level is called "understanding", "attainment". While studying "The Introduction to the Study of the Ten *Sefirot*", we read the well-known paragraph 155. It says, "The *Ohr Makif* shines upon the person who wants to attain the higher level. Such an attainment can only be achieved if we ascend to it and become a part of that level".

When we speak about spiritual forms, objects, conditions, actions and states, let us try to be on that level, and not on the level of this world. Leave your "head" in this world. You should simply try to rise there with your desire. This effort will stimulate the emanation, the release of the Higher Light that will elevate us there. One must learn to work with the heart, not with the head.

Sixth Inquiry

Our sages said that man is the center of reality, that the Upper Worlds and this corporeal world and everything in them were not created but for him (The Zohar, Tazriya, 40).

Man is in the center of the universe.

[The Kabbalists] obliged man to believe that the world had been created for him (Sanhedrin, 37). It is seemingly hard to grasp, that for this small human...

By his material size, and by his power in this world, in this universe, man is utterly insignificant. Whatever level we take (vegetative, animal or human), he does not represent something special. In comparison with his poor nature, he is more selfish and evil. So what is his advantage?

Moreover, for what does he need this entire Universe?

Concerning man's value in comparison with the Universe, Baal HaSulam says:

> He who grasps no more than a wisp of this world's reality, much less of the Upper Worlds, whose height is immeasurable, the Creator troubled Himself to create all this for him. Yet why would man want all that?

Vast, endless galaxies and spiritual worlds: why is all of this necessary? If it is made for man, at some point he has to use it, manage it, and somehow establish contact with it. However, where is he on this Earth with its various cataclysms? Where is he in our small (compared to others) galaxy, in this entire infinite universe? If we take our entire universe, our world in comparison with Upper Worlds, it is a tiny disappearing particle in the Infinity.

In the upshot, man, the only intelligent, yet the worthless being in our universe, is the center of all worlds! He is destined to command them in the future. It depends on man in what condition they will be. The Kabbalists say that he is directly connected with them. Is he in this state now? For what does he need it? What does he gain from it?

Why was it created for man?

Why did the Creator make it so that the person cannot comprehend what he can gain if he rules over the entire universe and all the Upper Worlds? He feels no need of this to be happy. However, all of this is created for man. Only by using it will he achieve the ultimate state.

This is the last inquiry we have to make. If we complete this research, we will be able to answer the questions that Baal HaSulam raised at the beginning of this Introduction and understand why we need the Book of Zohar. This is only the Foreword to the book.

Afterwards, while reading the Book of Zohar, we will know what we should do with the help of the book in order to attain all of these states.

4. In order to understand these questions and inquiries, one should start by looking at the end, i.e.,, at the purpose of creation. For nothing can be understood in the middle of the process, but only at its end.

This is a necessary condition. If we want to understand something, we should be sure to know what is going to be at the end. Yet how can we know this? In our world, we do not know about any state beforehand. Could we possibly harm ourselves if we had known the outcome in advance? How could we do anything if we had not anticipated some benefit?

Our problem is that we never know the end in anything. The only thing we know in this small animate world is to give advice to our children: "do this, don't do that". However, they do not listen to us. In our life, we cannot see the end of the next level or its consequences. We normally act without listening to others, and our children do not listen to us, even though we know exactly the right answer. In addition, the entire humanity does the same.

How can we agree with this thought of Baal HaSulam: *in order to understand these questions and inquiries one should start by looking at the end of the action, i.e., at the purpose of creation.* The purpose is the result for the sake of which the creation was created.

For nothing can be understood in the middle of the process, but only at its end.

This is true. The Creator looks at us from "the end of creation", not from its beginning.

He conceives all of His with regard to us and draws us closer to Himself. That is a perfect approach. I am unable to do that in our world. If I only knew in advance the results of what I am doing now and could make corrections to improve it; if I could know the result and see that I should not wish it, there would be nothing better. Yet how can I achieve that?

"The Study of the Ten *Sefirot*" describes in the following way: our spiritual advancement depends on the condition called "*Olamcha Tireh be Hayecha*" (lit. You will see your world in your life time).

It is said: "will see," and not "will receive". Even on this level, the person can see the future world (his future state) from afar. When he does, he can justify his path, receive energy, understanding and strength to rise above his egoistical desires, to acquire "the desire to bestow" and to work on his correction.

"Foreseeing the purpose of creation" and planning your actions and steps from that level is a compulsory condition. Without it, we will never make any correct move and our spiritual life would be exactly the same as our life in this world. The spiritual life does not tolerate things like that.

Every time I find myself in an initial position, I am obliged to ascend to the next state "plus one", to the next level. I have no clue how to do this and I do not know what my condition is going to be pertaining to this level. I need to see it in advance (1), and after that decide upon my actions (2). Only then can I work on it (3). This is the only way to do things right.

If I commence to act without knowing my next state, it will always be fallacious, because from the level I am on now, with my intellect and knowledge, I cannot possibly know what is on the next level, because it is higher. In the initial position, everything that I have in me is opposite to this level because here I am a big egoist. There I am a big altruist, but I do not desire it at all.

Based upon the prerequisites, principles, and desires that I have in me I cannot imagine my future. It is so opposite to me that whatever I imagine as being there is unattainable. My nature would not allow me to do this. However, even if it did, I would not aspire to it. I would keep away from it.

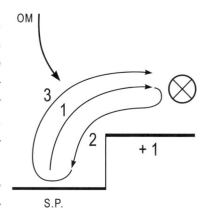

That is why I somehow need to see my next level. I need to understand and accept it inside of me. I should ask the Creator to help me from Above, to give me the *Ohr Makif*, so that in my third action I would move up to a higher level.

If I do not do that, I would advance in the spiritual world in the same way as in our world, making unsuccessful attempts all the time. Every next step of mine would be less successful then the previous one. Instead of ascending, I would go down more and more. Therefore, Baal HaSulam writes:

> One should start by looking at the end, i.e., at the purpose of creation. For nothing can be understood in the middle of the process, but only at its end. Moreover, it is clear that there is no act without purpose, for only the insane can be found to act purposelessly.

People always act with a purpose, so if I wish to ascend spiritually, this should become my purpose. I should acquire new strength, intellect, and properties, which I do not have. I cannot do this with my present properties.

I know that there are "know-alls" who scorn the method of Kabbalah (who believe that they know better ways), **saying the Creator created reality, but then left it to the mercy of fate;** *because of the worthlessness of the creatures, it is not fitting for the exalted Creator to watch over their petty* *little ways.* Had the Creator left me here, I would have never been able to rise to the next level. Why?

> *Indeed, without knowledge they have spoken, for it is not possible to comment on our nothingness and lowliness before we decide that we have created ourselves with all our tarnished natures. But while we decide that the Creator, who is perfect in every way, is the one who created and designed our bodies (our properties), with all their admirable and contemptible attributes, surely from under the hand of the perfect worker there cannot emerge an imperfect act, since each act testifies to its performer. What fault is it of a bad garment, if some no-good tailor made it?*

Of course, this is the tailor's fault. If we have some bad properties, it is clear to us that it is the Creator's fault. Here Baal HaSulam offers us a parable from the Talmud (*Ta'anit* 20).

> *This is a tale of Rabbi Elazar, the son of Rabbi Shimon, who came before a most ugly man...*

Rabbi Shimon wrote "The Book of Zohar". His son was one level higher than Rabbi Shimon was. Having reached the level of his father, he found an even uglier, lower level in himself. It was so ugly that he could not help saying (to himself): *"You are so ugly!"* The man replied, *"Go and tell the craftsman who made me – how ugly is this instrument you have made".*

If you have a grudge against some of your properties, turn to the Creator. He is the One who created them and He is the One who would correct them.

> *Hence, those who claim that because of our nothingness and lowliness, it is not fitting for Him to watch over us, and therefore He has left us, do nothing more than publicly display their ignorance. Try to imagine, if you had met some man who would create creatures precisely so that they would suffer and agonize their whole lives as we do. Not only that, but he cast them behind his back, not wanting*

even to look after them, to help them a little. How contemptible and low would you regard him? Can such a thing be thought of Him?

The paradox we see here remains a paradox so far.

5. Therefore, common sense... (Baal HaSulam tells us about it from the level he reached) *dictates that we grasp the opposite of what appears to be on the surface...*(what can be seen with the naked eye) *and decide that we are truly noble and worthy creatures...*

Indeed, we are so huge, so great, we can rule over our entire world and the spiritual worlds that are in absolute harmony with the Creator, in complete likeness with Him. We are truly in this state, but we feel just a tiny part of it that is called "this world". Indeed, we are now in a perfect, great state.

There is no end to our immeasurable importance; we are actually worthy of our Maker. For if you wish to find faults in our bodies, then behind all the excuses that you give yourself, it falls only on the Creator who created us and the nature within us. For it is clear that He created us.

He also knows all the ways that stem from our nature and the attributes He created in us. It is as we have said that we have to contemplate the end of the act. Then we will be able to understand it all. As the saying goes: "Do not show a fool an unfinished work".

Because of our lessons, you will see the answers to all the inquiries and questions and all that will be left for you to do is realize it all. I hope that it will be a result of our studying. What is necessary for that? I repeat, by no means should you consider Kabbalah as a usual science. Though Kabbalah is a science, it instructs you how to correct yourself and achieve eternity and perfection.

This is why the work of your mind is insufficient. You ought to desire your own changes with your heart and be on the level where Baal HaSulam is. He is teaching us now from that high level.

Question: I see my defects and try to correct them. I turn to the Creator, the only One who can correct them. I understand the method. The question is how can I speed up the process?

Everything you do is correct and, by the way, you actually do nothing. Why? It is because eventually, under the influence of suffering, and of contemplation, you would have found it necessary to turn to the Creator.

Our problem is in shortening time. In the chain that we should pass, we can only control time. All we can do is speed up the process with the help of a group. You need additional forces to turn to the Creator, so that the Creator would correct you more intensely.

This additional strength can come from your friends, who have the same purpose and agree to interact with you to join all forces to turn to the Creator. This is the only means available, and without it, you cannot accelerate your development.

In the end, the realization of all our actions comes to one thing: how to make our group more direct, more serious, and more intense. Strive to make your friends from the group like fighters who are always standing for our idea, for the Goal. You will then see how many states you go through in one day and you will have enough strength to do that. In just a few weeks, you will not recognize yourself. You will reach much higher levels!

It depends on all groups and on each separate group. Every group will get as much as it puts into the whole process.

Question: Can I see the next step?

I can see it, but only in a way that seeing it would not affect me negatively and I would not wish it selfishly, for myself. How can I adopt the next spiritual level in order to receive strength from it, to have the method of correction so that it will not obstruct my personal ascent? I want it to remain in me, as my own properties, as if I create this next level within myself. After all, I need to become similar to the Creator. This similarity means creating me on the next level, giving birth to myself.

To this end, I need to get the material for my birth from the next level. It means desires and strength to turn them into properties of bestowal. I am still very small, but I acquire my spiritual form. I can only obtain this from the *AHP* of the higher level. Hence, we perceive the *AHP* of the higher level in different variations; now luminous, now devoid of the light. We should stick to it, because it is our Creator. This is how we see Him. We should constantly cling to Him like a leech regardless of how bad or good, repulsive or attractive He may seem in our feelings; we simply must hold on to Him all the time.

A group can play a very important role in this. It always reminds me of what I need to do. I need a group alarm clock. This is not the kind of an alarm clock you carry on your wrist and fail to pay attention to. If your group were constantly thinking about it, you would always remember the goal and aspire to it. This way you would hold on to the *AHP* of the higher level so fast that it will pull you in against your will.

There is no other alternative. Our main task is to overcome this first level, because reaching it means crossing the *Machsom*. Afterwards, we already begin to feel the Creator. This is a very different kind of work.

Only group work can help, when all its members constantly strive to stay on this higher level. It does not matter how we imagine it. We should be obsessed with the Creator; only this will lead us to the Goal.

Question: Why did the perfect Creator have to create something? Was it perhaps in order to achieve even greater perfection?

He did it to bestow.

Question: How can we see our future state? Without seeing, there is no ascent, yet we cannot see!

We should accept it without seeing, because it comes from the Creator, not because we see and like it. In other words, we should accept it in our vessels of bestowal, in the intention "for the sake of the Creator", because He desires it. We need to ask for strength to accept it without seeing.

Question: My next level is opposite to me. Does it mean that what I can "see in this life" happens to be just a tiny part of the level closest to my properties? Otherwise, it will repel me and not attract me.

This is precisely why the revelation of the *AHP* of the higher level is defined as a spiritual downfall. If the person realizes that, he immediately finds strength to master this *AHP*.

> 6. *Our sages said: "The Creator created the world for no other reason, but to bestow delight upon His creatures (i.e., the sages, who attain the Creator, know His thoughts). Here is where we must place our mind and heart, for it is the final aim of the act of the creation of the world.*

Baal HaSulam says that one sentence *"The Creator created the world to bestow delight upon His creatures"* contains the thought, the act, and the end of the creation. Apparently, that is why he suggests that we should reflect on this phrase. What he actually means is that at the beginning, in the middle and at the end of all the actions that take place in the world, however noble or mean they may seem, on all their levels and in all their combinations, they pursue only one goal: to bestow delight upon the creatures. There is no other motive in any of the Creator's actions.

> *In addition, we must bear in mind that, since the thought of creation is to bestow to His creatures, He had to create in the souls a great amount of desire to receive that which He had thought to give. For the measure of any delight depends on the measure of the will to receive it. The greater is the will to receive, the greater the pleasure, and the lesser the will, the lesser the pleasure from reception.*

We know it from our own experience in this world. I may sit at a table beautifully laid with most exquisite delicacies, but I can enjoy it only to the extent of my desire. Therefore, we say that the Creator's light fills the entire creation. We are inside this ocean of light, and we shall feel it only in our desire for this light, for its property, for the delight of bestowal.

It is quite natural that if we do not feel anything now, it means that we have no desire whatsoever for this light of bestowal. Nevertheless, the Creator preinstalled in us an enormous desire to receive delight perfectly matched to His desire to bestow.

> *Therefore, the thought of creation itself dictates the presence of an excessive will to receive in the souls, to fit the immense pleasure that the Creator thought to bestow upon them. For the great delight and the great desire to receive must go hand in hand.*

> *7. Once we have learned that, we have come to understand the second inquiry to its fullness, and with complete clarity. For we have learned what is the reality that one can base clear decisions on, that is not a part of His essence, but constitutes a new creation. Now that we know for sure that the thought of creation is to bestow to His creatures, He necessarily created a measure of desire to receive from Him the bounty and delight that he had planned for them. Thus, we see that the will to receive certainly was not a part of His essence before He had created it in the souls, because He can receive from no one. He created a novelty that is absent in Him.*

> *Along with that, we understand, according to the thought of creation, that there was no need to create anything more than the will to receive. For this new creation is sufficient for Him to fulfill the entire plan – to bestow delight upon someone (if this someone exists as a will to receive pleasure). Since the Creator's desire is to bestow delight, He is in need of a will to receive delight. We happen to represent this will.*

However, all the filling in the thought of creation, meaning all the benefits He had planned to render us, stem directly from His essence. They are emanated from His very first thought – to create beings and bestow delight upon them.

He has no need to recreate them, since they are already extracted from the great will to receive that is in the souls. Thus, we clearly see that the whole matter of the renewed creation, from start to end, is only the "will to receive".

This is all we can imagine, except the perceived pleasure, i.e., the Creator Himself. Consequently, whatever or whomever we may speak about, on any levels of development (still, vegetative, animal and human nature), whether fields, bodies, emanations, spirits, or anything that exists in our world and in all the others (from tiny insects to vast galaxies), be it information, force, plasmic or other forms of creation – they are all created and constitute no more than a desire to receive pleasure.

There is nothing like it in the Creator; He made it out of nothing, sustains and fills all. Our life is but the Creator's microscopic filling. We are filled with one billionth of His light and we call it our life.

If we perceive Him clearer, we will feel Him, not what He emanates. We will then define ourselves as being in the spiritual world. That is, all that happens in us is a result of our sensation of the Creator. We should never forget about it, because our life, thoughts and everything good or bad in our hearts and minds is no more than the sensation of the Creator.

Therefore, if we wish to change our state, we just need to change our connection with Him, reach a different level of contact with Him.

8. After the previously mentioned, we have come to understand the third inquiry. We wondered how it was possible to say about souls that they were a part of the Creator, like a stone that is carved from a rock. There is no difference between them except that one is a 'part' and the other is a 'whole'. It seemed strange: it is one thing to say that the stone that is carved from the rock becomes separated by an axe made for that purpose, but can you say that about the Creator's essence? In addition, with what were the souls divided from His essence and excluded from the Creator to become creatures? From the above we clearly understand that, just as an axe cuts and divides a physical object in two, so the spiritual change of form divides it in two.

If a certain property of mine begins to change with regard to another property, this transformed attribute instantly (to the extent of the inconsistency between the two properties) begins to move away from the original one and may even become opposite to it. This is how the souls are separated from the Creator.

That is, the Creator originally created a desire, filled it with Himself, whereupon it started moving farther and farther away from Him, until it became completely opposite to Him.

For example, when two people love each other, we say that they merge with each other as one body. When they hate each other, we say that they are as far from one another as the east is from the west. However, it is not a question of near or far in this case.

We define people in our world as close or distant to one another by the proximity between their bodies. On the other hand, we may speak about affinity or estrangement between the souls.

Here the matter concerns the equivalence of properties, when each loves what the other loves and hates what the other hates (i.e., if they refer to all of their qualities in the same way), they become lovers (similar in their properties) and merge with one another. If there is some change of form between them, meaning that one of them likes something that the other hates, then to the extent that they differ in form, they become distant and hateful to one another. And if, for example, they are opposite in form, meaning that everything one likes is hated by the other, and everything he hates is liked by the other, they are deemed as far away from each other as the east is from the west, meaning from one end to the other.

There is not a single common property that would connect them. No contact is possible unless these properties partially coincide. Sometimes people quarrel, then they make up. This way they test the contact between them, share various properties, both similar and dissimilar.

If they are opposite, there is not even the slightest chance for a contact. Such is our initial contrast with the Creator today.

The revelation of the Creator within us is the purpose of our studies.

9. Thus, in spirituality, the dissimilarity of properties acts as an axe in our world, dividing the material. The degree of divergence is determined by the measure of dissimilarity of properties.

I need not pay attention to anything else - neither to my parameters, nor to the parameters of the Creator, nor to any additional conditions. I should think only of one thing: "How can I more closely resemble Him? To that extent I shall discover Him and I shall feel His filling in me. In that measure I shall receive the sensation of pleasure, light, life, eternity, and perfection".

And from here we will understand that, since the [egoistical] desire to receive pleasure is inherent to souls, and as it is already discovered by us that this property is not completely present in the Creator, we can conclude that precisely this dissimilarity of properties (egoistical desire to receive pleasure), which the souls acquired - acts as an axe, separating them from the Creator. Therefore, it is through this difference of properties that the soul separated from the Creator and became to be known as "created".

Until the soul feels its complete separation from the Creator, it is impossible to speak of the existence of creation. At that point, it is still simply the desire to take pleasure, which has not left the Creator and was not separated from Him to become something existing quite independently. Therefore, looking at the world around us, at the 7 billion "homo sapiens ", we cannot say that these are creations (and even more so, we can neither say that about the inanimate, vegetative, and animal levels, because they do not have a sensation of contrast to the Creator).

At present, we also lack this property, this analysis. The first thing we must accomplish is this so-called "comprehension of evil" (*Akarat HaRah*), as it is the comprehension of the polar inverse to the Creator. This is where the creation begins. As soon as we reach it in all our primordial properties, we shall feel, together with the property, how opposite it is to the Creator. Then this property is discerned as independent, completely remote, cut off, chopped off from Him with this axe (this change from the Creator). It therefore already considers itself the creation.

However, everything that souls attain from the light of the Creator is received from the essence of the Creator, from what is existing. In the light of the Creator that is received in the Kli (the soul, the will to receive), there is no difference from the Creator's essence. In fact, it comes directly from the Creator as from something existent. The entire distinction between the souls and the Creator's essence is no more than that the souls are just a part of the essence of the Creator. That measure of light received inside of the desire to take pleasure, (that part which was torn off from the Creator since I am not completely similar to Him), separates from the Creator by a dissimilarity of properties, takes the form of being separated from the whole, and is referred to as a soul. In fact there is no difference between them except that one is the whole, while the other being its part, is as a stone chiseled from a rock.

Ponder upon the depth of the above-mentioned, since it is impossible to explain further this exalted matter.

Nonetheless, we shall try to add a few words regarding the matter.

The most harmless perception about creation is to perceive ourselves existing in the most perfect final state, because that is the only thing created by the Creator, the only one in which we exist. It is only for us that the perception is the final state, as though there were an initial state and an intermediate state. Actually, it is the only existing condition. That is, when the Creator conceived to create creations, His idea instantly became action.

The fact that we are inside of the Creator, completely filled with the light of Infinity, is a concealment. Actually, this is our natural, unique, and true condition. If this is how we perceive it, then another relationship becomes clear - how to discover the measure of connection between us. I am in a static condition completely filled with the Creator, and what separates me from the Creator (prevents the feeling of closeness to the Creator) is my egoism, my internal desire, which is opposite to His desire. Only to the degree in which I can change my internal desire, my direction, will I at once start to feel the Creator, to feel myself as filled with another kind and measure of life.

The small measure of the sensation of the Creator which is in us, named "*Ner Dakik*" ("*Ner*" - "candle", "*Dakik*" - from a word "*Dak*" - very thin, minute part), is a portion of light that enables us to exist in the biological, animal state we are in.

If we can change a measure of light in us, we cardinally change our life - it takes life to the next level, and the greater measure of light in us, the higher the level. The only thing we should do is to let the light that is in us do its work, open ourselves and let it shine in us. We can facilitate this process only from our attitude to the Creator, from our likening to Him. Therefore, ascending spiritual levels is no mechanical movement. Rather it is an inner increased likening to the light, a sensation of a full, perfect, and eternal life.

One should not merely receive that small particle of light that only supports the animal condition of existence. Rather, we should receive the large portion of light that would sustain one in a condition of life above the biological body; that is the challenge to us.

The following step, the next portion of the light that we receive, will already be spiritual light, and it will already take us on a level of spiritual existence. That is what one should imagine clearly today.

> 10. Now the opportunity presents itself to understand the fourth inquiry. How is it possible that the system of impure forces and Klipot come from the purity of the Creator? Since in fact it is extremely distant from His purity, how is it possible that the Creator would fill and sustain it?

Moreover, we can imagine the worlds from top down, AK (the world of Infinity), then *Atzilut, Beria, Yetzira, Assiya* (the pure worlds) and *Beria, Yetzira, Assiya* (*Klipot*). The *Parsa* is under the world of *Atzilut*, and our world is under the *Klipot*. That which enters from *Malchut* of the world of *Atzilut* through all the worlds and comes to the impure worlds, refers to *Ner Dakik* (a small candle, a small luminescence). When the *Ner Dakik* descends to the *Machsom* and reaches us, we receive what is referred to as "our life".

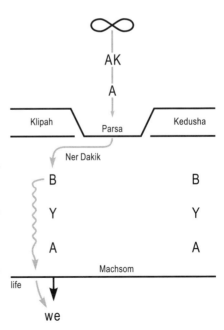

125

That is, all that fills, supports, revives and pulls us forward in our world, we receive through the system of impure forces.

Baal HaSulam asks, "How can it be that a property at such a spiritual level as the Creator's - complete bestowal - creates impure desires, including us, who are the lowest, and the most insignificant of them? Not only are they created by Him, but He also fills them, albeit with small light. Furthermore, He constantly sustains them and maintains contact".

Let us clarify the question; How can it be that the Creator acts this way? This question arises from the point of view of our previous definition. If we say that in the spiritual world such categories as merging, separation, rapprochement, and remoteness occur to the extent of the similarity of properties, it means there is no connection between the Creator and this system, since the system of impure forces is absolutely antithetical to the Creator. So how could He have created it?

Suppose there was a non-recurring act of birth. However, there is no such concept in the spiritual, since everything exists there permanently, (i.e., born, filled, and sustained permanently). This is unlike our world where there is an event of creation after which the body exists and subsequently dies. It exists and dies precisely because the act of creation has ended. In the spiritual world, it is different. Everything that occurs there is constantly sustained, and therefore eternal. All actions exist constantly at all levels.

Therefore, if the Creator has created impure forces, sustains and supports them, this would contradict the previous conclusion. How is one to reconcile this?

First, it is necessary to understand the essence of the system of impure forces and Klipot. Know that the huge desire to receive that we spoke about is the essence of the created souls. This desire is ready to receive all the fulfillment that is in the plan of creation; and, it does not remain in the souls in the same form, for if it remained in them permanently (in a form which is antithetical to the Creator) the souls would be forever separated from the Creator. This difference of properties would forever cut them off from the Creator.

To correct this initial remoteness from the Creator, He has created the worlds and has divided them into two systems: the four pure worlds of ABYA and the four impure worlds of ABYA.

Moreover, He has positioned the soul between them.

In our ascent, we constantly choose the middle line - the overlapping of pure and impure forces. The soul ascends to the Creator precisely on this middle line.

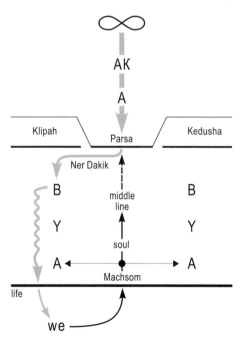

Having created the system of impure and pure forces, this initial huge, impure egoism opposite to Himself, He also creates a system with which we can transform this egoism - having retained all the same desires and only having corrected their intention. Therefore, it turns out that, while ascending the middle ladder from one level to another between the two systems of pure and impure forces (egostical and altruistic), we choose how to act.

We take from the egoistical system, from our essence, whatever we can, to adapt all our desires to the Creator and to ascend.

Let us consider a simple example.

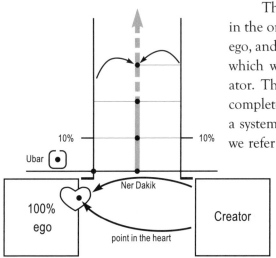

There are two systems: "I" in the original form - an absolute ego, and a system opposite to me, which we agree to call the Creator. They are opposite and are completely divided. Between us is a system of communication that we refer to as the system of pure and impure forces.

What does it give me? To exist, I receive from Him only a small portion of the light, the *Ner Dakik*. Besides, I receive from it a so-called point in the heart. By receiving *Ner Dakik*, I revive my heart.

Having received a point in the heart, after a number of efforts, I arrive at a certain baseline level. On this zero level called "*Ubar*" (embryo), one can compare himself to all the properties of the Creator only as a tiny point. It is in the middle of these properties, and it signifies that everything that I can attach to the Creator's attributes is no bigger than a point.

If I can take 10 % of my desires and assimilate them accordingly to 10 % of the Creator's desires, then the midpoint between them will be my next level. And so on. That is, I always ascend along the middle line, where I compare my egoism with the properties of the Creator, until I completely work through 100 % of my desires. Only then do I achieve 100 % likeness to the Creator.

It transpires that the system of pure and impure forces has neither bad nor good in it. It only exists relative to the observer who needs these graduated levels of his own comparisons, associations, unions (exact terminology is unimportant) with the Creator. Such an internal system exists in me for this sole purpose. These worlds do not exist outside; they are the essence of my internal structure.

With the help of such levels – these thresholds of sensitivity – one feels either more remote from the Creator or closer to Him. One cannot sense a half or a quarter of any level. Internally one is graduated in such a way that one feels only certain threshold changes in sensations, and they are referred to as steps of the worlds. Naturally, these are inside the person, for nothing exists outside. In general, we do not know what exists outside; hence, it will never exist for us. We address only that which is present inside us. This is what we feel; it is our world, our life.

Therefore, Baal HaSulam says that the Creator has created egoistical desire to receive ...and He has given over to the system of pure worlds His property to impart, and has withdrawn from them the desire to receive for the sake of oneself, and has given it over to the system of impure worlds. As a result, this system became completely separated from the Creator and from everything pure.

The Klipot are, therefore, referred to as dead and so are sinners (we, who are under them), because our desire to receive, which is opposite to the Creator, does not allow the light of a life, the light of pleasure, to manifest itself in us (therefore we only experience a small portion of this light's influence upon us, namely our animal life). In addition, we are extremely remote from the Creator, as there is no trace of a desire to receive in Him, only the property of bestowal. However, in the Klipot (and in us), there naturally is no concept of bestowal; there is only a desire to receive, the desire for selfish gratification.

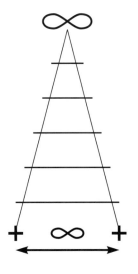

Our spiritual separation from the Creator begins with a small dif-ference of properties with the above and ends up as a complete op-position.

We emerge in the spiritual worlds and then gradually diverge. At the level of our world, we are completely and indefinitely opposite to the Creator. By bridging the chasm between the Creator and the creation, we reach the Higher Infinity, boundless sensation of the Creator.

11. The worlds descended to the level of this world's reality, i.e., to the place where the body and the soul exist. This is the time of being uncorrected and the time of correction. The body is a will to receive, which stems from its root in the thought of creation. While passing through the system of impure worlds, it remains under the influence of this system until its correction begins.

As you know, in Kabbalah the body the body of the *Partzuf* means a will to receive pleasure. As a rule, the Kabbalist will interpret the body as the *Kli* and the soul as the light.

Quite often, both the light and the *Kli* are implied by the word "soul", or sometimes the word "soul" is offhandedly used as the *Kli* without the light. However, normally, while studying our higher spiritual states above the level of this world, we should never think about our biological body, because it is in no way connected with our soul.

All of our properties and desires, all that we can use to influence our soul and our spiritual advancement have nothing to do with our body. The powers we wish to develop in ourselves are not biological; they are spiritual. We must receive them from Above, for only then will we be able to help our soul to ascend to the Creator. We cannot influence the state of the soul by our animal properties.

Therefore, man's properties are quite irrelevant. He may be healthy or sick, intelligent or mentally retarded, or he may possess any character traits. This does not matter at all. Nothing of what refers to our physical body, nothing we may characterize in man as his human property concerns the spiritual. It neither affects our inner egoistical desire, which is opposite to the Creator, nor the revelation of the light in us.

In order to expose my soul, my inner part that is yet non-existent in me, to such an influence, I need to acquire new *Kelim* that would help my soul to grow and enable me to reveal the Creator in it.

The instrument for the development of my soul is called a screen. I should receive it from Above. I cannot achieve the goal with the animal properties I possess today.

The comprehension that I cannot use the instruments at my disposal, i.e., my mind, will power, even my great desire and total inability to change spiritually, are referred to as the realization of evil, awareness of the insignificance of my own nature. It is not evil in itself; I consider it faulty because it prevents me from discovering the Creator and merging with Him.

In fact, it cannot be regarded as evil; "the realization of evil" is merely a definition. When I reach this state, I really discover a miracle. I see that there is Someone I can turn to, that I can receive the Creator's power – the light, which corrects me by endowing me with a screen.

On the one hand, the sensation of my own insignificance is called "the realization of evil", on the other hand, it leads to the reception of a screen from Above.

Here is another definition demonstrating the absence of evil. The Kabbalists call us sinners because we exist under the system of impure forces. Actually, we are not sinners at all. How can we possibly sin, if we are absolutely unaware of it? In other words, this name is used in a purely figurative sense.

The worlds descended to the level of this world's reality, to the place where the body and the soul exist (the Kli constitutes the impure, egoistic desires, the body and the soul are some essence, a tiny particle of the light, a point in the heart, the nucleus of the soul). *This is the time of being uncorrected and the time of correction* (in our world we perceive the levels of correction as a temporal factor).

Because the body, which is the egoistical will to receive, is extended from its root in the thought of creation (from the Creator – Yesh mi Ayn, something from nothing), *through the system of impure worlds, and it remains under the influence of that system for the first thirteen years, which is the time of corruption.*

What does it mean "the time when a person remains under the influence of the system of impure forces"? This refers to thousands and thousands of years, when we pass through certain unconscious corrections in our consecutive incarnations.

From 13 years of age and on... That is, when the desire for the spiritual ascent begins to manifest in man *through commandments*, i.e., with the help of correction of his desires. We have 620 desires within ourselves. Of course, we do not understand them at this time. Where are these desires? Perhaps we can count 10 or 20 desires, but certainly not 620. Later on, we will discover that the correction of each desire from the intention for one's own sake to the intention for the sake of the Creator is called fulfillment of the Creator's commandment.

If man observes it, he begins to purify his will to receive, and slowly turns it into the desire to receive delight for the Creator's sake. Thus, the upper soul descends from its root in the thought of creation, passes through the system of pure worlds, and "dresses" in his soul.

What does it mean? *Thus the upper soul* (i.e., the true spiritual light) *from its root in the thought of creation passes through the system of pure worlds* (begins to manifest in us through the system of our gradual corrections). By correcting ourselves, we build our pure *Kli*. The light that will be revealed in it already fills it, but we cannot feel it yet.

This is described by the words: *It passes through the system of pure worlds and "dresses" in his soul. This is called the time of correction.*

There is a preliminary period called the uncorrected state that lasts until the person receives the point in his heart. It starts pushing him towards the spiritual. From this time on the period of correction begins.

Thus, man ascends and attains the levels of the thought of creation in the Creator's Infinity, until he can turn his desire to receive for himself into the desire to receive for the sake of the Creator.

Man gradually receives new portions of the correcting light. With the help of this light, he gradually reveals his soul and the degree of its similarity to the Creator determines the extent of this revelation. In other words, as much as he can create the screen within himself, so can he reveal his soul, his *Kli*. Man feels the light inside of this *Kli*. This is what Kabbalah defines as man's degrees of similarity to the Creator, the levels of his spiritual ascent.

These levels help one another: the lower one helps the higher one, and the higher one helps to reveal one's soul completely with the emerging of the Upper Light in it.

Man's properties become equivalent to the Creator's, since reception for the sake of giving is a "pure" form, a bestowal.

What is a revelation of the *Kli* and the light that fills it? If I wish to reveal and feel this light not for my own enjoyment, but to please the One Who filled me (when I see what delight my revelations bring to Him), then my attainment will be considered bestowal and will take place.

Man achieves complete merging with the Creator... Where does he achieve it? Inside of what he reveals. There he discovers himself, his *Kli*, his intention and the Creator who fills him. He no longer needs to look at the Creator and reveal the *Kli* - now he sees both himself and the Creator within this common thought.

Man achieves complete merging with the Creator, because the spiritual merging is nothing but equivalence of properties. Our sages asked, "How can one merge with the Creator?" – and answered their own question: "By merging with His properties".

In other words, it can be expressed this way: "I will know You from my similarity to You". That is, if I gradually reveal the Creator in accordance with my growing similarity to Him, then I will finally become exactly like Him. It turns out that the Creator's revelation, similarity to Him, correction of the *Kli*, and reception of His light are the same action.

Because of this, man discovers that there is no division between him, the action he performs and the Creator. All of this is a single, undivided whole (as if a vessel is one thing, the light filling it is another, the reaction of the vessel to the light, and that of the light to the vessel is the third). Nothing like that exists. One suddenly realizes that all of this is a single whole, indistinguishable in any way. This condition is called merging with the Creator.

12. Thus, we have clearly explained the correction of the will to receive that is imprinted in the souls by the thought of creation (imprinted in the egoistic desire to receive, which is initially inherent in us). *The Creator has prepared for them two systems of worlds, one against the other, through which the souls pass and divide into two aspects, body and soul, and dress one in the other. With the help of the Kabbalistic method* (that includes a gradual correction of one's desires), *defined as "observing commandments", they convert the property of "reception for himself" into the property of "bestowal".*

They become blessed with all the pleasures in the thought of creation. And along with it (with the sensation of this blessing) *they completely merge with Him.*

That is, a person neither receives the Creator's bounty nor gives Him anything, but reaches the level of the Creator, rises up to the essence - up to the Creator. The result is a paradox, but that is what happens.

"By Your actions I will know You". I receive an example (of how I should act) from Him, the screen (what to operate with), a desire and strength. By following His example, I perform the same actions that He does. This way I build the middle line: from the left side I take my egoistical desires, from the right side - His light and the screen. As much as I can make one similar to the other, I build this combination and create my middle line from it; I perform my own action.

Finally, it leads to a surprising consequence: I do not liken myself to the Creator in action, but by making my actions similar to His, I begin to understand His intention, His thoughts, and the so-called secrets of the Torah. This is called: "By Your actions I will know You". As a result, we discover that the Creator's thought is not just to fill man with some pleasure, and it does not matter that the pleasure is infinite, eternal, and perfect.

The Creator's goal is to elevate man to His Own level, higher than the initial point of his creation. As a result of becoming similar to the Creator, man ascends above the point of his birth. He rises to the higher level and reaches the Creator's thought that had existed even before He created the desire to receive pleasure from nothing.

This is the End of Correction. Since there is no longer a need for the system of impure forces, it shall be eliminated from the earth and death shall cease forever.

These allegorical expressions can seriously spoil our picture, but if we interpret them correctly and immediately apply them, then they only strengthen our knowledge and enrich this internal image.

The word "ground" alludes to the egoistical desire to receive pleasure, since it takes in, imbibes, absorbs, and decomposes all that enters into it. On the other hand, if the ground (the property of reception) is combined with water (*Bina* – the property of bestowal), and a grain is planted into it, these two properties can create the condition for the emergence of a new life.

Later we will be studying all these spiritual roots and why our world is built this way because of it.

The system of impure forces shall be eliminated from the earth (i.e., the intention for one's own sake will disappear from the egoistical desire) *and death shall cease forever* ("death" means the gap between the light and the desire to receive pleasure; and as soon as the light enters the desire to receive, it gains life).

And all the work in the Torah and commandments (i.e., drawing the light, Torah comes from the word "Ohr", "Ohra'a" – "the light"; a "commandment" means the correction of an egoistical desire) *is given to the world during 6000 years of its existence...*

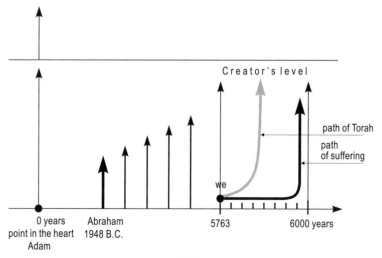

It is 5764 now (according to the Jewish calendar), i.e., a few hundred years from "the end of the world's existence" according to this chronology. In the future, we will clarify what "the End of the world's existence" means.

Let us consider into what periods these 6000 years are divided. Let us follow the development of the two axes – the spiritual and ours.

Adam is the first person who has discovered the point in his heart. What we mean is not the spiritual Adam, but a human being in this world. In about 1948 B.C. Abraham appeared. This is the period when the point in the heart did not merely appear inside a human being; it awakened and began to lead him to the Creator. Until this time, human beings existed like animals, without any aspiration to the Creator.

For the first time, the point in man's heart manifested in Abraham. He strongly desired to merge with the Creator and revealed Him. Now the year is 5764.

During the period of 6000 years, all of humankind is obliged to reach the level of the Creator. Even before Abraham, there were some actions taken in this direction, but at that time, only the preliminary method existed. After Abraham, thousands of people have done it.

Today we can do it to enable all humankind to accomplish it quickly and without suffering, by way of Kabbalah, i.e., by way of the light. If we do not help humankind quickly to pass through the period of realization of evil and to aspire to the Creator, humanity will advance by way of suffering.

Baal HaSulam writes, "These few hundred years may be very critical. They might bring terrible destructions, nuclear wars and immense calamities as a result of which only a small number of people will remain on the Earth. But they will execute the program of the creation; they will include all the other souls."

We can help the rest of the people to accelerate this process, to pass through this period painlessly and comfortably.

And all the work in the Torah and commandments that are given to the world during 6000 years of its existence and to each person for the duration of his seventy years of life, are only in order to bring them to the end of correction, to the equivalence of form and merging with the Creator.

So we have clarified how the system of impure forces and the Klipot (shells) emerged from the Creator's purity and exists at His expense. It was bound to happen for the creation of bodies (i.e., egoistical desires) that will later be corrected by the light (the Torah) and with the help of the screen (observing the commandments).

Unless our bodies had been created with the uncorrected (egoistical) desires by the system of the Klipot, we would have had no opportunity to correct them (i.e., man would never have been able to realize his own "I" and reach the Creator's level by himself).

Instead, it would be the same solitary point existing in this infinite light, not as an independent being, but as a desire made by the Creator that does not exist by itself.

Question: Is there any practical method for strengthening the contact with the Creator? Is it possible to merge with Him during this life?

Kabbalah is a practical method of increasing contact with the Creator called a revelation. While existing in our world as we are, a chance just to hear about this idea, this method, already enables us to implement it in this life, i.e., to merge completely with the Creator. We can reveal the entire reality in such a way that we will stop feeling any transition between life and death of our biological body. We can now ascend to the world of Infinity and exist on its highest level.

This is not only the question of increasing our contact with the Creator; we are talking about becoming similar, equal to Him.

We have all the prerequisites for it. Unlike previous generations of Kabbalists, we do not have to wait for ten years. We can do it in ten months. It only depends on our unity and common aspiration. Let us join our forces!

We continue studying item 13 of "The Introduction to the Book of Zohar". Baal HaSulam wrote several introductions to the Zohar: "The Introduction to the Zohar", "The Foreword to the Zohar" and "The Introduction to the Commentary on the Zohar".

"The Foreword to the Zohar" is the most profound and summarizing of all. It touches upon the general system of creation, penetrates its depths. "The Introduction to the Commentary on the Zohar" describes the mechanics of the spiritual ascent. "The Introduction to the Zohar" expounds the peculiarities of the book and explains how it should be approached

Let us have a closer look at the most important of these introductions in order better to understand the scope and power of the universe. We also need it to prepare ourselves for the actual reading of the Zohar.

> 13. *However, we must still understand: if the will to receive* (i.e., egoism, a desire to receive for its own sake) *is so bad and corrupt, how could it be planned and stem from the Thought of Creation in the Infinity and Perfection of the Creator Himself, whose wholeness is unspeakable?*

That is, how can there be a root to all that happens to us and in us within the Creator, the root of the imperfection we are in?

The thing is that when the thought of creation had only just begun, everything had also ended. This is because unlike us, the Kli needs no actions. All the souls and their future states immediately emerged in their completeness and utter perfection (in their final, best, ultimate state). *They appeared exactly as the*

INTRODUCTION TO THE BOOK OF ZOHAR

Creator had conceived them. Only at the end of correction will the souls achieve this exalted state (from the Creator's perspective it already exists. He is already merged with us in the final, perfect state). *After our will to receive is completely corrected and becomes "pure" bestowal* (with the intention for the sake of the Creator), *it* (the will to receive) *attains complete equivalence of properties with the Creator.*

With regard to the Creator, we have existed in this final state from the moment of our conception. He sees us in this perfect state and appeals to us from it. If we consider those, we will better comprehend His attitude to the creation, to us. We will also know how we should appeal to Him.

The Creator's attitude to us can be compared to the way a mother treats her child. While knowing that her child can be in various states, her love for it is complete. On the other hand, the child is bound to experience the "developmental diseases" and finally achieve complete equivalence of form and correction.

Why does creation go through this transformation with regard to the Creator?

Because the past, present, and future exist as a single whole in the Creator's infinity.

Time does not exist relative to the Creator, because there is no difference between an action and its consequence. They all unite into one.

The same applies to people. While entering the Upper World, a human thought becomes an act, and time contracts to the point of non-existence. As man ascends the spiritual levels, time begins to disappear. In the realm of his sensations, where man is equal with the Creator, he exists beyond time.

By making his properties similar to the Creator, the person begins to feel that his desires, actions, and his ultimate state are the same. There is no chain of cause and effect. It exists only where something needs to be corrected. Where it is already corrected it ceases to exist, time stops and everything freezes in a state of perfection.

Hence, there was no corrupt will to receive (regarding the Creator) *separated from His Infinity, and vice-versa, the equivalence of attributes that is destined to appear at the end of correction appeared immediately in His eternity* (with the thought of creation).

This is what our sages meant when they said, "even before the world was created (the Hebrew word "Olam" (world), comes from the word "Ha'alama" (concealment). This word refers to a descent from the level of infinite perfection), *He and His Name* (the Creator, His Light and all the creatures) *exist in the "only perfect state", because there was no separation of the will to receive in the souls, but rather they were merged with the Creator in their attributes* (they were completely identical). *That state is described in the words "He and His Name are One."*

"He" designates the Creator; "His Name" means a vessel (*Kli*), the creatures that were created in their perfect, eternal, final state.

When we speak of imperfections, impure forces, suffering and the various states we are to go through from the Thought of creation to its end (from the first state, through the second and into the third one), we should understand that the transition from the first to the third state exists only for us. For the Creator they all merge into one. To the extent of our correction, the corrected part also merges with this one perfect and infinite state.

14. From here stem the three states of the souls:

The first state is in the world of Infinity, in the Thought of creation, where the souls already have the future form of the end of correction.

The second state is called the period of 6,000 years. With the help of two systems (the pure, altruistic system and the egoistical, impure system), *the souls divide into body and soul* (meaning the light called "soul" (*Neshama*) and the body (*Guf*) known as a vessel (*Kli*), which is an egoistical uncorrected desire). *We were then given the work in the Torah and Commandments in order to turn the will to receive into the will to bestow.* (This work is performed through corrective actions under the influence of the Upper Light; by drawing the Light upon ourselves, we turn the egoistical intention of our desires into to the altruistic ones).

We do not change the desires themselves. They were created in us. Only the intention to use them selfishly is considered the "will to receive." The intent to use them for the Creator is called the "will to bestow."

Hence, we exist between the pure and impure systems of forces. We can receive forces for correction from the right side, while the left side constantly adds corrupt desires. Thus, we attain our correction.

The corrupt desires that come from the left side, from the impure forces (*Klipot*), are not completely alien to me. Those are my own corrupt desires that are always at my left side, while the lights that correlate to them and correct them are on my right. I ought to take the next desire that corresponds in size to my ability to correct from my left. I then take from the right the appropriate Light to correct that desire (i.e., its egoistical intention). Thus, I create within myself a corrected desire with the intention for the sake of the Creator. This will be defined as my "middle line".

Neither the right nor the left lines are my own. They were given to me from Above by the Creator. They were both created by Him. I only connect them by taking the impure force from the left and correct it using the pure force from the right. Only this singular act is mine. This means that neither the egoistic desires from my left nor the Light that comes from the right are mine. So what is mine? Mine is the action!

What does it mean, "my action?" If the Light affects the desire and consequently corrects it, then it is the action of the Light and not my own. I am only the character that performs it. It is more accurate to say that what depends on me is to wish that my egoistical desires collide with the Upper Light from the right, and be corrected with its help.

It can also be expressed in another manner (as we read in § 155 of "The Introduction to the Study of the Ten *Sefirot*"). While studying, we have the only opportunity actually to perform a correction in its pure form, in action. During our studies, we concentrate on our desire to be exposed to the influence of the Surrounding Light that would correct and elevate us to the level we read about. At that particular moment, we expose our egoistic desires to the Upper Correcting Light.

Souls may be in two states. The first one relates to the world of Infinity, to the Thought of creation. The second one relates to the relative period of 6,000 years (though it can take less time). During that time, we correct ourselves. This means that under the influence of the Light we gradually correct all of our 620 egoistical desires.

"Gradually" means a consecutive ascent of the 6,000 levels. The entire way can also be divided into 125 levels. It does not really matter how we divide it. What is important is that we must go through all of them. The order in which we progress is as preordained as our actions.

The only thing that is not preordained is our desire for it to happen. Without our desire there will be no correction; the right and the left lines will neither come into contact nor interact. That can happen only if we want it to. This desire is called "*Aliyat MAN*" (raising of MAN), i.e., raising our desire. It appears the moment we want it.

This desire is exactly what we should reach during our studies. As we study, we should only think that this correction will come to each and every one of us. We ought to long for the tremendous Upper Light to descend upon all of us. There are many of us; we have a large group all over the world. We go through many different states and live in different conditions. With our combined effort, we can draw a very intensive Upper Light that would correct us; we should only want it.

It all depends on the intensity of our desire. If it reaches its maximum (it is really in our power), we will be corrected and achieve the first spiritual level.

While we are in this state (of 6000 years), **only the souls are corrected, but not the bodies. This means that we must relinquish all the desires to receive for ourselves called the attributes of the body, and remain only with the desire to bestow known as a spiritual desire.**

Plainly speaking, we do not correct the body itself during the six thousand years. This means that we are unable to correct "*Lev HaEven*" (heart of stone), our original egoism. We can only do it by ascending to the higher-level called "*AHP de Aliya*".

Even the souls of the righteous cannot be in the Garden of Eden (a specific level in the world of *Atzilut*) *after death* (when one's egoism dies), *but only after their bodies rot in the ground.*

We have talked about the meaning of the "bodies rotting in the ground". We know that it constitutes a complete revocation of our egoism (we perform *Tzimtzum*). Egoism becomes completely detached from us and we only work with the properties we receive from Above - GE (desires of bestowal).

All of our *Kelim de Kabbalah* (vessels of reception) are restricted. By refraining from using them, we seemingly bury them in the ground to rot. What does this "rotting" mean? It is as though we examine each of those desires and acquire *Kelim de Ashpa'a*, GE (vessels of bestowal). Abstaining from the use of these desires is called "decomposition" of these desires. We will discuss it later.

After the acquisition of all the altruistic desires (GE), we begin to raise the previously rejected AHP. Such a return of the AHP to the corrected level by retrieving it from the state we put it in is called "resurrection of the dead". We raise the "dead" desires that we did not want to use, revive them with their flaws, thus correcting our egoistical AHP. That is the meaning of the dead that have completely rotted rising from their graves. This way the vessels of the AHP join with the vessels of GE.

One should by no means imagine that this happens with our physical bodies in the material world. We can burn or bury the physical body, perform implants and do whatever else we want with it. We are not talking about this body; it has nothing to do with spiritual terms, and the soul is completely disconnected from it.

> The third state is the end of correction of the souls after the "resurrection of the dead. (When the GE are already acquired, and the AHP are corrected and connected with it, this means that the vessel (Kli), all the Ten Sefirot, the 620 completely corrected desires, are complete), when all the bodies (egoistical desires) are corrected. In that state, reception for one's self (original), which is the property of the body, is overturned and adopts the form of pure giving, thus becoming worthy of receiving all the bounty, pleasure and delight that is in the thought of creation.

This means that before the Kli has corrected all the Light that comes to it, it is felt as darkness because of the dissimilarity of properties. And vice versa, to the extent that we acquire equivalence of form with the Light, with the Creator, we begin to feel Him. We feel this Light in its true form, as a Giver of perfection, infinity, love, and goodness. It all depends on how similar we can be to the Light that comes from Above.

Therefore, our today's world will begin to expand and to be filled with the Upper World to the extent of our similarity to the Light. This world will be gradually "disappearing" from our sensations. The more we correct ourselves, the clearer we will see the laws that exist around us in the Upper World. This is how we will feel the universe.

> At the same time, souls merit complete merging with the Creator through equivalence of properties with Him. That is because they do not take pleasure in their own will to receive, but rather in the desire to give to the Creator (they become equal to Him). Consequently, He enjoys when they receive pleasure, because they also receive pleasure from Him.

The souls rise to the level called the "Thought of creation". They become equal with the Creator, and they are granted the sensation of unbound infinity. It is said: "The thought of creation is to delight the creatures." They feel endlessness in each of their feelings, pleasures, and attainments, timeless and flawless existence.

Many states follow the correction of the vessels. We are just talking about achieving a state when our Kelim (desires) are corrected. Once we are corrected, the Creator begins to elevate us to His own level and higher. We cannot even speak about these states; there are no words in our language to describe them. We can only discuss something that precedes the end of correction, when everything enters the state we refer to as Infinity (Ein Sof).

We are unable to understand what follows, because what we feel, understand and attain, what we can absorb and analyze, can only exist because it consists of opposites: black and white, pain and pleasure, or any kind of limit. It is only in the transition between two opposite states that we can feel. We use the opposites to create symbols, express our inner feelings as letters, black symbols against a white background.

As we enter the world of Infinity (Ein Sof), where there are neither opposite attributes, nor contrasting sensations of good and evil, our language becomes useless. Consequently, we can read nothing about those states, because Kabbalists have no means to convey them to us.

It is therefore said: "Taste and see that the Lord is good." It can only be verified by tasting, by drawing Inner Light called flavors (Ta'amim). There is no other way.

Kabbalah is a purely applied science. By using its methods on themselves, Kabbalists achieve correction. Unlike those who study it theoretically and therefore can never understand what these books have to say, Kabbalists receive their attainments within themselves and understand what it is all about.

For the sake of brevity, we shall refer to the three states of the soul as states one, two, and three. You should remember them well.

Baal HaSulam uses these names quite frequently, referring to them as the first, second and third states. The first one is the Thought, the second is the 6,000-year period of correction, and the third is the final state.

15. By looking at these three states, we find that they necessitate one another. If one of them did not exist (even a tiny detail in any of them – action, cause and effect), *the others would disappear as well.*

These above three states are interwoven, support one another, and exist simultaneously in the present. We should perceive them as initially created, existing relative to us. It depends only on our desire to be included in this or that state and be in it.

This desire is called "Aliyat MAN" (raising of MAN). It is the sending out of a prayer and depends only on how much we perceive the greatness of the Upper One as well as the lowness of our own condition.

For example, unless the third state, in which the property of reception turns into the property of bestowal, existed, the first state would not have been able to exist in the world of Infinity (in the primary thought). Perfection in the first state could only manifest, because it already exists in the third state in the future. Because of the Creator's eternity, the third state exists as present, and the perfection of the third state is seemingly copied onto the first one (this way, the first state becomes as ideal as the third one). *Hence, the third state necessitates the existence of the first one.*

In other words, if the Creator had not created the perfect state, the first state would also have been unable to exist regarding Him.

Unless something existed in the second state, where occurs all our work in correction (during 6,000 years), *in reaching spiritual levels, then how could the third state come to pass* (with regard to us)? *In this way, the second state determines the existence of the third one.*

It is not enough for something to exist in the Creator, because it exists in Him even without us. He is in a perfect and eternal state. However, for us to feel that we are in the third state, we should go through the second one.

It is the same with the first state in the world of Infinity, where the perfection of the third state exists. It definitely necessitates the existence of the third state, i.e., the second and third states should manifest in complete perfection. Thus, the first state necessitates the emergence of two opposite systems in the second state. This brings forth the body (egoistical desire in the second state), *enabling us to correct it with the help of the impure forces* (and attain the third state that would ensure perfection in the first one).

This leads us to the conclusion about the necessity of the impure forces. We cannot attain the third state unless we fall under the influence of impure forces and receive the material with which we can work and correct ourselves.

Had there been no system of impure worlds, we would neither have had the will to receive (the enormous egoistical desire that matches the Creator's desire to bestow), *nor could we have corrected it and achieve the third state, for "man cannot correct that which is absent in him".*

The system of impure forces is necessary as storage of all the corrupted desires. We extract and correct them one by one, and ascend the ladder from the first state to the third one, getting closer to the Creator.

Thus, we need not ask how the impure system emerged from the first state (which is perfect and eternal, because *Malchut* in the world of Infinity performed the first restriction [*Tzimtzum Aleph*] and, having no other desires, was merged with the Creator). These impure forces appeared so that we would be able to correct them, and consequently attain the third state.

The gap between the first and the third states makes the impure system necessary. It is expressed in our falling to the full depth of the impure forces and subsequently ascending and correcting them in accordance with the first state. This becomes the third state, because we have now acquired the impure forces and corrected them.

Therefore, the difference between the first and the third states lies in the correction of the impure forces and not merely in the reception of additional forces, desires, and possibilities.

Malchut of the world of Infinity is but a point in the Light. In order to fill the entire Infinity, the greater, outer circle, *Malchut* should acquire impure desires that match the size of that circle. *Malchut* itself is just a point in the circle that is surrounded by impure forces. It first acquires and then corrects them, so they become pure forces of *Malchut*. Thus, it fills up the entire circle, acquires the upper nine *Sefirot* and the point turns to *Partzuf*, the *Kli* the size of *Infinity*.

The first state, *Malchut*, is just a point merged with the Creator. It is perfect, albeit only a point. *Malchut* in the third state is a huge circle. You might say that it is 620 times bigger than the first point. In truth, it is impossible to measure just how much greater the circle becomes with these 620 desires after it connects them to itself and uses them for the sake of bestowal. This is the actual difference between the first and the third states.

16. *But the above words should not lead us to the conclusion that we have no freedom of choice because we are compelled to come to the third state, being that it is rooted in the first one.*

It appears that if the first, second, and third states exist, one might ask where my freedom of choice is? Are we just marionettes "tramping" from the first state to the third without any say in the matter? No! We do have freedom of choice. Then, how is it expressed?

The fact is that the Creator has prepared two paths for us in state two.

This means that there are two ways for us to proceed from the first state to the third one: a short way and a long way.

1. The Path of Torah and Commandments

A Commandment (Mitzva) is an act intended to correct a desire. When we correct a certain egoistic desire, the act of correction itself is the Mitzva. In other words, the act of correction is what the Creator commanded: to correct the egoistical use of a desire to the altruistic one.

The Light does it. The Light is the "Torah" (from the Hebrew word "Ohr" - light). There exist many types of light, such as the Light of Hassadim (Mercy), the Light of Hochma (Wisdom), Light of AB SAG, the descending, ascending, and surrounding Light, and the NaRaNHaY. However, the Torah is the general Light that descends from Above.

We learned that correction is made by way of Torah and Mitzvot (actions influenced by the Light). This way is called the path of Torah, or the path of Light.

2. The Path of Suffering

Suffering refines the body and eventually compels us to turn our (egoistical) will to receive into the will to bestow and merge with the Creator. Our sages said, "If you repent **(i.e.,** if you follow the Path of Torah)**,** *then it is fine, but if not, I will place over you a ruthless king, and he will make you repent"* (allusion to the Pharaoh).

In other words, terrible sufferings will compel us in spite of everything to understand that we should only progress spiritually. Mere development of technology, ethics, or any other field will eventually degrade us more and more, with each passing generation.

It is written: "By good or by evil. If you merit, I will hasten it (I will lead you to the third state); *if you do not, then by pain and sufferings." It means that by observing Torah and Commandments, we hasten our correction and do not need the harsh agony and the prolonged time to compel us to correct ourselves* (with the help of the Light, through Torah and Commandments). *If not by way of Torah and Commandments, our correction will in any case be completed through the path of suffering; it will be forced upon us. The path of suffering entails the punishment of the souls in Hell.*

What in fact is "Hell"? In a word, Hell is the feeling of absolute lowness, smallness, and baseness of the egoistical attributes compared to the Upper Light and perfection. It is the difference between the Upper One and me. This is the contrast between the egoistical sensations and the sublime altruistic ones. Hell is a terrible, endless abyss that is felt between these two states.

Be that as it may, the End of Correction (i.e., state three) is a must for all and is preordained by the first state. Our choice is only between the Path of Suffering and the Path of Torah and Commandments.

Thus, we have made clear how the three states of the souls are connected to one another and necessitate each other's existence.

It is not quite correct to say that there are only two paths, namely the path of Torah and the path of suffering. In fact, it is impossible to be corrected through the path of suffering. Only the Light corrects. We learn in the four phases of the Straight Light: The Light begets the will to receive, i.e., *Behina Aleph*, and then it awakens the will to bestow in *Behina Aleph*, which forms *Behina Bet*. Afterwards, the Light continues acting in the desire to bestow of *Behina Bet* and creates *Behina Gimel*, then *Behina Dalet* and so on.

The Light affects the *Reshimot* in all the worlds. It elevates and lowers, corrects and develops. It is therefore impossible to be corrected by suffering. The only thing that can be achieved through pain is the realization of the necessity of correction. We can either suffer or quickly awaken (before the most terrible calamities befall us), and with the help of studies and a group expose ourselves to the influence of the Surrounding Light.

We must regain our sight before we plunge into real anguish, because eventually we will still have to return to the starting point. We should both grow smarter and do what we must, or wait until sufferings compel us to do the same. There is no other way. Therefore, our freedom of choice is in becoming smarter and taking advantage of the opportunity provided.

This is the only choice we have. We need quickly to realize what we should do. In that case, our journey will be peaceful, comfortable, and quiet. We will know and look forward to everything that awaits us. Thus, we will constantly attain better and better things, feel pleasant feelings, and attract the Surrounding Light upon ourselves.

The alternative is to stubbornly stay put and wait until terrible pain forces us to climb the same steps towards our already existing third state.

We normally err in our interpretation of the concept of free will. We perceive it as an ability to do something freely. However, nothing is free! We are given a desire to work with, and we can do it either the right way or the wrong way.

My desires are pre-instilled in me. I can work with them exactly as they are within me, in their corrupt way. This means that I do not inspect them in view of the purpose of creation without first checking what I should do with them, what the Creator wants of me. I simply follow them. This situation is regarded as living in this world. In other words, I choose a slow and painful road.

However, there is another way. I can examine my desires, compare them with the future, with my corrected state, know what form they must eventually take, and try to draw the Surrounding Light. This light will correct them and equalize them with the Creator so that I will begin to feel Him.

This is the difference between a senseless existence in the desires of this world below the *Machsom*, and an existence in contact with the Upper World, in aspiration to it, in matching my desires with those of the Upper World. That is the manifestation of our free will.

17. From all the above, we understand the third inquiry: when we examine ourselves, we find that we are as corrupt and as despicable as can be...

There is no need to explain to every person what he really is. The meaning of not knowing one's self entirely is that he must still go through a period of recognition of evil (my individual evil). Then he will see that all of his desires and intentions are only for his own benefit, that he is ready to give up everything to satisfy even the most inconsequential desires that he does not care at all about what happens around him. This is the meaning of baseness, opposition to the Creator.

When we examine ourselves, we find that we are as corrupt and as despicable as can be. However, when we look at the Creator, we must be similar to Him, for there is no one higher than He, as is

becoming of the Creator who created us. That is because the nature
of the Perfect One is to perform perfect acts.

How could something imperfect create something perfect, and
vice versa, how could something imperfect be emanated by something
perfect? That is impossible, for if the Creator is perfect, and He creates
something imperfect, it means that this imperfection existed in Him to
begin with.

Now we can understand that our body with all of its insignificant
egoistical desires is not our real body (it is what we are given from
the impure system). *Our real body, eternal and perfect* (corrected),
already exists in the third state.

The impure thoughts and desires that we receive from the left line
(our so-called "impure body), are only given for us to correct. While
climbing by means of our corrected desires, as if on the rungs of a ladder, we ascend to the third state. That is where we receive our complete
form, in reception for the sake of bestowal. All of the 620 impure desires
given to us must be turned into a perfect and pure body.

Thus, state one (in which *Malchut* is merely a point) *necessitates our*
reception of a corrupt and loathsome shell (*Klipa*, the will to receive), *of the*
egoistical desire. State two separates us from the Creator, (we do not feel it,
because it covers all our feelings) *so as to correct it and allow us to receive our*
eternal body in state three. We need not angrily protest it (such a loathsome
body) *because our work cannot be done except in a body as transitory and as*
wasteful as ours (in these detestable and egoistical desires)...

We need something to work with. Unless we had these desires,
what would we have to correct? We need somehow to comprehend the
acts of the Creator. Why do we need this metamorphosis? Why do we
have to go through all these phases of correction? Could we not have
been spared this forced correction? We really could, but then we would
remain a point, a mere fetus inside the Creator.

When we examine the 620 desires that are opposite to the Creator, correct them, and make them similar to Him, we become equal with the Creator. That is because He created those 620 desires by His will to bestow. When we correct them, we become similar to His bestowal, we acquire the necessary properties, intention, power, and knowledge. We learn what happens inside the Creator Himself and become equal with Him.

Therefore, it is impossible to receive those 620 desires corrected in advance. If that were the case, we would not be able to adopt them in us without turning them from negative to positive, until they become similar to the Creator.

Thus we are already in a perfect state, in correspondence with the perfect Creator who has made us in the second state (it does not matter that the second state is low, because it is not our own). *Since our body is going to die, and since it is here only for the time necessary for the reception of its eternal form, it can cause us no harm.*

The Creator gave us a loathsome, base, and egoistical body by dropping us into infinitesimal negativity. He did this so that we might have a way to ascend. For that reason, these properties were created artificially. They are, in fact, a backward reflection of His attributes, allowing us to make them similar to the Creator.

If we invert them from reception to bestowal, the past intentions die, rot, and disappear, making room for the intentions to bestow to emerge in their place. Hence, this body *is only here for the time necessary for its cancellation and reception of our eternal form.*

18. That resolves our fifth inquiry, which was – how could it be that from the Eternal (like the Creator) *transitory, wasteful actions would be extended* (concrete, discrete and of limited size)?

How can something transitory, limited, low, and flawed, stem from something eternal? We do not fully understand these questions because we do not feel any kind of eternity. That is how opposite it is to our condition.

However, the difficulty still stands. We will understand what Baal HaSulam is saying only when eternity begins to shine on us from Above. It will happen slowly as we begin to attain the Surrounding Light that creates the complete and perfect universe around us and creates this picture in our mind's eye. Only then will we begin to understand this contradiction, how this flawless eternity and perfection, without even a trace of limitation, contrast, or opposites, in which all the points are perfect and eternal and continuous, can come from a source where states and actions are passing, transient and low.

We see that we are indeed in a state worthy of His eternity, meaning that even now we are eternal and perfect beings.

The only thing that obstructs us from feeling this eternity is the shell that wraps us, this being our egoistical impure intention. We are like a magnetic field that reflects everything we project outwardly. When we stop turning inwardly and can turn the current from inside out, we will instantly feel the eternity and perfection we are actually in. We must only neutralize the shell.

And our eternity necessitates that the egoistical shell of the body will have been given to us only for a transitory, wasteful work (in order to turn it to altruism and increase it from being a point to being a circle, meaning the level of the Creator), *for if it had remained eternal, we would have remained separated from the Life of Lives for all eternity.*

As we have said in item 13, this form of our body, which is the will to receive for ourselves alone (with the intention for our own sake), *is not at all present in the thought of creation, for there we are formed as state three* (to begin with), *but rather appears* (to us) *only in the second state* (so that we acquire it by ourselves in the third state).

It should not appear as a paradox, or something unnatural. We are in fact in the third state, and only exist in the second one with our subjective feelings, in order to correct them to correspond to the real situation.

We must not ponder (there is no question) *over the state of other beings in the world* (they are inconsequential for us), *since man is the center of creation.*

We think that humankind cannot be the center of creation, because we are lost, even on this planet. We exist on a thin layer of the planet, sitting on a vibrating, steaming, and erupting volcano. We are in a vast universe, dependent on some negligible star called "Sun".

If we measure ourselves with respect to the nature of the still or the vegetative, which are so abundant, it will seem that we are a tiny insignificant minority. You can also say the same thing with regard to animate nature, which is thousands of times greater than we in numbers are.

If we exist on this planet as animals, completely disconnected and detached from the Upper World, without accepting upon ourselves the purpose of creation, we naturally become tiny fractions in space and in this world. If we begin to acquire the attributes of the Upper World, we will become lords of the universe. During the ascent to the Upper World, we begin to absorb it into ourselves, to the point of Infinity.

It turns out that without connection with the Upper World we are insignificant. In fact, this is our actual strength. To the extent that we acquire these Upper Forces, being the Light that controls, creates, sustains and fills everything, and come to own that Light, we will rise higher than all of nature.

We must not ponder over other beings in the world, since man (a person who attains the Upper World) *is the center of creation.*

All other creations (still, vegetative, and animate) *do not have their own value, but only as much as they are useful in bringing humanity to completeness. Thus, they ascend and descend with man without any regard for himself.* They all depend on us, on how much we draw them to ourselves for the purpose of our ascent.

When one begins to ascend in spirituality, one finds a wondrous interdependency where one's every inner trait is not one's own, but rather a reflection of an external nature. My animate nature contains the entire nature around me. My vegetative degree is more internal, meaning it is a higher reflection of the entire vegetative nature. My still desires are a higher reflection of the entire universe, of the entire inanimate nature around me.

Once I discover this dependency, I begin to use nature through perception of it, consequently understanding its language and sensations. That is the reason Kabbalists are said to understand the language of the birds and the animals, and feel and understand everything around them. It is metaphorically described as man containing everything within.

After that, while ascending to the Upper Worlds, we discover the entire surrounding nature within us, in our new attributes. Our inner vessels, our perception of the surrounding world, become incomplete. As a result, we are separated and severed from our surroundings.

The absence of the screen, which produced the second restriction, created a division of internal worlds and external worlds. The parts of the *Partzuf* were created from the innermost to the outermost.

Immediately after the conclusive and collective screen is created, everything will unite into one structure of Ten *Sefirot*, and our entire world will be contained in each and every one of us. Then we shall all unite into a single soul, and become *Adam*, the only *Adam* (*Adam HaRishon*), containing everything within.

Therefore, we need not ask about the rest of nature, for it depends on us alone. We now discover how badly we influence it. As we spiritually correct ourselves, we will discover fantastic changes for the better in our surrounding nature. We will not need any genetic engineering to be able to provide for ourselves. Nature will independently create in us everything we need.

Let us continue studying "The Introduction to the Book of Zohar," where we have carefully examined the first three points. Here Baal HaSulam approaches the fourth question.

19. If the Creator is kind and only brings goodness, how could he intentionally create his creations so that they are bound to suffer and grieve during their lives?

It is said that all this suffering is predetermined in our first state, in which our perfect eternity will be achieved from the future third state, that obligates us to follow the path of Torah or the path of suffering

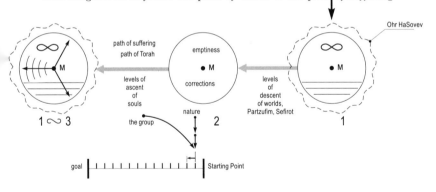

in order to achieve eternity in state three.

What is Baal HaSulam talking about? Let me remind you with the help of a little sketch.

We say that state one, created by the Creator, the state of Infinity, is completely filled with the light and this is *Malchut*. In state two,

Malchut performs a *Tzimtzum*, becomes empty, and during this state it is being gradually filled with the light, performs corrections, which finally lead to the third state, when *Malchut* returns to being completely filled with the light.

This third state is equivalent to the first one, the only difference between them being that the third state was achieved by *Malchut* itself. According to the above sketch, the first state is created by the Creator from outside, by the surrounding light called *Ohr Sovev*. The third state – the world of Infinity - is achieved by the correction of *Malchut* itself, which absorbs all these previous properties. They become the properties of *Malchut,* which fills the entire volume of Infinity by attracting the outer light.

It is not that the Creator governs and fills the world of Infinity, but rather *Malchut* fills this void from within its own desire. We are going to examine how these three states predetermine each other.

There is an opportunity to pass from the first state to the second and then from the second to the third in the following way: from the first state, we pass to the second by descending the so-called levels of descent (the worlds, *Partzufim* and *Sefirot*). This process is usually depicted as one unfolding from up downwards, from the World of Infinity to our world. The passage from the second state to the third constitutes the levels of ascent (correction) of the souls. Naturally, we do not exist between the first and the second stages; there are no created beings yet. The path of creation starts between the second and the third states.

There are two paths: *"the path of Torah and the path of suffering"*. The difference is only in time. From the beginning until the end of every path, I should go through a certain number of levels. Every time, while passing from one level to another I need to feel the evil and corruption of my current state and the perfection expected at the next one. I can evaluate the corruption of the current level and the perfection of the future one either under the influence of my group, books and the Rav or under the influence of blows that I will be dealt. These blows act slowly; they are stretched in time and therefore I prolong my passage on the path of suffering.

However, with the help of books, the Rav, and my group, I can quickly realize the corruption of my current condition and the perfection of the following state and thus move forward of my own free will. That is, the path itself does not mean escaping from a corrupted state to a better state by necessity, but rather it means to be in a state of attainment and exaltation. The path itself becomes an ascent and time spent in each state will literally shrink to a minimum. Here lies the difference between the path of Torah (light) and the path of suffering.

Only with the help of a self-created outside source can I start advancing along the path of Torah instead of the path of suffering. I myself create my group; the group is most important. Only with the help of my complementary element, by switching the natural factor of influence on me with my group's influence, do I start moving much faster. This is the most important factor at our disposal. Our studies cannot guarantee us any advancement. The essence of what we study is to create forces around us that would influence us and move us forward faster than those natural forces that move the rest of humanity. This is the reason we gather; this is why we study and try to understand why Kabbalists, who have already attained this, advise us on how to accelerate our development, our passage from the second state to the third.

So, Baal HaSulam says that *all this suffering is felt only in the Klipa of our body,* (i.e., in our still uncorrected desires), *which was created for nothing else but to die and be buried.*

This means we should bury these desires for the purpose of not using them. The desires that have not been used by man are called dead.

> *This points out that the will to receive* (egotistical desire to obtain everything, to fill oneself) *was created only to be destroyed in the mode in which it exists, in its initial mode, to be wiped out and*

turned into the will to bestow. Suffering is only given to us to discover the insignificance and harm of the will to receive.

In other words, there is a goal in suffering, some causality, and the people who try to follow the right path, replace bodily suffering (from their unsatisfied egotism) with purposeful ones.

When the whole world agrees to set itself free and annihilate the will to receive for its own sake, everyone will only have the desire to give to others. This transformation will happen under the influence of enormous suffering of which Baal HaSulam writes in his article "The Last Generation," and which the ancient prophets predicted to us pointing at our time as a beginning of this period.

When the whole world agrees to set itself free and annihilate egoistical desires, when it chooses to acquire the will to bestow, it will annihilate all the evil in the world and everyone will be sure of a healthy and full life, because each one will have the whole world taking care of him and his needs. However, when everyone only desires to receive for his own sake, this becomes the cause of suffering, atrocities, and wars, from which we cannot escape. This desire weakens the body with disease and pain.

That is, on all our levels suffering is determined by our common egoism. Naturally, as humanity evolves, this suffering will only increase up to the point of becoming so unbearable that everyone will want to get rid of his own egoism just to stop suffering. It is therefore called the path of suffering. Imagine how much suffering every person and humanity, as a whole will have to go through in order willingly to get rid of egoism as a source of suffering. How much of his own evil should each one of us realize? Just imagine what a horrible future is ahead of us in such a case!

On the other hand, by attracting the Upper Light into this world, even our small groups relieve people from suffering, although they know nothing about Kabbalah as a method of achieving happiness. We already give them some subconscious inner factors that help them quickly find correct answers to their questions about suffering. We see how a new person comes to a group and without knowing or understanding what the group is doing, in no time adapts himself to what is being taught there.

It took those who have studied for a long time months or years to reach this level, whereas the newcomers are so quick in the uptake. This happens because we have paved the way for them. Moreover, every generation that is engaged in spiritual work similarly influences all the consecutive generations.

So we should not be thinking of the enormous sufferings awaiting us. By increasing the number of people studying Kabbalah, we help the world to reach the realization of evil faster. In the near future humanity will clearly understand that egoism is the source of every evil. All we will have left to do is to show that there is a method of turning this evil to good.

Thus, we can see that all suffering in our world exists only to open our eyes, compel us to get rid of the evil egoism of our body, and attain the perfect form of desire to bestow. The path of suffering is quite capable of pushing us towards this desired condition.

That is, the sooner the person realizes the reason for his suffering, the sooner his group will be able to help him, the faster he will attain the Upper World, eternity, perfection and wisdom.

Know that the commandments pertaining to relations among people are more important than man's relations with the Creator are, because giving to others leads to bestowal upon the Creator.

That is, where and how can I recognize evil? Where is it and what is its purpose? I can understand it faster by working with my friends in a group.

This is why it is said that relations among people are more effective for finding evil than relations between man and the Creator. Since man's relations with the Creator are hidden from him, he can imagine them in all possible variations, but none of us will know for sure, until our eyes open and we see our true relations with the Creator.

At the same time, the relations among the members of a group as with opponents, antagonists or as real friends moving towards the mutual goal, agreements and disagreements among them - all of this is a testing ground, a laboratory in which the person can quickly discover the reason for his terrible states. He will understand how by making necessary changes he can attain the Upper World.

This is precisely why we are given this world and our life among other people. A huge society is purposefully created around every single one of us. On the other hand, every one of us has an opportunity to create a small society in which he can work on his inner changes. We have it all, so we just need to accomplish it.

20. *After all the research we have done so far, we can now answer the first question: "What is our essence?", because it is the essence of all the realms of Creation, which represent no more and no less than the desire to receive.*

It follows that we are a "desire to receive pleasure" created by the Creator.

Not in the way it appears to us in state two (in the uncorrected condition, far from perfection, after all the stages of descent of the worlds and *Sefirot*), *as a will to receive for oneself alone* (egoistical desire), *but in state one, in the world of Infinity, in our eternal form, as a desire to bestow, to please the Creator.*

But even though in reality we have not yet achieved state three (in our sensations) *and still remain within the limits of time* (i.e., we are still ascending the levels of correction), *it does not in the least diminish our essence* (the question was - what is our essence. The fact that we are now in the state of imperfection, does not diminish our inner essence), *because our third state* (the future state) *is guaranteed by the presence of state one. The one who will receive it in the future is similar to the one who has already received it* (if he knows exactly what he receives and is absolutely confident in his future state).

If we had "faith", i.e., not egoism, but a desire to bestow, we would then feel our third state in advance. It would already be shining upon us from afar, even in our uncorrected states, as the *Ohr Makif* (the Surrounding Light) is shining upon us.

In this case, we would not feel any problems, any imperfections, even in state two, because we would receive the luminescence from our future state three. This resembles a person who, with all the responsibilities and tasks he needs to do during the day, awaits the evening when he will receive something extraordinary, something wonderful. You live in the anticipation of the evening. You are confident that it will be something really special, something exciting, and enlightening. Your whole day completely changes. Why? It will only happen in the evening! You draw upon yourself that future state in advance. Therefore, if we could only see our future state (it is only possible in the Reflected Light), it would already be shining upon us today, and it would be like being within that Light.

Oftentimes, when the person is controlled by his egoistical desires, anticipation of a better state is sometimes much more powerful then the actual state, when we achieve it. This is because anticipation is caused by the Surrounding Light, and it is not limited by my *Kelim*, by my desires. It is unlimited because I receive the light from afar; it is not inside of my *Kelim*; it comes from outside; it is around me. It is as the light of Infinity, so anticipation of it is always much more promising and exciting than the feeling of the actual pleasure.

Therefore, even now we can be in that state (although we really are in state two) by receiving the luminescence of state three, but only if we possess the Reflected light. Baal HaSulam says that even though in reality we have not reached state three and remain confined within the bounds of time, this does not in the least diminish our essence, because our future state three is guaranteed to us by the present state one. And he who will receive in the future is similar to the one who already received.

> The time factor becomes a problem when the person has doubts (i.e., when there is a lack of faith) whether he would complete everything he is supposed to complete in the given time. Since the person achieves such a state when he has no more doubts, it is as if he achieves state three.

So what is our task today? What is the most important thing to do? We should immediately feel Infinity, eternity, the state of absolute attainment and omnipresence. Life and death of the body become irrelevant. Everything depends on acquiring the attributes of *Bina* (faith). As soon as that happens, the light of state three will start shining upon us.

> The evil body (our uncorrected desires) that we received at present does not diminish our essence, because the body with all of its acquisitions will disappear together with its source - the system of impure forces. The one that disappears is similar to that which has already vanished, as if it had never existed.

This is what the Creation looks like from the next level, and if we rise above it and look behind and ahead of us, then egoism disappears and the perfect state begins to shine upon us.

> However, the essence of the soul dressed in the body is only the desire to bestow, which is rooted in the system of four pure worlds: Atzilut, Beria, Yetzira, Assiya. This desire is eternal, because it is the property of the Source of life. It is invariable and therefore eternal.

In order to have a better understanding, let us look at the following picture.

The Creator created, from top down, the will to receive pleasure. This will to receive is the desire to feel Him. If the Creator is the light, then the desire to receive is the desire to feel the light.

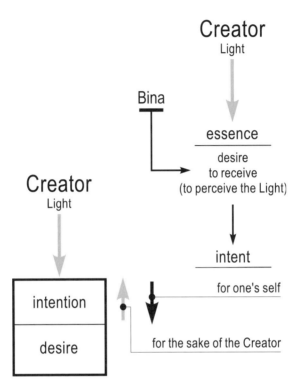

This desire is neither good nor bad; it is the essence of Creation. Because of the breaking of the vessels, it received from *Bina* the intention on how to use the desire: for oneself alone or for the Creator. That superstructure appears above the desire. Therefore there are the desire, the light or the source of the light (the Creator), and the intentions on how to use that desire. That is all.

21. Do not be led astray by the philosophers who say that the essence of the soul is a substance of the mind and that it only exists through the concepts it learns and from there it grows and they are its essence. The question of the continuance of the soul after the departure of the body depends solely on the extent of concepts it has acquired, until in the absence of such concepts, there remains nothing to continue.

Philosophy states that man's existence depends on his knowledge of nature.

What is contained in this knowledge? It is just an understanding of what exists outside of me. First, is this knowledge absolute? Even through research, we understand that the world we feel around us is nothing more than the result of our subjective perception. If we had different senses, we would feel the world quite differently, not as air, solid bodies or liquid, gaseous and plasma states of matter. The world would have a completely different degree of density and other perceived qualities.

The way the world exists around us is merely a consequence of our internal states. That is why philosophy's stipulation that man's life is dependent upon his conception of the outer world cardinally contradicts the opinion of Kabbalah.

It is also unaccepted by the heart, and anyone who ever tried to acquire some knowledge knows and feels that the mind itself is a possession and not the possessor.

Nevertheless, as we have said, all the substance of the renewed creation, both the substance of spiritual objects and the substance of corporeal objects, is no more and no less than a will to receive.

Our essence is the will to receive. Moreover, any difference between one essence and another lies in their respective desires to receive that generate needs within every essence, which in turn create certain thoughts and knowledge that are sufficient to satisfy those needs. Therefore, desires are the very core of whatever is within us. Our mind is created to satisfy these desires. Our essence is not the mind; it is the will to receive.

Just as human desires differ from one another, so are their needs, thoughts and ideas. For instance, those whose will to receive is limited to beastly desires, their needs, thoughts and ideas all aim to satisfy those desires.

People only differ in the combinations of their desires. Moreover, we cannot do anything with people. We cannot affect them from outside, no matter what pressure we put upon them. Somehow, we should indirectly find a way to speed up their development and transition from the animate level to the human and from the human to the spiritual. Unless the person's desires change, we would not be able to give him anything that is out of tune with his desires, because his essence is a desire. The current level of development of his desires constitutes his true state.

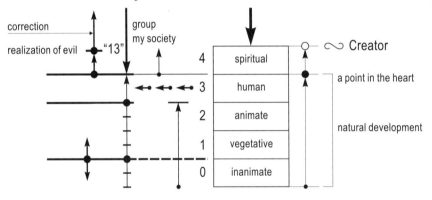

In every one of us, there are five levels of desires: still, vegetative, animate, human, and spiritual. Zero, one, two, three, and four are five types of desires (or five types of *Dargot Aviut*), five kinds of ego. This is the way people evolve. However, if the person reaches a level where he passes from human desires to spiritual ones, a point in his heart emerges and he starts to feel something. This point is a beginning of the spiritual desire, while the end of it is similarity to the Creator. Such is the way of correction.

Desires evolve naturally up to the spiritual level, whereas the development of the point in the heart may follow either the path of Torah or the path of suffering. We live in a society where everyone has his own desires. Consequently, every person exists at a certain level of development: still, vegetative, animate, human, or spiritual.

If people come to us, we need to determine whether they already reached the necessary level. In other words, has the point in their hearts awakened? If yes, then this is my society, my group. I seek such people to build a force around me that would help me to advance in the right direction. Some people come to us with their desires being only on the still, vegetative, animate, and human levels. Human desires include cravings for wealth, honor, fame, and knowledge. Any desire below that level is considered natural.

Therefore, the people whose level of desire is below the level of the point in the heart will never understand us. Nevertheless, as we attract the Surrounding Light upon us, we gradually elevate them as well. More and more people have come to us recently with greater inner readiness to adopt our material at an ever-accelerating pace.

However, until the person's desires change, he will not be able to understand anything. In other words, everyone understands only through the point of his desire. The one who reached a certain level only wants to fulfill the desires at that level. He is neither interested in desires below this level, for he has already overgrown them, nor does he understand the desires above, for he perceives them as quite unreal.

For instance, take a simple person from a village, start telling him how good it is to write music, to paint and discover nature's secrets. Having no such desires, he will simply not understand. Similarly, an ordinary person does not want to be a millionaire. Therefore, each of us acts only from the level of desire that is developed in us; hence, we should relate to it correspondingly. Therefore Baal HaSulam says that the most important thing is not human knowledge or thoughts, but desires. The only thing we can do for people and for ourselves is to stimulate a rapid evolution of desires. This will lead the world towards a perfect state, quickly and painlessly.

For instance, those whose desire to receive is limited only to animal types of pleasure, their needs, thoughts and reasons are directed to fulfilling this desire in his animal entirety. Even though they use human reason and knowledge for this purpose (in fact, it is time for them to grow up), their mind is as the mind of an animal, since they are enslaved to animal desire and its service.

Sometimes we see influential and very self-confident individuals, who, apparently, understand what they are living for. However, in spite of their self-confidence and understanding, what are their real desires? In fact, they only want to acquire something in this life and content themselves with it.

On the other hand, those whose desire to receive demands by and large human delights such as honor, power (control) over others, which is not available to the animal type, their main needs, thoughts and knowledge are intended only for the completion of their desires, as much as possible. Again, those with the desire to receive generally require all their needs, thoughts, and knowledge only to fulfill entirely this desire.

Mind, thoughts, and knowledge are meant to serve the desires, to fulfill them.

22. These three kinds of desires predominate in every man, but everyone combines them in different proportions. All differences between people come from this point. Speaking about material properties, you can draw an analogy to spiritual properties, according to their spiritual value.

23. Thus, the souls of people with their spiritual investing the Reflected light (Ohr Hozer), which they receive from the Upper Worlds and from which they descend, find only the desire to bestow, the intention for the sake of the Creator. This is the essence of the soul. After its investing into a man's body, it bears in it the necessities, thoughts, and intellect that are aimed at giving, pleasing the Creator according to the value of the soul's desire.

Baal HaSulam says that as we advance and work in contact with the Creator, we begin to understand the Creator and enter Infinity and Perfection. We attain the true creation breaking free from our present existence, rise above the level of life and death. However, we continue working with our desires, investing them with the intention for the sake of the Creator. The same desires remain; they just acquire an opposite direction.

In addition, with the change of direction, they obviously acquire different filling.

> 24. Thus, the essence of the body is only the desire to receive for itself in all its manifestations and with all its acquisitions. Everything it gets is just for filling this depraved desire to receive that has been created only to be destroyed and to disappear from the world (the intention for one's own sake is meant), in order accomplish state three at the End of Correction.

> That is why it (our egoistical intention) is mortal and, of course, imperfect, for all its acquisitions are slipping by like a shadow, without leaving anything after them.

This can be compared with our own experience in this world. We have already lived here for a few decades, but where are all those achievements and pleasures that we so enjoyed some time ago? All of them disappear and the person is left with nothing at the end of his life.

Why are they not accumulating in us? Why do we not feel greater satisfaction every time? Why, in our egoistical state, do we need always to loose the previous one to get a new fulfillment?

The fact is that such is the law of impure forces called Klipot. They cannot receive more than a small spark of light and are therefore unable to get the next fulfillment before they get rid of their previous tiny portion.

This is the essence of our life: exhalation and inhalation, emptying and filling. This continues at the same level, like small vibrations: up and down, up and down. Moreover, our entire life is made of such periods of intermittent emptiness and fulfillment.

Therefore, Baal HaSulam says:

That is why it is mortal and, of course, imperfect, for all its acquisitions are slipping by like a shadow, without leaving anything after them.

At the same time, the essence of the soul is just the desire to bestow. All her manifestations and acquisitions are filled with the desire that exists already as in the eternal state 1 and in the future state 3.

What does the second intermediate state mean? This is my starting point from which I should attain my true state three. In fact, we are already in that state. We just need to feel it. Thus, our gradual advancement towards state three and its gradual manifestation represent the stages of the path that we have to go through.

Nothing new ever happens in the world. My eyes begin to open and I gradually reveal the Infinity in my sensations. If the person tunes himself up this way, he will eventually start feeling it.

Try to tune yourselves to this feeling: we exist in the world of Infinity, of which we perceive only a tiny fragment. We just need to discover it. This is what Baal HaSulam says. This way, the shroud will disappear along with all of its manifestations and the eternal, infinite world will emerges.

But what should disappear? By the shroud, we mean our egoistical body that is destined to die, be buried, and completely disappear. The egoistical body is our intention to receive for ourselves.

On the contrary, deliverance from the uncorrected body makes her stronger, so that she can rise up to paradise (Gan Eden).

Paradise, or the Garden of Eden, is *Malchut* of the world of *Atzilut* that acquired the properties of *Bina*.

> *Thus, we have made plain that the eternity of the soul does not depend on the knowledge it has, as philosophers consider. The eternity of the soul is in her essence, that is, in her desire to bestow.*

The soul is eternal; it is the desire to receive initially created with the intention for the sake of the Creator.

The knowledge that she obtained is her reward, and does not represent her.

The true knowledge is the *Ohr Hochma* that enters into the corrected intentions.

> *25. From this, we will find a complete solution to the fifth analysis, where we asked if it is the case that the body is so imperfect* (by body we only mean the egoistical desire with the intention for oneself) *that, unless it is decomposed, the pure soul* (by soul we mean the Upper Light that enters into the intention for the sake of the Creator) *cannot enter into it, why does it come back and revive by rising from the dead? As it is said by the sages, the dead* (i.e., all these egoistical intentions for oneself) *are resurrected with all their shortcomings, so that nobody could say that they are not the same bodies.*

Why do we have to struggle through these purposely-confusing ideas in the texts of Kabbalists? According to what we saw in previous articles, the soul and her correction depend not on knowledge, but on a change of desires and intentions. Therefore the Kabbalist, even though he writes such articles as we study now that are supposed to shed some light on our state, is least of all concerned about our understanding of what he wants to say. His intentions with regard to us are very different.

He wants us, half-asleep, lost, unconscious and confused to follow his thoughts. He does not demand from us an understanding of the text we are reading now. What he does demand is our presence in that chain of thought, which he unfolds before us. Hold on to him like a small child. It does not matter how much you understand. The most important thing is your desire to go along with him.

Just be with your teacher, go along with him and he will lead you forward. The person can never understand a higher state with the mind of a lower state, because very different desires, functions, and laws rule on the higher level. He will never rise to the next level before he understands it. It is utterly impossible. The Kabbalist purposely muddles his texts, because he wishes us to feel the need to cling to him. He wants us to follow him in the dark, as if we are small, helpless, and blind.

Hence, this state of confusion, incomprehension and ignorance is good. We just need to realize that it is not the mind we have to use, but our intention to merge with the Creator. We should use our desires, not the intellect, because our intellect cannot function there. It functions only in our world. It is of the animate level, not spiritual. When we make our desires spiritual, going hand in hand with the Kabbalist who guides us, our desires will change. They will generate very different thoughts aimed at fulfilling these new, spiritual desires, to correct them, elevate them even higher, absorb and understand them.

That is, the mind is a pure consequence of our desires and evolves together with them. Therefore, it is said that suffering makes one wiser. It is truly so! Because the mind, the intellect is the consequence of the necessity to escape suffering. You should never hope first to find out something about the spiritual and then rise to the level of your knowledge. Never! The mind only develops in accordance with a change of desire. We always advance this way.

That is why I am saying it again: it does not matter at all what your condition during the lesson is, even if you do not know the language or cannot "switch on" your brain today. The only thing that matters is you desire to follow the author, lecturer, teacher. If you do, then you advance. And vice versa, when you come to the class relaxed, able to catch everything with your sharp intellect, with your inquiring mind, you basically rob yourself, because you switch all of your energy from obtaining the spiritual information to gaining purely intellectual fulfillment.

> *You have to understand that this is from the plan of creation itself; thus, from state one. We said that, as soon as the plan becomes to delight the creation, it without fail creates in souls a huge desire to receive this pleasure, which is in the plan of creation, for a great pleasure requires a huge desire* (the Creator wished to delight us with Infinity; hence, He created in us infinite desire).

> *We also said that this huge desire to receive is the only new creation, which has been created, so there was no need at all for something bigger to fulfill the plan of the creation. With his perfect nature, the Creator does not do anything superfluous.*

One thing the Creator needed for bestowing delight is the will to receive delight.

> *We also said that this huge desire to receive had been completely expelled from the system of pure worlds and was given to the system of impure worlds. They are the source of the bodies' provenance and existence, with all their acquisitions in this world, until a man reaches the age of thirteen* (i.e., egoistical desires).

It is just an arbitrary number used by Baal HaSulam to confuse us. When he mentions certain numbers, such as 40, 13 or 70 years, he implies a certain inner condition of the person.

Thus, our development can be divided into two periods: first, when we are under the power of egotistical desires – conventionally, this period is called the age before 13, before coming of age. After the age of 13, a person with the help of higher light begins to comprehend his soul, which is to correct his desire from egotistic to altruistic. This transition is conventionally called "13 years".

That is, from this level the person starts to take interest in Kabbalah. He completes the first stage of his development (realization of evil) and starts to correct himself and acquire pure intention. He already exists at the expense of the pure worlds in accordance with the attainment of the soul. That is, before he reaches the state called "13 years", the person exists under the power of impure worlds. In this state, he is constantly given more and more egoism, and he absorbs it to the point when he finally begins to realize how harmful, vain, and evil it is.

Finally, the person comes to a turning point where he feels the need to begin correcting his egoism. This point is called "coming of age". From this point on, he is considered an adult, i.e., he begins to obtain the screen that gives him the ability to work with his desires in the altruistic mode.

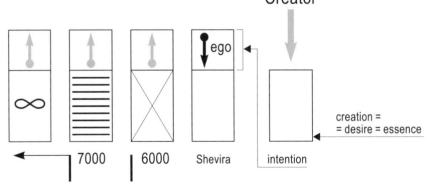

It was also said that during 6000 years that were given us for the work on corrections, the body, i.e., the huge desire to receive, remains uncorrected. All corrections that are the result of our work happen only with the soul (with the intention). The soul ascending to higher levels of purity and sanctity merely increases the desire to bestow.

That is why the body is predestined to die, to be buried, to decay, because it does not make any correction and cannot really exist like that. Alas, if that huge desire to receive from this world should disappear, the plan of creation will not be fulfilled. Created beings would not receive all the great pleasures that He planned for them. An enormous desire to receive delight and great pleasure correlate to one another. As soon as the desire to receive diminishes, the enjoyment from receiving diminishes as well at the same level.

What is Baal HaSulam trying to say?

He talks about the stages of our development. There is the original desire - *Malchut* and the light. At the next stage, the same *Malchut* acquires egotistical intentions for itself. The next stage is uncorrected. We call it *Shevira*. After that, *Malchut* "destroys" itself, since it wishes gradually to acquire the desire for the sake of the Creator. The work during 6,000 years is a gradual transition from the intention for its own sake to the intention for the sake of Creator. At that, the body is not taken into consideration. It is being constantly destroyed. When the intention for the sake of Creator is fully obtained, the will to receive is resurrected. This constitutes the seventh millennium, when the so-called "dead" rise from their graves and gradually join with the pure intention for the sake of Creator. The next stage marks the achievement of final and complete correction, when the intention for the sake of the Creator prevails.

There exist only the Creator and His Creation. Creation is a desire and everything that is above it is intention. The Creator created desire, and this is what our essence is. Intention is a superstructure built above desire, and it only appears to correct this desire and make it similar to the Creator.

At first, we receive an egoistical intention that is directed towards ourselves, our ego. We then transform it into its opposite. This transformation takes place during the so-called 6,000 years. The end of that period marks a complete acquisition of the altruistic intention. In the seventh millennium, the desire is corrected together with the intention. After that, the *Kli* exists in its infinite form. What is "infinite form"? It means no limitation for any of the original desires. The intention for the sake of Creator makes Creation entirely similar to Him. We do not study what happens with the creation after that.

> *26. As was already said, state one obliges state three to exist. It has appeared in all its completeness, as in state one, according to the plan of creation; nothing less was planed*

Baal HaSulam says that the Creator created *Malchut* in the center of the world of Infinity. *Malchut* is inside the light called the world of Infinity. This is state one.

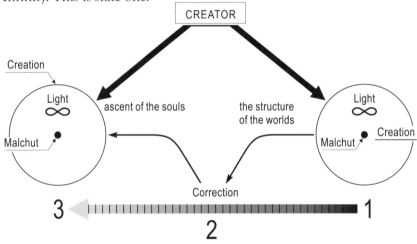

He also created state three, in which *Malchut* exists in the state of Infinity, filled with the light, where all is inside it. So what is the difference? The difference lies in the fact that in the first case only *Malchut* constituted creation; now it expanded and filled the entire volume of the world of Infinity.

This is because having gone through the so-called period of correction it passed from state one to state three. *Malchut* became similar to the entire volume, which we refer to as "the world of Infinity" or the Creator. We can achieve state three either by taking the path of Torah (i.e., correction with the help of the light) or the path of suffering.

In any case, both states are identical as regards the Creator. Time and correction do not exist for the Creator, because with regard to Him both these states are quite obvious and real. Only we, who are moving along this path, gradually pass from one state to the other.

This transition consists of several stages. The first one is called "construction of the worlds", the second – "correction" and the third – "ascent of the souls". The first stage necessitates the existence of the third one.

> So, state one obliges the resurrection of the dead bodies. That is, their huge desire to receive that became worthless, ended, and decayed in state two (during correction). It must again rise from the dead, in its enormous proportions without any reduction, that is, with all its former shortcomings.

> Work begins anew in order to turn the enormous desire to receive into the desire to bestow for the sake of the Creator. Here we win twice: First, we have an opportunity to obtain the abundance and pleasure that is in the plan of creation. We already have a huge desire to receive, which ascends together with these enjoyments.

> Secondly, receiving in this way will be equal to the desire to delight the Creator and will be a "pure" bestowal. In other words, we gain the equivalence of properties with the Creator, which is complete merging of our state one with state three.

Baal HaSulam wishes to tell us that state one, in which the will to receive pleasure was created, is a minimal natural desire. At a later stage, this desire is complemented with a huge "makeweight" – the intention for oneself. This negative intention goes through a period called the "realization of evil", and is completely rejected by the person (considered "dead"). The person who studies Kabbalah acquires the intention for the sake of the Creator with the help of the Upper Light.

That accomplished, the person attaches his desires to the acquired intention and "resurrects" them. When desires are used with the intention for the sake of the Creator, the person becomes completely similar to the Creator.

There are several stages in our development. At first, we only have one desire. Later we acquire the egoistical intention called our "ego". Being our natural properties, our desires are not taken into consideration regardless of what they are and what form they take. The intention (for what purpose we use our desires) is critical.

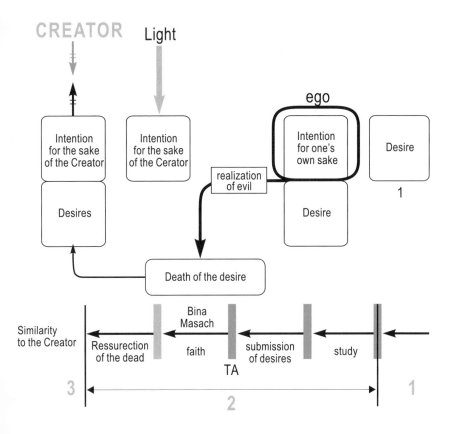

Whatever desires our children may have, we do not consider them egoists. In our view, they resemble small animals, and we treat them with kindness. If a child takes something that does not belong to it, we do not consider it as theft, as something evil. We judge every action by the intention that stands behind it.

Evil begins when I acquire the egoistical intentions. I then recognize them as "dead" and refrain from using them. I detach myself from my previous intentions, neutralize my desires, and acquire the intention for the sake of the Creator under the influence of the Upper Light.

The first stage continues as we study Kabbalah. During our studies, the Surrounding light descends upon us. At some stage we begin to perceive ourselves as egoists, mean, evil people totally opposite to anything spiritual. This happens because under the influence of the Upper Light, we begin to feel our own evil. As we reach a state when we can neither use the intention for our own sake, nor our desires, we will make a kind of *Tzimtzum Aleph* and be ready to receive only spiritual properties. The next stage is the reception of *Masach* (or "faith"), a new *Kli*, the intention for the sake of the Creator.

As soon as we receive it, we proceed to the next stage called "resurrection" and "similarity to the Creator". Baal HaSulam writes about these stages in item 26.

27. *Indeed, resurrection cannot take place before the End of Correction; that is, at the end of state two.*

Baal HaSulam says: resurrection of the dead (i.e., our desires and intentions we refused to use) takes place when we acquire the intention for the sake of the Creator (*Kelim de Ashpa'a*). At the next stage, we add *AHP* to *Galgalta ve Eynaim*. This is the *AHP* that we ignored, considered dead before, and now revived. Thus, we form a complete *Partzuf* consisting of Ten *Sefirot* similar to the Creator.

Reception of the *Galgalta ve Eynaim* is called "acquisition of the intention for the sake of the Creator". The subsequent adding of the *AHP* occurs when we resurrect our old previously unused desires. So the revival of the dead desires, or as Torah describes it, "resurrection of the dead" happens right before the End of correction. Naturally, not a word of what we say refers to our biological bodies. We only speak of desires. Whatever is found in our world has no continuation.

Therefore after we achieved the eradication of our huge desire to receive and earned the desire to bestow, we were privileged to attain the levels of the soul that are called Nefesh, Ruach, Neshama, Haya, and Yechida. We gained the greatest perfection so that the body arises from the dead in all its enormous desire to receive. Now it does not threaten us any more with a separation from our merging with the Creator. On the contrary, by adding the desires of the body (AHP) we get over it and give it the form of bestowal (similarity to the Creator). This is true about any particular bad property.

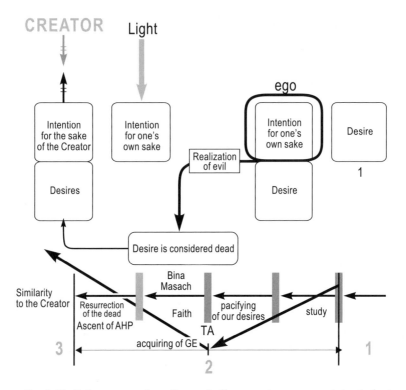

Baal HaSulam says that first of all, we reject our original desires and make a *Tzimtzum* on them. Secondly, we acquire a new desire. Our third action is the resurrection of our old desire.

He says that we apply the same method in our world.

> It deals fairly with any individual bad property that we want to get rid of. At the beginning, we have to give it up completely so that nothing of it remains (i.e., completely neutralize it). Then you can come back (by gradually attaching the AHP), get it over again, and bring it (AHP) to the middle line.

This period is very long. At the beginning, we just study and gradually conclude that all we are made of is evil. We then obtain Faith and the *Kelim* of *Galgalta ve Eynaim* and ascend them. Starting with the period of "resurrection of the dead" we begin to attach to ourselves the *AHP*. The similar process takes place in the worlds as well.

We exist in this world, cross the *Machsom*, acquire the *Kelim* of GE (Aviut 0 and 1) and finally reach the *Aviut* 2 (absolute Faith), three and four (resurrection of the dead). The seizure of evil occurs when the *Machsom* is crossed. "Resurrection of the dead" is the *AHP de Aliya*. By acquiring the *GE* we gradually attach to ourselves the *AHP*. Only when the person can start raising his *AHP*, does he become similar to the Creator, because only reception for the sake of the Creator is considered bestowal.

When the *Kelim* of GE are all I have, I only learn how to bestow. Real bestowal can only be at the last levels three and four, when by receiving pleasure the person pleases the Creator.

Hence, the resurrection of the dead takes place right before the *Gmar Tikkun* (End of Correction). Only at this level can the similarity to the Creator be achieved.

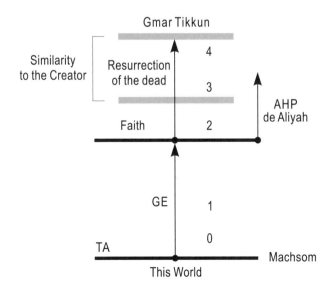

185

28. As it is said by the sages, "In the future, the dead will rise with their defects and then will make a complete recovery". That is, at the beginning, the same egoistical body rises from the dead. It is a huge, limitless desire to receive, one that was nurtured by the system of impure forces before it was honored to be purified by the light with the help of Kabbalah.

Of course, this is an allegory. No dead bodies are going to rise from their graves. When we begin to work with our previously dead *AHP*, it appears in all its original vileness (*Aviut* 3 and 4). We begin to correct the emerging egoism on the last levels of similarity to the Creator. Prior to that, it was only the period of preparation. Although we are in the spiritual world, these are just the *Kelim de Ashpa'a* (vessels of bestowal). However, at the levels three and four, we achieve reception for the sake of bestowal, which is equivalent to absolute bestowal.

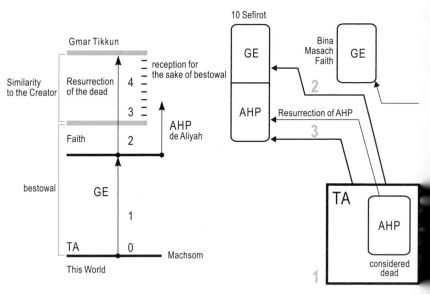

We completely rid ourselves of egoistical desires, acquire altruistic intentions, and begin to resurrect our dead desires from the smallest to the biggest, while attaching them to the altruistic intentions. Such is the order of correction.

> *Thus, all of our desires recover and achieve the similarity of properties with the Creator.* From this, we can understand why the dead must rise from their graves with all their defects. *The expression "Nobody would say that these are different bodies" means: no one would say that this form is different from the one that was in the Thought of creation. The huge desire to receive the abundance of the plan of creation was only temporarily given into the power of the Klipot...* (the intention for oneself).

As a result, the desire is given to the person to correct with the intention "for the sake of the Creator". He not only becomes similar to the Creator in his actions, he becomes equal to Him in that he achieves the ultimate level of existence. He not only enters the Creator's sensations, but also attains the Thought of creation, eternity, perfection, infinity, and absolute freedom.

At that, our world loses its significance, disappears from the sensations of the person who now includes all the other souls.

We should reach this state while living in this world. We should attain and feel all the spiritual levels while being in our biological body. Everyone has this opportunity.

> *29. From all we have explained, it is possible to answer the second question: What is our role in the long chain of reality in which we are small links throughout our short life?*

We come to this world to spend some 60-70 years and have no clue how we are going to live them or what we can make out of this life. The first 20-30 years are spent to reach adulthood. The last years do not count, because we grow too weak, indifferent, and tired. All we have left is a few years to ask a question about the meaning of life and understand something.

What are we and what is our purpose, how can we do or influence something, if our conscious existence is so brief? Why are we so sensitive to this question that animals never ask themselves?

This is what Baal HaSulam says:

> *You should know that our work during the years of our life consists of 4 periods. In the first period, the person acquires a huge, limitless desire to receive in all its depravity, while remaining under the power of the system of the 4 impure worlds of ABYA. This is the AHP, which we gradually destroy. Why does man first acquire enormous desires from all the Klipot? Unless we had that uncorrected desire to receive, we would not be able to correct it, because you can correct only the properties that you have.*

Our first steps consist in acquiring as many desires as we can, although we aspire for the spiritual! Actually, we do not strive to satisfy our egoistical desires. Yet, as the person's spiritual aspirations grow, his egoistical desires awaken and develop as well. Hence the words: "He who aspires higher than others has bigger egoism" are very true.

Do not be surprised by the growing feeling of our egoism. This happens not only because we understand ourselves better, but also because bigger egoistical properties are revealed in us. This way, we acquire the *Kelim* of the *AHP*, the egoistical vessels in their egoistical form (with the intention for oneself).

> *Hence, the desire to receive, which our body has from its birth in this world, is not enough...* For a certain amount of time we should be under the influence of the *Klipot*, i.e., we unconsciously and unwillingly let the egoistical desires grow in us.

The period during which the egoistical desires grow in the person is called "13 years". *This means that impure forces should control the person and give him some of their light under the influence of which his desire to receive would grow, because the pleasures which impure forces supply the desire to receive extend and increase his demands.*

Affected by the Upper Light, egoism grows day by day, because we need more and more of this light. By His purposeful influence, the Creator causes our egoism to grow.

For example, when man is born, there is a desire only for one portion, no more. When the impure forces fill the desire with this portion, the desire to receive doubles immediately. When the impure forces satisfy the increased desire, it extends and wishes to receive four times more pleasure.

Unless the person begins to limit himself and acquire the intention for the sake of the Creator (the *Kelim* of GE), unless he purifies himself, severs all ties with egoism and makes a *Tzimtzum Aleph* (does away with his *AHP*), he will continue chasing various pleasures of this world. Every time he receives some satisfaction from the *Klipa*, his desire would become twice as big as before. Hence, it is said:

If the person does not purify the desire to receive in order to turn it into bestowal, it grows during his lifetime, until he dies without gaining the desired objective.

This is what happens with us during all our incarnations, until we really understand that the pursuit of pleasure never leads to fulfillment.

I was asked by a local TV station to comment on Madonna's visit to Israel and her plans to make a video clip about Kabbalah. People want to know why she decided to do it in Israel. The presenters were genuinely puzzled asking why would someone who has seemingly everything, millions of dollars, influence and fame, all of a sudden seek Kabbalah, come to Israel, although the situation here is rather volatile. Why would Madonna be promoting Kabbalah?

I told them that the person comes to a state, when he or she ostensibly achieved in this life all he ever wanted. Nevertheless, he suddenly realizes that he in fact has nothing. He understands that by increasing his desires he will only intensify his suffering, i.e., he will increase the emptiness of his *Kelim*, his sensations. So instinctively, he begins to search for an alternative method of fulfillment and discovers that this method is at a level that is higher than the usual pursuit of pleasures.

We see that, after satisfying their big desires, people like Madonna suddenly feel that it is not the end, that there is more pleasure waiting to be received. These desires are purely egoistical, but unfortunately, the hosts of the TV show do not feel that way. Everything depends on the level of development of egoism.

> *Thus, the person is under the power of the Klipot and impure forces. Their task is to extend and increase his desire to receive and make it limitless in order to show him the material (all of his AHP) which he should work on and correct.*

Until the person receives this *AHP*, until he perceives it as dead, unfit to be used for receiving pleasure, he will continue reincarnating repeatedly.

By feeling his dead desires that are totally unable to give him a genuine fulfillment, the person will begin to soar and acquire new, sublime *Kelim* of GE. This only happens after the realization of evil.

This process can be accelerated. We should not try to get everything in the world, while receiving blows each time something is achieved with no fulfillment. We do not have to go all the way to the end, when we can save time and avoid suffering with the help of the Upper Light.

By attracting the Upper Light, we see how defective all of our *Kelim* (AHP) are. We have not yet used it, but we see how evil and opposite to the light it is. Therefore, we need not spend many more lives to discover the fallaciousness of the egoistical fulfillment.

This is what we call time contraction; this is what the method of Kabbalah is about. We need to draw the Surrounding light, and by using it, quickly go through the period of realization, correction, and ascent to perfection.

All the stages of this path are predetermined. The only thing that depends on us is the acceleration of time. Without plunging into negative sensations and clashing with our own egoism, we can see the vileness of egoism in advance and avoid its blows.

This is achieved by the most intensive drawing of the Upper Light, which is only possible with the help of a group, of friends who aspire to the Goal together. I can attract the Surrounding light that affects all of us.

If we join our forces, we will make a breakthrough towards the end of state one. If we accumulate the light that everyone can attract, we all would feel its influence and realize our own evil so intensively that we would desire to obtain the Kelim of GE (properties of bestowal). Therefore, everything depends exclusively on our intention, on how much we are prepared to adopt this method.

30. *The second period is from 13 on* (after we come to the realization of the dead state, AHP), *when strength is given to the point in the heart of man. It is the opposite side of the pure soul clothed in the desire to receive from the moment of his birth.*

That is, from the moment of birth, we possess the egoistical *Kelim* that keep growing until we wish completely to reject them. Only then does our point in heart awaken. Even before we reach the level of "13 years", we feel it as an aspiration for the Creator, but it is still suppressed by our egoistical desires. As soon as we see their evil and vileness and relinquish them, the point in heart emerges and manifests.

Awakening does not come before one reaches the level of "13 years". After that, a man begins to pass into the power of a system of the pure worlds because of his study of Kabbalah. The main purpose during this period is to obtain a spiritual desire and to increase it (to reach GE, i.e., the properties of Bina, the screen, Faith, Kelim de Ashpa'a). From his birth, the person only seeks to satisfy his material desires. Therefore, notwithstanding that during 13 years he gains a huge desire to receive (feels his AHP in this first period), his development is not finished yet. The end of development of the desire to receive is an aspiration to spirituality. If for example, during 13 years his desire to receive aimed at receiving wealth and honor in this material world, it is known that this world is not everlasting and that, like a fleeting shadow, everyone appears in it for a brief moment and then disappears.

When he gains the huge desire to receive spirituality, he wants to absorb all the abundance of the eternal world to come for his own pleasure. Therefore, the essence of the huge desire to receive is to gain spirituality.

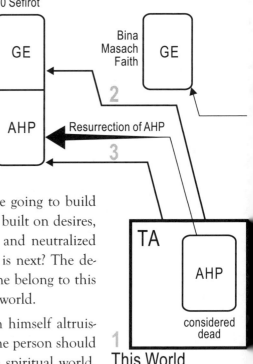

Thus, he acquires the eternal, enormous AHP.

After the first period, the person makes the First Restriction (*Tzimtzum Aleph*) and starts working with the vessels of bestowal in order to acquire a screen. What is he going to build his screen on? The screen is built on desires, yet he restricted, destroyed, and neutralized them in state one. So what is next? The desires he restricted in state one belong to this small, simple, and egoistical world.

In order to develop in himself altruistic intentions in state two, the person should lean on new desires for the spiritual world.

First, he grows his desires of this world up to the level of "13 years". They in turn separate into animate desires and the desires for wealth, honor, fame, and knowledge. This happens in all of our previous incarnations.

Feeling them as evil, he restricts them (makes *Tzimtzum Aleph*) and begins to acquire other desires that develop on spiritual levels.

He builds his altruistic *Kelim* (GE) on the enormous egoistical desires zero and one, which are much greater than "our world". This state is called "*Katnut*" (small state). Now he has GE, or as we say, he achieves the states of *Bina*, the *Masach*, or Faith. Here he begins to build his new desires: two, three, and four. When he reaches the level of "*Gadlut*" (big state), he attaches to himself the *AHP* (levels of *Awzen, Hotem* and *Peh*). At this stage, he becomes similar to the Creator.

This is what the entire path of man is like.

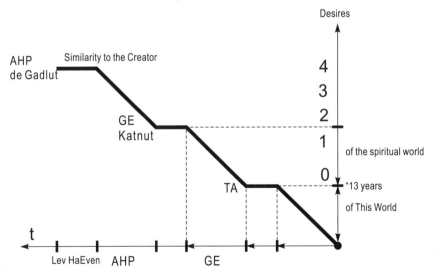

We are now in the middle of the process of realizing evil. After that, we will be building our GE and working with the "dead bodies", i.e., with the *AHP*. This stage will be followed by the correction of the *Lev HaEven* when we achieve complete similarity to the Creator.

Baal HaSulam describes these stages of our development in a different way, uses a different language. We can look upon the states either from the point of the light (the *NaRaNHaY*), or from the point of the *Kelim* (the *Sefirot*). We can also divide them into periods that presumably correspond to a human life. This is because all the spiritual roots have their reflections in our world.

Baal HaSulam may use the language of the Torah (the Bible or Talmud) to demonstrate that all the sacred books write about the same topic: the path man must traverse and how he will do that. He says that the problem starts not in this world, but at the stage that follows, because man's desires begin to grow. The *Klipot* (impure forces) emerge and enable the person to transform their influence into something opposite and pure.

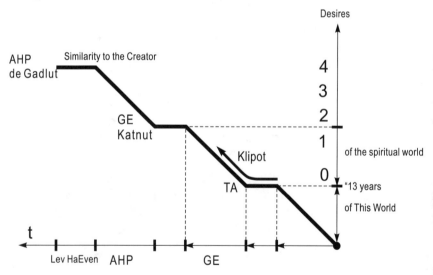

How does it happen? Here is what the Kabbalist says:

31. Our sages say: "The leech has two daughters, crying, give, give (Proverbs 30, 15)": "A leech means Hell (hell is a forced use of the egoistical properties). *The sinners, who fall into the trap of hell, bark like dogs: "Bow-wow" ("Hav-Hav" – Heb.: give-give), meaning – "give us the wealth of this world and the wealth of the world to come".*

The level at which the person works with the *Klipot* is very important, because this way he obtains the material for his work. He acquires the desires without which he cannot become similar to the Creator. Therefore, there must be periods when we receive uncorrected desires and correct them.

Therefore, the level that comes after 13 years is defined as "pure", which is the meaning of the writing, "the house-maid serves her mistress", that is, to serve the Holy Shechina. It means that the maidservant symbolizes egoistical desires that lead to the spiritual level of bestowal, when the person is awarded "the light of Shechina".

It is the person's responsibility to do everything he can in order to gain the state of "Li Shema" (desire to bestow). If he does not make every effort to reach the state of "Li Shema", he will fall into the garbage bin of the "impure" maidservant, who is the opposite of the "pure" one.

Unless the person who studies Kabbalah begins to purify the acquired impure desires, he falls more and more into the *Klipot*.

The zero level corresponds to our natural petty egoism. Below is the area of the *Klipot*; above is the place of *Kedusha*, the intention for the sake of the Creator. Unless the person makes an effort to apply the right method of spiritual ascent, unless he turns the property "-1" into "+1", "-2" into

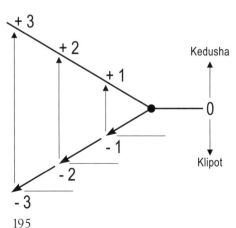

"+2", etc., he falls deeper and deeper under the power of the *Klipot*, until his study of Kabbalah is for his selfish enjoyment, with an intention to pass himself of as an important Rabbi, in order to lock people to him and to turn them into zombies. Thus, he plunges into absolute impurity.

> *This means that the maidservant takes the place of her mistress and prevents the person from approaching the Holy Shechina. The last level of this period is the desire to enjoy the Creator. This resembles man in this world whose passionate desire is so great that it is burning in him day and night, as it is said, "A constant memory does not let me sleep".*

> *It is also said about him, "The tree of life is full of passion", that is the five levels of the soul form the Tree of life for 5oo years. Every level lasts 100 years that brings the person to the reception of all these five levels of NaRaNHaY that become revealed in the third period.*

Why are there exactly 500 years? 500 years is a complete level. Every level is called "100 years", because it consists of 10 *Sefirot* and each *Sefira* in its turn has ten sub-levels. Therefore, the number "100" is considered a complete level. If *Nefesh* is a complete level, it is called "100". This means that man created the *Kli* and acquired for it the inner light called "100". This is how the corrected *Kli* filled with the light is designated. It is defined similarly on all the levels: *Nefesh, Ruach, Haya, Neshama,* and *Yechida,* which totals 500 years. However, this is attained in the third period.

> *32. The third period is in Torah and Commandments Li Shema, that is, for the sake of bestowal and not for receiving a reward. This work purifies man's desire to receive for himself and turns it into the desire to bestow.*

After man acquired all the egoistical desires, not only the *Galgalta ve Eynaim,* but the AHP as well, he begins to work for the Creator. I would like to remind you that "the desire to bestow" and "the desire to receive" are just names. Human beings do not have pure desires to receive or to bestow. The desire to bestow is the Creator's attribute, while the desire to receive is man, creation. This is his property and there is nothing else in him.

If man wishes to become similar to the Creator, he uses his desire to receive for the sake of bestowal, i.e., he receives pleasure to please the Creator. However, he still receives. Desires remain unchanged, only the intention, the method of using the desire is modified. Therefore, when we say that man passes from the "desire to receive" to the "desire to bestow", we ought to understand that he acquires a new intention for the same old desire. This is why old desires with the intention for one's self are considered dead. At a later stage, they rise and become pure and eternal, if man acquires the intention for the Creator's sake instead of the intention for himself.

Let me say this again: although Kabbalah is called a science, it is attained not in the mind of our world, but in the Upper mind. This world is attained in its *Kelim*, in the mind of our world. To start attaining the Upper World above the *Machsom*, one should acquire the mind that corresponds with the Upper World.

The mind of the Upper World is called "faith above reason"; it is the property of bestowal. This property is exactly what constitutes the mind in the Upper World. You may be sitting at the lesson and understand nothing. It does not matter. Just make an effort and this will attract the Upper Light. The Upper Light will create in you the Reflected light, the correct intention. This intention is where you will feel the Upper World and receive the Upper mind.

This will happen not because you will be racking your brain, but because while being confused, irritated and exhausted, you will continue to aspire to Him. You will succeed not because you slept well and came to the lesson in good spirits, with pen and paper, eager to research the

Upper Realm as the scientists of our world. This will only happen because of your effort.

Quite the contrary, everything will work out from the state of confusion, disillusion, detachment, and weariness. When spirituality seems insignificant and unreal, it means that you are in the most correct state with regard to the Creator. If, while being in these states, you continue aspiring to the Upper World, the necessary spiritual *Kelim* (spiritual mind) will be formed in you.

Man rises to the level where so much light descends upon him that he can already transform his desires into spiritual, altruistic.

> As soon as man purifies the desire to receive, he becomes worthy and ready to obtain the five parts of the soul that are called the NaRaN-HaY. They are in the desire to bestow and cannot be clothed into the body until the desire to receive has a power in him.

The soul has two components: one is the *Kli* that consists of five parts: *Keter, Hochma, Bina, ZA* and *Malchut*. It is alternatively called the body of the soul, or the Partzuf. Inside it there is the light called the *NaRaNHaY* (*Nefesh, Ruach, Neshama, Haya, and Yechida*).

As soon as the egoistical intentions become altruistic, desires begin to fill with the Upper Light to the extent of the *Ohr Hassadim* (or the Reflected light, or the screen – the definition is of no consequence). *Keter, Hochma, Bina, ZA,* and *Malchut* are the five *Kelim* that are filled with the five lights of the *NaRaNHaY*.

> However, when man is honored to become entirely a desire to bestow without receiving anything for one's self, he earns the same properties that he has in his upper NaRaNHaY (descending from its source in the world of Infinity from state one through the pure worlds of ABYA). These properties descend upon him immediately and clothe in him in accordance with the level.

The fourth period is the work after rising from the dead. It means that the desire to receive that completely disappeared, died and was buried, rises from the dead in its biggest and worst appearance, as it is said, "In the future, the dead will rise with all their defects", and then turn them into receiving for the sake of giving.

Some special individuals are given this work during their lifetime in this world.

Baal HaSulam says that there are people, who complete this work and reach the levels that are above the "resurrection of the dead", when *Lev HaEven* becomes completely corrected. This is the level we are destined to achieve.

33. Now, there is the sixth analysis left to understand. As it is said by the sages, all worlds, upper and lower, were created only for man, not for anything else. At first glance, it seems very strange that the Creator has tried to create all of this for such an insignificant creature like man, who is like a grain of sand in this world in comparison with the whole universe, let alone with the spiritual worlds.

The matter concerns man's feelings, his mental and spiritual parameters. How can we compare ourselves with the Upper Worlds, when even our world, our universe is a tiny grit in the great cosmos with regard to the smallest level of the Upper World?

We are told that man is created to become the master of all the worlds, to include all of them within him, and that nothing exists except for man with all the worlds within him. How can this be? It utterly contradicts our ideas about ourselves, and the universe that we know by our sensations.

It is even stranger to realize why man needs all these Upper spiritual worlds? What is this universe for? How can we use it? We do not even properly know our own planet. We have no idea of what is a couple of miles below us, or a couple of parsecs above us. Why do we need all that is created around us? Here is what Baal HaSulam answers:

You should know that the Creator receives joy just from the gratification of those whom He has created, but only to the extent in which creation feels Him, feels that He is giving and wishes to delight them. He starts amusing Himself with them as a father who is playing with his beloved son. As much as the son feels and recognizes the greatness and power of his father, he shows him all the treasures that he prepared for him.

Read this again; *As much as the son feels and recognizes the greatness and power of his father (the Creator)...* This means man acquires the properties of the Creator, for how else would he be able to understand?

Think carefully about what was said and then you can understand and know the great amusement of the Creator with those perfect souls that were honored to feel and understand His greatness throughout all the ways He has prepared for them, until they come up to the relationship between father and son. Everything that was written is for those who perceive the spiritual worlds.

Until we reach these levels and establish the same contact with the Upper Force, we will not be able to understand the purpose of all that was prepared for us. As much as we can feel the greatness of this power, realize it on ourselves, and adopt its properties, we will begin to comprehend how we can rule over the universe and all the Upper Worlds in place of the Creator. Only then shall we discover why He created such immense and awesome worlds for us.

There is nothing more to say about it. It is enough to know that for those pleasures and amusements, it was worth it for Him to create all the worlds, both the Upper and the lower, which we are yet to reveal.

*34. In order to prepare His creatures to reach the aforementioned
exalted level, the Creator thought of four levels that evolve one out
of another. They are called still, vegetative, animate, and human,
and they are indeed the four phases of the will to receive that each of
the Upper Worlds consists of. For although the vast majority of the
will is in the fourth phase of the will to receive, it is impossible for it
to materialize all at once, except by the preceding three phases that
gradually expose and develop it, until its form has been completed.*

Man gradually enters into the sensations of the Creator, becomes
similar to Him, masters the system of creation, and begins to rule over
the heritage that the Creator prepared for him. Man gradually ascends
the four levels still, vegetative, animate, and human, while attaining the
four degrees of comprehension of the universe.

These four levels exist in our will to receive and, by correcting each
of them, we ascend to the next level of sensation of power over the surrounding world.

*35. In the first phase of the will to receive, called still, which is the
preliminary exposure of the egoistical desire in this corporeal world,
there is but a general movement that includes the whole of the still
category. But in particular items there is no apparent movement.
That is because the will to receive generates needs and the needs
stimulate movement that is sufficient to attain what it wants.*

It is the same with us; the most important thing is desire. If there
is a desire, I will be able to make a move to receive what I want. If I feel
that I am too lazy, (What does it mean, to be lazy? – It means that my will
to receive is insufficient), I have to work on increasing my will to receive,
and then I will not be lazy anymore.

How can I make this happen within myself? Only with the help of
studies, contacts with others like me, by receiving the Kabbalistic method from the books, listening to what Kabbalists advise us.

Our will to receive is small. To increase it to such an extent that we break through the barrier into the spiritual, we need to turn our desire from being small into being an all-conquering one. One can do this only under external impact, under the influence of a group, when I have 35 people around me.

If all of us out there are given the opportunity to unite, then each of us will receive the will that is 200, 300 times greater, according to the number of people now present at our virtual lesson. It will be quite enough to cross the barrier and enter the Upper World right now. We lack only one thing: the union of our aspirations for the spiritual.

Since there is only a small will to receive, it dominates the whole of the category at once, but its power over the particular items is indistinguishable.

This refers to the first phase – the still level of the will to receive. Each subsequent level appears as a superstructure above the preceding one.

36. The second phase of the will to receive that is called vegetative is added to the first. Its desire is larger than in the still phase, and it dominates every item of the category. Similarly, in the vegetative world we see a germ, a spark of life in every plant.

Each one has its own private movement that spreads up and down and to the sides, and moves where the sun shines (reaction of each part to the Upper Light); **the manner of nourishment and excreting waste is also apparent in each item.** There is already a recognition of what is "good" and "evil"; useful things are attracted, harmful are repelled. Already the vegetative type of will to receive exists in us, but is nonetheless a very small, general desire.

A group appears and, in general, it aspires to something. You may say, "Well, isn't it good that the group aspires to something?" Everyone in the group must be an individual, but at the same time, all of them must be united, merged in a single whole, despite their outstanding individual qualities.

Only then will this gathering of individuals become a group. If they are not prominent individuals, but simply people united on their small level, it is not a group, but an amorphous mass. This difference separates a Kabbalistic group and an ordinary mass of people. A group is made up of people who are developing themselves individually to the maximum, while uniting in one whole to the maximum despite their individuality.

Thus, individuality starts from the second vegetative level, when each of us begins to feel inner movements, to comprehend and distinguish between the notions of "evil" and "good", "to the Creator" and "to myself", "to friends" – "away from them", and so on.

37. In addition, we also have the animate level, the third phase of the will to receive that is so great that it generates in each of its parts (that is, in every individual who reaches the animate level) *a feeling of freedom, which represents a special life of each part that is distinct from the others.*

Plants and trees in the field shed their leaves at the same time, and then begin to grow. The leaves fall because there is no sun; the sun shines for all of them. Conversely, they wake up when the sun rises, turn in the direction of the sun, and so on. That is, there is a common life for all, different from that of the still nature, but it is common for each species.

Each individual animal leads a separate life; each can move around freely, even though there are periods common to specific animal groups, such as mating, development, growth, and rearing. Animals are at the intermediate level, but they have freedom of movement.

In the same way, as we reach the animate level of development where free inner movements awaken within us, work begins on our egoistical desires that are unique for everyone. Yet what is still negative and insufficient on this animate level? Why is it not final? Baal HaSulam says:

> However, these desires yet lack the sensation of their neighbor (this is most important), *that is, they are yet unprepared to feel compassion for others' suffering or joy over their good fortune.*

He does not write, "to feel joy over others' suffering or joy over their good fortune", but puts it in the right, altruistic way: "*to feel compassion for others' suffering or joy over their good fortune.*"

This is the fourth degree of the will to receive. Why do we need it? Why is it something that distinguishes man (by man we mean his spiritual category) from an animal?

> 38. In addition to all is the human level, the fourth phase of the will to receive. This is the complete, fully developed will to receive, because it includes feelings for others.

> If you wish to know with absolute accuracy what the distinction between the third (animate) phase of the will to receive, and the fourth (human) one is, I shall tell you that it is as the worth of a single creature against the whole of reality.

What does the feeling of someone's joy and suffering give me? Why should I feel another's *Kli*, another's desire?

The person who finds himself at the third level of development is an ordinary person. If he reaches the fourth level of the will to receive, he includes in himself all the worlds. Only the quality of feeling his neighbor enables man to grow his will to receive to such a degree where he attains and absorbs the whole universe. This is what he gets from the sensation of others, something that animals lack.

A feeling for others is an altruistic feeling! Animals possess an egoistical sensation of others; they help one another, have families, prides, packs and herds, i.e., groups of all sorts. They have developed mutual aid on a very high, animate, instinctive, egoistical level.

Baal HaSulam writes in paragraph 37, "to feel compassion for others' suffering". Compassion means to feel someone's suffering as one's own or to be happy for his good fortune. When someone else receives, I feel as if I receive.

If man can reach such a level of his will to receive, he rises above nature, above all the other worlds, starting from phase zero, where he is still at the animate level of development. If he rises to the human level, i.e., absorbs in him all the negative and positive desires of those around him and identifies himself with them, then he turns into an immense vessel that includes all souls, all worlds, including the world of Infinity. This whole circle enters inside his large, common soul.

> *This is because the will to receive at the animate level, which lacks the sensation of others, is unable to beget desires and needs other than what is imprinted in this creature alone. Whereas man, who can feel others, acquires their desires and properties as his own, absorbs them, becomes needy of everything that others have too, and is thus filled with envy wishing to acquire everything.* He then acquires additional egoistical desires, the *Klipot*, that he can now correct.

> *When he has a certain share, he wants to double it.* (He sees that someone else has something and craves it). *Therefore, his needs multiply until he wants to swallow all that there is in the whole world.*

He desires all that exists in the world, including the desire called "Pharaoh". He wants the Creator to fill, delight, and serve him. Only owing to our inner quality of envy, meaning sensation of others, can we evolve and reach the level called "man". The rudiments of this opportunity exist outside us. How can we prevent them from leading us to the *Klipot*, away from the Creator? We shall discuss this at length later...

We continue studying "The Introduction to the Book of Zohar." In this Introduction Baal HaSulam tells us about the development of the human soul – from a small Reshimo, which awakens in man, up to the moment when he enters the spiritual world. First, in the form of a spiritual embryo, then as a child, and later on – as an adult, man becomes similar to the Creator and enters the sensation of eternity, infinity, and perfection. He rises above life and death, feels life as an endless process. Therefore, he naturally perceives his state in this world quite differently.

Each of us aspires to achieve such a state because the people who feel good do not come to Kabbalah. All of us need something, but mostly we are restless because of the tormenting question about the point of our life. The point of life can be attained as a result of the revelation of the Upper World, the Creator, the entire universe in which we exist (it is called the Creator on the highest level with regard to us). The remaining lower levels are called the worlds.

Kabbalah explains how man can go through all these intermediate states and rise from the level of this world to the Upper World, and then reach the highest level of merging with the Creator. Since it reveals the most important concerns in our life, man's purpose, what he is going to achieve from his efforts in this world, this wisdom is vitally important for man. Because Kabbalah not only theoretically explains the existing reality, but also ushers the person into the Upper World, it is also important for the entire humankind.

We are just beginning to understand it and hope that others will soon realize it too, thanks to our efforts. The only means for entering the Upper World is the spiritual light that corrects us. We should expose ourselves to this light, so that it will pull us out of this reality into the sensation of the Upper World. Only during the studies can we tune ourselves up to this Supreme force (the so-called *Ohr Makif* – the Surrounding light). Being surrounded by the Upper Light is the most favorable state. We just need to prepare ourselves, be more sensitive to it, and wish to be influenced, corrected by this light.

The influence of the light depends on our desire, which can be increased at the expense of desires of other people. The way we receive desires for something in this world, from our environment, the virtual group, all of us should tune each other to the reception of the Upper Light and to spiritual ascent. When this becomes the most important thing in our life, when we need the influence of the Upper Light more than anything else, it will reveal itself to us and elevate us to the next level.

Therefore, during our studies we should imagine huge virtual groups with hundreds of people who gather and listen to us in Russian, Hebrew, and English all over the world. We should get to know each other well and encourage it in every way possible. We need to create a common webpage, post our photographs, and share our impressions. You should join this virtual group so that our spiritual aspirations will merge. Then the light of correction will shine upon all of us and elevate us to the Creator.

As a teacher and a guide, I only direct you to the Creator. Do not lock yourselves to me. Your opinions, desires, requests, and demands should be directed to the Creator alone. Even the questions you ask me on the forum, in your letters and in phone conversations should first be turned to Him. You may receive the answer and find the necessary solution within yourself. This will be the Creator's reply to you.

After such attempts, when nothing is clear to you and it makes you suffer, you may turn to me. However, even in this case you may not receive my answer, because the answer to such questions should come from Above. As a teacher, I will not answer them.

Our advancement is directly connected with the higher spiritual level. We should try to demand the *Ohr Makif* from it, address all our questions to it and only from it receive the answers. The group, the teacher, and the books are only the means that help us to advance. This is the attitude we should adopt. Do not replace the Creator with Rav or the group, because they are only auxiliary instruments on our path to Him.

Now we will find out how to advance towards the Creator. Baal HaSulam says:

> 39. *We have shown that the Creator's purpose is to bestow upon His creatures, so that they may know His genuineness and greatness, and receive all the delight and goodness He had prepared for them.* We do not yet understand His purpose, but it will gradually transpire. It is most clear to the Kabbalists, on whose behalf Baal HaSulam speaks. They attain the purpose, the meaning, and the final result of the entire creation.

> *After that, we* (i.e., the Kabbalists) *clearly find that this purpose does not apply to the still and the large planets such as the Earth, the Moon, or the Sun, however luminous they may be.*

> *The Creator's intentions refer neither to the vegetative nor to the animate level of nature* (although they live some form of a biological life), *for they lack the sensation of others* (they cannot even develop it on their own level, let alone on the higher one).

They lack the sensation of others, of jealousy, envy, and real pleasures, even of the animate kind. Animals do not feel pleasure. All they do is dictated by their inner instincts. Since they are unable to absorb the desires of others, they naturally cannot enjoy the pleasures of others either. An animal may be either hungry or not, but it cannot get hungry by simply looking at another hungry animal.

Even on a primitive animate level, desires do not pass from one animal to another, even more the desire to attain a higher spiritual level, which is initially absent in us. Suppose I have no idea what it means to be a scientist, a professor, or an actor. However, I look at them and see how they enjoy it, so I want to be like them. With the help of "*Kinah, Ta'avah ve Kavod*" (envy, craving for pleasures and the desire for honor and fame), I can acquire from others the tastes that are totally unknown to me. This way, my *Kli*, my desire, can constantly grow, and I can infinitely develop it in our world by absorbing all the desires existing in the universe and even on the spiritual level. It resembles a hypothetical situation where, with the help of certain actions, a plant could turn into an animal, or an animal into man. However, only humans can rise to the Divine level. This is possible because the root of such a property is present in us – the sensation of another human being. This property is absent in the inanimate bodies, plants and animals.

We are born with only animal desires, purely animal instincts that existed in primitive people. These are our bodily desires for such natural pleasures as food, sex, home and family. Besides, as a result of envy man develops a desire to receive something that another person has, even if he does not really need it. Even if I have all that my heart desires, but there is someone who enjoys something else; then I want to receive that pleasure too.

Finally, the desires for power and honor bring me pleasure, because I feel people's submission and respect. These are man's ultimate aspirations in this world. It does not matter to me that I do not have it in my pocket; I enjoy people's attitude toward me. This makes me bigger, more significant.

Envy, craving for pleasures, and the desire for fame and recognition develop man to such an extent that he can attach additional egoism from others to his own and begin to advance spiritually.

Man does not receive his desires only from the level of this world. He has a "point in his heart" – the egoistical spiritual desire. In Hebrew, it is called "*Achoraim de Nefesh de Kedusha.*" This is the egoistical desire of the upper level. I come to desire to control this Upper level, the Creator. I want Him to do what I wish. The attainment is not limited by the desires of this world; the process continues in the Upper Worlds. Always, my Upper level begins with my desire to enslave the Creator.

When I discover His properties and gradually reveal His perfection, it transforms me in such a way that I already wish him to enslave me, my egoism. I want Him to pass His properties to me, so that I may absorb them and become similar to Him.

However, everything begins with huge egoistical desires. Hence, it is said: "He, who is higher than another has greater egoistical desires." One should not be afraid of that.

Therefore, a few months after the person begins to study Kabbalah, he suddenly notices that his egoism has grown. For example, he never dreamed about millions of dollars before, and all of a sudden, he realizes what the passion for money is. He never thought of honor and recognition, for why would he need that and from whom? From other two-legged creatures? Yet suddenly he begins to crave it; he wants people to pay attention to him. The person who was quite moderate in his animal instincts (food and sex) suddenly loses his mind. It becomes his inner obstacle, which gave him no trouble before.

Everything that happens to the person in the process of his spiritual growth is based on the development of egoism. It is said in the Babylonian Talmud that, since the destruction of the Temple (when we spiritually fell to the level of this world), the real taste for sex and the genuine egoistical desires ("sex" being the core of our animal pleasures) can only be enjoyed by those who aspire to the Upper World (*"Ta'am Biah Nishar Rak le Ovdei HaShem"*). We need to correct additional egoism for advancing spiritually.

Having realized that the Creator's desire, the purpose of creation, is in bestowing pleasure upon created beings, we now clearly see that this purpose refers neither to the inanimate bodies nor to huge planets, since they have no sensation of others. Neither does it concern the plants and animals in our world, because they also lack such a sensation. How will they be able to feel the Creator's goodness if they cannot even feel their own kind?

When we develop and reach the spiritual level called "man", i.e., when our egoism is so developed that we want much more than others, we begin to envy them and desire whatever they have, although initially we never had such desires. We envy their pleasures, honor, fame, and wish to conquer the whole world. This is called the real man. He is still uncorrected, yet he is ready for it because he already has what to correct.

Man alone, after having been prepared with the sensation of others who are like him, after delving into Torah and the commandments, will turn his will to receive (egoistic, enormous desire acquired from outside) into the will to bestow, and come to equivalence of form with his Maker. Then he reaches the levels that had been prepared for him in the Upper Worlds. This is the way we ascend the Upper Worlds.

As we receive additional portions of egoism (from the left line), we begin to correct it with the help of the Upper Light by raising a request (commandment) and receiving the Torah (the light of correction) from Above. The correction occurs with the help of the right line, the descending light. Thus, we create ourselves in the middle line. Our egoism of the left line becomes similar to the Creator's properties of the right line.

We build ourselves between the two lines, while receiving the *NaRaNHaY* on all the 120 levels of our ascent to the world of Infinity. The *NaRaNHaY* in the world of Infinity is referred to as the light of the Torah; its parts on the preliminary stages between our level and the world of Infinity are called *Nefesh, Ruach, Neshama, Haya,* and *Yechida.* While ascending the five worlds we receive the light of *Nefesh* in the world of *Assiya*, the light of *Ruach* in the world of *Yetzira*, the light of *Neshama* in the world of *Beria*, the light of *Haya* in the world of *Atzilut* and the light of *Yechida* in the world of *Adam Kadmon*.

As we ascend from the world of *AK* to the world of Infinity, we simply are included into the common light already called, not the *NaRaNHaY*, but the Torah. There are no distinctions or subtle nuances in it, just the perfect light.

Thus, rising from our world to the world of Infinity, we pass through the following levels: first "secret", then "allegory", after that "hint" and finally "simplicity". It is called *PaRDeS – Pshat, Remez, Droosh*, and *Sod*. The *Pshat* is the simplest light in the world of Infinity; the *Droosh* (the light in the worlds of *AK* and *Atzilut*) is below it; then the *Remez* is like a hint in the world of *Beria* and *Yetzira* and the *Sod* in the world of *Assiya* and in our world, the secret, concealed light, which we neither feel nor understand.

Therefore the attainment of the *PaRDeS* occurs in the reverse order (from down upwards). This is what the *Gaon* from Vilna says in his prayer book: "The *PaRDeS* constitutes four different levels of attainment: first the simple, then a little deeper, then deeper still and finally very profound knowledge".

Thus, we ostensibly attain the *PaRDeS*, but in fact, we just mechanically study what is written in the book, staying within the bounds of a simple learning of the text on the level of our world. In reality, the attainment of the *PaRDeS*, i.e., of the Torah in the world of Infinity is simple, like the light that is shining there, because even the *NaRaNHaY* becomes one simple light on that level.

Here Baal HaSulam says that the common people who study the Torah think that everything is studied on our level and that the knowledge of the laws of the universe requires no spiritual ascent. He calls such people "philosophers" or "*Baalei Batim*" (house owners), or sometimes "false sages".

40. *I know that it is completely unaccepted in the eyes of some philosophers. They cannot agree that man, whom they think of as low and worthless, is the center of the magnificent creation.*

In other words, man should not ascend and absorb the entire Creation. Everyone except for Kabbalists thinks this way. Kabbalists, however, are convinced that just with the help of his egoism, and not through its suppression, man should take in this whole world and become similar to the Creator in his attitude to the universe.

Baal HaSulam says: *I know that it is completely unaccepted in the eyes of some philosophers...* He speaks about "the know-it-alls" among us, who are not willing to grasp the universe and rise above it. *They are like the worm that is born inside a radish and thinks that the Creator's world is as bitter and dark as the radish it was born in. However, as soon as the shell of the radish breaks and it peeps out, it wonders and says: "I thought the whole world was the size of my radish..."* This is what we say to ourselves today. Each of us feels this way before crossing the *Machsom*. "I thought the whole world was the size of my radish, and now I see before me a grand, beautiful, and wondrous world!"

So too are those who are sunk in the shell of the will to receive; they were born with (that prevents them from feeling something beyond themselves), *and did not taste the new means, new sensations and the divine properties* (that would enable them to transcend the bounds of their egoism and feel the world beyond themselves) *that can break this hard shell and turn it into a will to bestow contentment upon the Maker* (i.e., become equal to Him). *It is certain that they must determine their worthlessness and emptiness, as that is what they really are like, and cannot*

213

comprehend that this magnificent reality had not been created but for them.

Indeed, if they had delved into Kabbalah in order to bestow contentment to their Maker (if they had transformed their egoistic desires into bestowal upon the Creator). *They would try to hatch from the shell they were born into and receive the will to bestow, their eyes would immediately open to see and attain all the pleasant and sweet, beyond words, degrees of wisdom, intelligence and clear mind, which have been prepared for them in the spiritual worlds. Then they themselves would say as our sages said: "What does a good guest say? Everything the host did, he did for me alone".* We should attain this level and see all that the Creator is doing for us. "All" implies the level of the world of Infinity.

We learn that the last level of man's attainment is called the "Thought of creation". The first, the second, the third, and then the fourth levels descend from there, from the four stages of the Straight light. The highest level consists of two parts. The lower part of this root level, *Behina Shoresh*, refers to us. The Upper Light descends from it and gives birth to *Behina Aleph*, the first stage of the Direct light, but this is the lower part of the root level. The upper part of the root level is the Creator's Thought, where all that was created is inside Him, on His level. We should reach this level.

Although we are born on the lower part (zero stage), we have to achieve the Creator through our own effort.

Behina Shoresh consists of two parts. The first stage (the will to receive) is born from the lower part. Then the second stage (the will to bestow) emerges. Here the Creator's action manifests with regard to us. His Thought is in the upper part (the zero stage).

We are born in the third stage, and then the fourth stage follows. *Malchut* transforms itself, performs *Tzimtzum Aleph*, acquires a screen,

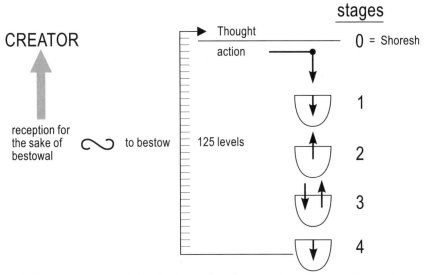

and then ascends 125 levels through a long series of corrective actions. Although it was born because of the Creator's action, by imitating His actions, it rises, achieves His Thought, and merges with Him, since "similarity" in the spiritual world implies likeness to the Creator's actions – the desire to bestow. Our will to receive for the sake of bestowal is equivalent to the Creator's bestowal.

It is said: "*I will know You by Your actions*", (i.e., we reach the Creator's level. "I will know You" means I will rise to the level of Your thoughts). This is what similarity gives us. Only after reaching the level of the Creator's thoughts can we really say: *Everything the host did, he did for me alone.*

41. However, there still remains a need to clarify why man would need all those Upper Worlds the Creator built for him? For what use has he of them?

Bear in mind, that reality is generally divided into five worlds, which are Adam Kadmon, Atzilut, Beria, Yetzira, and Assiya. Indeed, in

*each of them there are an infinite number of details, which are the
five Sefirot...*

Each world consists of five parts, called *Sefirot*. I would call them
five *Partzufim*: Galgalta, AB, SAG, MA, and BON, alternatively, Atik, AA,
AVI, and ZON. It is not so important how we name them. Baal HaSulam
calls them *Sefirot* instead of *Partzufim*: Keter, Hochma, Bina, Tifferet, and
Malchut. He does not wish to divide the worlds into *Partzufim*: five worlds
with five *Partzufim*, five *Sefirot* in each *Partzuf* amounts to 125 levels. He
wants to explain that:

> *Because the world of Adam Kadmon is Keter, and the world of
> Atzilut is Hochma, and Beria is Bina and Yetzira is Tifferet and
> the world Assiya is Malchut. And the lights that dress in those five
> worlds are called YHNRN, as the light of Yechida shines in Adam
> Kadmon (the most powerful common light of the Torah,
> which shines in the world of Infinity), the light of Haya shines
> in Atzilut, the light of Neshama shines in Beria, the light of Ruach
> shines in Yetzira, and the light of Nefesh shines in Assiya.*

> *All these worlds and everything in them are included in the holy
> name Yud Hey Vav Hey, and the tip of the Yud. In the first world,
> Adam Kadmon, we have no perception. Therefore, the tip of the Yud
> of the name indicates it; we do not speak of it and always mention
> only the four worlds ABYA. The Yud is the world of Atzilut, the Hey
> is Beria, the Vav is Yetzira, and the bottom Hey is Assiya.*

> *42. We have now explained the five worlds that include all the spiri-
> tual reality that extends from Infinity to this world. Indeed they are
> included one in the other and in each of the worlds there are the five
> worlds, the five Sefirot - Keter, Hochma, Bina, Tiferet, Malchut,
> where the five lights - NaRaNHaY are dressed, which correspond to
> the five worlds.*

Besides the five Sefirot, in each world there are the four spiritual categories - Still, Vegetative, Animate, Speaking - where the soul of man is regarded as the Speaking in that world, and the Animate is regarded as the angels in that world. The Vegetative are called the clothes, and the Still are called the halls.

They are all dressed one into the other - the Speaking, which are the souls of people, are dressed in the five Sefirot: Keter, Hochma, Bina, Tifferet and Malchut - in that place. The Animate, which are the angels are dressed into the souls, the Vegetative - which are the clothes – dress into the angels and the Still - which are halls - encompasses them all.

The world of Assiya includes our world. The initial point of the Yud is in the world of AK and in the world of Infinity. That point is the beginning of the whole creation and the little tail beneath it points at what emerges and spreads from the point. This corresponds to Shoresh.

Why are these four letters used? This is because the point is a source of the light. If the source of the light moves to the right, it means the light of *Hassadim*. If it moves to the left, it is the lack of *Hassadim*. If this point goes down, it means the spreading of the light of *Hochma*, if it goes up – the light of *Hochma* disappears.

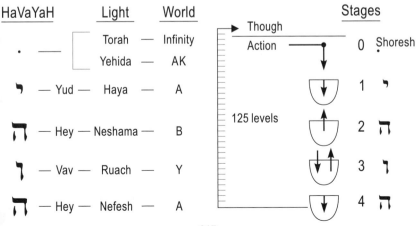

HaVaYaH		Light	World		Stages	
. ─		Torah ─	Infinity	Though Action ─	0	Shoresh
		Yehida ─	AK			
י	─ Yud ─	Haya ─	A		1	י
ה	─ Hey ─	Neshama ─	B	125 levels	2	ה
ו	─ Vav ─	Ruach ─	Y		3	ו
ה	─ Hey ─	Nefesh ─	A		4	ה

217

All kinds of combinations occur inside the construction of the *Kli: Keter, Hochma, Bina, ZA,* and *Malchut.* Each of these five desires has its own property and interrelates with the rest. In addition, we act with the screen and see how we can fill ourselves, so it turns out that there is never a "pure reception" or a "pure bestowal".

"Pure receptions" and "pure bestowals" only exist in the world of AK. It is from there that the light spreads through the world of Infinity down to our world. The light, which descends from the world of Infinity to the world of AK splits, into *Nefesh, Ruach, Neshama, Haya* and *Yechida,* where they descend to us in their pure form.

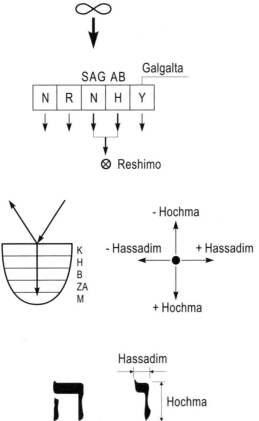

The *Galgalta* is the light of *Yechida,* the AB is the light of *Haya,* and the SAG is the light of *Neshama.* When the two lights AB-SAG come to us, they correct and purify us with all their power.

They influence the *Reshimo* and the *Reshimo* (depending on its structure) chooses how much of the light of *Hochma* and *Hassadim* should affect it. Therefore, the *Reshimo* (its inner structure) determines to what kind of influence it will be exposed. Perhaps, *the* influence of the light on the *Reshimo* would be in the form of the letter "*Vav*" – a little of the light of *Hassadim* and much of the light of *Hochma*, from up downwards. Alternatively, perhaps it is in the form of the letter "*Hey*", where in the "*Reish*" (the massive spreading of *Hassadim* on the light of *Hochma*) there is a small "*Vav*" inside. This letter consists of the two *Partzufim*, the inner and the outer, like a mother with a fetus (the tiny inner *Partzuf*) inside her womb. This characterizes *Bina* when it is the first (upper) "*Hey*". We will discuss the structure of the letters later on. They constitute the complete spreading of the light in all of its variations; hence, the name HaVaYaH implies the influence from Above.

The inanimate, vegetative, animate and human levels are divided into the *Heichalot* (Baal HaSulam calls them halls, sometimes we call them houses), the *Levushim* (clothes), the *Malachim* (angels) and finally the souls (man).

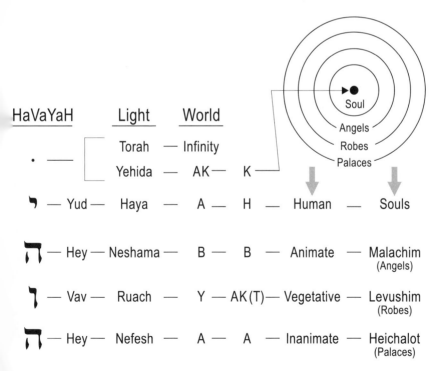

As you may see, there is nothing regarding *Keter* because this is the Creator. If we begin to analyze how these spiritual levels are inter-related, we will discover that the soul is in the center, the angels dress on the soul, the *Levushim* dress on the angels and the halls dress on the *Levushim*. Inside the soul, a part descends from *Keter*. It consists of the Ten *Sefirot* of the Straight light, the Ten *Sefirot* of the "*Kav*" ("line").

Since the soul "dresses" on the Creator, it is in turn surrounded by the angels, the clothes, and the so-called halls. It is preferable to use the Hebrew names, because in Hebrew their structure and inscription include many different elements. These words are very meaningful and they include many levels of information.

> *Since the soul "dresses" on the Creator and the angels, the clothes and the halls dress on the soul, it becomes clear that the angels, the clothes and halls, i.e., the outer universe regarding the soul is only necessary for bonding this soul with the Creator, who is inside it.*

Now we begin to deal with ourselves, and Baal HaSulam speaks about our path from the lowest level. You will not find the things he so clearly and laconically explains in this Introduction anywhere else. He writes openly about the things that are normally ignored. How much of it can we grasp?

While reading these lines please let us think of each other, of how we can help each other by simply joining our desires. Let us assume there are 1000 men and women in the world, who simultaneously listen to me about the Creator's revelation to man. Let us all together want it to happen to us. This is called the raising of prayer, of desire, that will be answered with the Surrounding light. It will, by all means, generate this action in us.

> *43. When man is born, he immediately receives a "holy soul", Nefesh...* Oh! If he only could have it... But he does not. So what do we actually have when we begin to aspire to the Creator? *However,*

not an actual soul, but the posterior of it, meaning its last category, which is called a "point" because of it smallness. It is inserted in man's heart, in his will to receive, which is found primarily in man's heart.

Heart means all our egoism. There is a point in the heart – the reverse side of the soul, its beginning, its root. It is a tiny part that is destined to become the soul and will have to go through inversion in order to become a true point of the soul.

We feel it as opposite to our egoism. Even if I wish for the spiritual, my desire is absolutely egoistic. My point is called "a point in the heart", because it is in the midst of my egoistic desires. It is in the center of my heart. For example, after satisfying all my egoistic desires of this world, I now want to grab the spiritual delights (I can think of no better word).

Know this rule, for all that you will find in reality in general, you will also find in every world, even in the smallest particles of it.

The same laws that rule in the universe influence the very last, microscopic part of it. The Hebrew phrase "*Prat u Klal Shavim*" (the common and the individual are equal) explains the idea. This is because there cannot be even a slightest detail that would not consist of five stages of the Straight light. All that is concentrated in these five stages only spreads through the worlds from our first state to the third. Actually, nothing else was created except for these stages of the Straight light. Every minute detail consists of them. Therefore, "*Prat u Klal Shavim*" is the general law of the universe, even its smallest part.

The smallest soul and the sum of all the souls are equal. There is nothing in the spiritual that would be bigger or smaller than something else would. Moreover, if one is against all the rest of the 599,999 souls, this one is equal to all the others. This is a marvelous property of the spiritual world.

Just as there are five worlds in reality, which are the five Sefirot, Keter, Hochma, Bina, Tifferet and Malchut, so too are there five Sefirot, Keter, Hochma, Bina, Tifferet and Malchut in, each and every world, and there are five Sefirot in the smallest particle of that world.

Everything is divided into five parts.

We have stated that this world is divided into the still, vegetative, animate, and human levels. They correspond to the four Sefirot, Hochma, Bina, Tifferet, and Malchut; or rather in the reverse order, Malchut, Tifferet, Bina, and Hochma.

Indeed, even in the smallest particle of each species in the still, vegetative, animate, and human levels, there are four inner categories: still, vegetative, animate, and human. The same exists in a single species, i.e., in one person..., in all of us.

Now let us understand what man is. Why should we think about anything else? We are the most active part of the universe, that which is destined to bring everything to the Creator. If we (the soul) merge with the Creator, then the halls, the clothes, and the angels will merge with Him together with us (i.e., the entire universe ascends to the Creator's level). This depends only on our desire and our work. Therefore, we study the level of "man" and the way he ascends to the Creator.

So even in one person, there are also four levels (still, vegetative, animate and human), which are the four parts of his will to receive.

In all, there are five kinds of desires. We call them *Aviut* zero, one, two, three and four. All of these egoistic levels of a desire, still, vegetative, animate and human, exist in our world and are characterized by the general notion of a man's heart.

The still level is represented by the bodily desires for food, sex, family, and home. The vegetative level is the desire for riches. The animate level is the desire for honor and fame. The human level is the desire for knowledge. Above it, there is only the spiritual desire.

We can see the same inside us. Even on the level of the biological and physical-chemical structure of the body, there are various minerals, non-organic compounds (the still level). Then there are nails and hair (the vegetative level). The next to follow is our flesh (the animate level) and finally, our inner psychology (the human level). Yet all of theses parts are of the animate level. Above them is also the Divine nature that is called a point in heart. Man begins to study Kabbalah only because this point prevails in his heart. Instead of craving this world with its food, sex, family, its chasing after money, fame and even knowledge, man becomes interested in something bigger, even without knowing what it is. This point makes him restless.

> 44. Earlier than the "thirteen years of age" (a relative level in man's development) there cannot be any detection of the point in his heart. However, after "thirteen years", when he begins to delve into Kabbalah, even without any intention for the Creator's sake, (i.e., without any love and fear, as there should be with someone who serves the king), even not For Her Name, the point in his heart begins to grow and reveal its action.

Man, who begins to feel an aspiration for the spiritual world is considered to have come of age. From then on, he willy-nilly begins to develop the point in his heart, because this desire prevails over the others. He tries all kinds of ways until he finds a group, a book, and a teacher. The point in the heart leads him to the place, to the source that can fill him. We believe it to happen by chance, but it is not so.

However, man should constantly check the source from which he receives. I advise all of you who are sitting before your monitors not to trust me, to check for yourselves where you are. Perhaps you may find a better company, a wiser teacher who will provide you with a more powerful influence and lead you to the Purpose of creation. This is our main task. The rest is a means for achieving the goal.

You should have no other image before your eyes except for the Creator. You should say to yourself, "Only in order to achieve Him, am I ready to listen to some wise man, read some books, be in some company of people, make a sacrifice, etc. The Creator should constantly be in front of me; He alone should determine what I do.

This is the correct development of the point in the heart. Even if my desire for the Creator is egoistic, I still aspire for Him and nothing else. By no means should I join someone in order to feel more secure and comfortable.

I once asked my Teacher: "How can I be sure that I am in the right place? I have only one life, so I wish to realize everything I need by my-self". His answer was very simple: "Keep looking. This is your free will".

The freedom of will is in a constant search for the right group. Only after you have checked everything, may you begin to work on its improvement. You are obliged to do it because your future depends on your environment, on your books, and teachers. Do not take anything on trust. You should check everything because this is the only way you can grow. Unless you put your effort into the group, unless you try to make it stronger, you will not be able to grow.

The realization of my freedom of will consists in exerting influence on the teacher, the books, the group, and consequently the Surrounding light, so that it will develop me. If man relaxes and wants to get under the wing of some wise person, some Rabbi, he confines himself to the still level and stops growing. Try to avoid such aspirations, although our body desires them very much. We should force ourselves every second to shake them off and realize our free will. Thus, we will only shorten the period of our correction because all the levels are predetermined. We will not reach the next level until we have corrected this one.

Even if man begins to study Kabbalah without any intention for the Creator's sake, the point in his heart begins to grow.

This is what we partially feel and hope that it will continue to develop. The actions performed by the beginning Kabbalist so far do not require the intentions. Man always acts with a certain intention – with the egoistic intention for his own sake. However, regarding the spiritual, these actions are considered to be without intention. We can influence something in the spiritual only in accordance with our altruistic intention. Therefore, at the beginning of our development, even an egoistic intention is good enough. It is important to have a huge desire to conquer the spiritual world and the Creator, even if it is egoistic.

In his book "*Pri Hacham*", Baal HaSulam says in one of his letters on page 70, "This should be similar to the sensation of a man overwhelmed by passion for his beloved. He can neither see nor hear anything; it fills his whole world, he ... loses his mind". In Hebrew, it is called "*Metoraf*" (crazy). There is no other pleasure that can fill his empty *Kli*.

This is exactly the state we have to achieve with regard to the Creator. Only He can fill my vessels. I do not want anything else. This is the final level of this world after which we pass on to the spiritual one.

Man purifies, corrects the still level of his egoistic desire ...

That is what we do today. We do not know anything on this level. We cannot see the difference between the elements. They are still. As a result, we pass through all 613 parts of the point in heart. Actually it consists of 620 parts, but we agreed on 613 parts that exist in every spiritual organ, shell, *Partzuf*, both in the general structure of *Adam* and in each of its individual parts. It does not matter what we speak about, whether it be the five stages or the 10 *Sefirot* or the 613 parts. There can be neither more nor less than that.

To the extent that man aspires for the Creator, he purifies the still part of the desire to receive. He builds the 613 organs of the point in the heart, which is the still level of the pure soul. When all the 613 actions called the commandments are completed, he creates the 613 organs (the corrected parts) of the point in the heart, which is the still part of the holy soul.

Let us imagine our big egoistic heart with a tiny point consisting of 613 desires. I should develop each of them to the maximum and direct them to the Creator. I neither know nor understand any of these 613 desires in the heart. I do not feel the difference between them because these desires are of the still level. However, this is not important. Like a still body, I automatically aspire to the Creator with my might.

Two hundred forty-eight spiritual organs are built through the observance of the 248 actions of "do" (precepts that you have to perform in), and its 365 spiritual organs are built through the observing of the 365 precepts of "do not do", until it becomes a whole Partzuf of pure Nefesh.

What does it mean? I have the Partzuf that consists of two parts – 248 and 365, in all – 613.

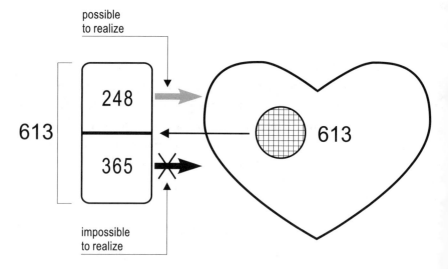

Two hundred forty-eight actions out of 613 that I perform with my desires are those with whose help I can act. Basically, these are my actions in the group, with all the people, friends, and family – the desires in which I can express and realize myself.

However, there are actions in which I cannot realize myself. I have no idea how to work with them correctly. These are not simply desires to kill or to steal. These are all of my desires that I cannot connect with the spiritual in any way.

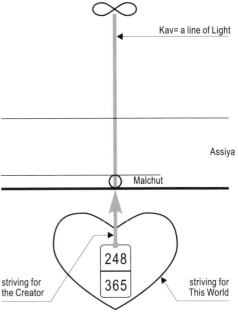

This is a natural process. We should not think: "Now I want something, so how am I to deal with this desire, satisfy it or refrain from it?" When I aspire to the Creator on the level of my point in the heart, I still do not have the inner definitions and cannot make this inner analysis. It is not necessary at this point. Consequently, my level is defined as still. I have not yet received the light from Above that breaks my point into 613 tiny squares where I know what properties each of them represents and that they are connected with the Creator. I cannot do that yet. However, when I do it... "*my level of Nefesh rises and dresses Malchut in the spiritual world of Assiya*".

Below the level of the spiritual worlds, inside my heart (the heart is all our desires, but you should on no account imagine the biological heart) the *Partzuf* emerged (my aspiration to the Creator as something

227

distinct from the aspirations of this world). If I aspire to the Creator, I rise to the level of *Malchut* of the world of *Assiya* on the first still level.

All the worlds form a descending line ("*Kav*"). "*Kav*" is the line of the light descending from the world of Infinity down to this world. When my *Partzuf* is complete, it rises and "dresses" from Above onto the *Malchut* of the World of *Assiya*, on the light that is there.

In other words, my soul "dressed" on this line with the angels, the clothes, and the halls enveloping my soul. They are added because these are my auxiliary desires that I have realized in order to ascend to this particular level.

> All the spiritual parts of the still, vegetative and animate levels in the world that correspond to the Sefira of Malchut of Assiya serve and aid the soul of man who has risen there. To the extent that Nefesh (the soul, the very first level) uses them, they become spiritual nourishment to it...

All of these halls, clothes, and angels are our desires, except for the aspiration to the Creator. These are the desires of our world that strengthen my aspiration to the Creator. Even the hindrances in the form of a bad boss or problems with the children, everything that surrounds me in this world, are all the positive and negative influences that aspire together with me and "dress" on my soul, on the *Malchut* of the world of *Assiya*.

This means that, if I carry out a spiritual action and there are people who help me to do that, then as I ascend to a certain spiritual level, all those who helped me, "dress" on me with their inner parts and receive the light. This reception is still unconscious because they have not yet prepared their inner spiritual *Kli*. However, they do take part in the process. This is what makes the connection between all the people in the world so important. Through mutual aid, communication, and trade, our world has now become a small village. The world, as it exists with regard to the ascending man, rises together with him and enters the clothes of the *Malchut* of the world of *Assiya* and then even higher.

> To the extent that Nefesh uses them (the auxiliary desires: the halls, the clothes and the angels) they give it strength to grow and multiply until it can extend the light of the Sefira of Malchut of Assiya in all the desired perfection to shine in man's body. That complete light aids man to add toil in Kabbalah and receive the remaining higher levels.

> Just as immediately at the birth of man's body, a point of the light of Nefesh is born and dressed in him, so it is here, when his Partzuf of "pure Nefesh" is born. A point from one level higher is born with it, meaning the last degree of the light of Ruach of Assiya, and fills the inner part of the Partzuf Nefesh.

As soon as we ascend to that world, instead of it, what remains? The next part forms the so-called "naked" *Partzuf* – the next point in the heart. It has changed and has now divided into its own 613 parts. This second point in the heart is not of *Aviut Shoresh* (0). In order to ascend and dress on *Malchut*, it has to have *Aviut Aleph* (1). This happens because, as the *Partzufim* emerge, one is always born inside another and after completing its own development, pulls the next one after it similar to the forming of a garland.

Therefore, as soon as the *Partzuf, Nefesh,* completes its ascent and dresses on the *Malchut* of the World of *Assiya,* that very instant the point of the following *Partzuf* emerges and begins to push this whole process forward. Like cars of a train move one behind another, the point of the next *Partzuf* will push them up to the level of Infinity. This is an ascending movement, because man should reach the world of Infinity while living in this world – in his body, with his heart and with the point in it.

Here I would like to end this lesson and remind you again that we should unite. It will save much time and effort in our advancement.

None of us will be able to gain individually what we can gain collectively. The growth of our group by just 10% shortens our path by many months. As we grow sufficiently and the members of the group learn to understand one another, even very different people will have much to discuss. We will know how to advance together to the Creator.

In the process of reading "The Book of Zohar", a person gains the sense of the upper world. In any case, reading this book creates internal prerequisites, *Kelim*, with whose assistance we begin to feel what we could not feel before, something that seemed non-existent to us, but now becomes real. Something that could not be felt in our senses suddenly comes into the field of their sensitivity, and the world starts opening up, slowly developing like a photograph, until we enter into this common whole world. "The Book of Zohar" should do this to us. "The Introduction to The Book of Zohar" helps us to understand what stages we should go through.

The conception of a *Partzuf* occurs in such a way that there is an upper *Partzuf*, half of which is above the *Parsa* (so-called GE), and another half (AHP) is below the *Parsa*. We, the broken souls, broken *Kelim* (*Kelim Shevurim*) exist below the *Parsa*. The little crosses on the picture mark all of us. This does not mean that I gave up on us, but quite the opposite; those who are marked here have a bright future. Now we can raise all the AHP. Where? To me. Your upper *Partzuf* is me. Raise all your desires with me and through me get up to the GE. From this picture you can clearly see how important it is for us to join together and cling to the AHP whose GE is above the *Parsa*, above the *Machsom*.

This world below is where we exist and where the AHP of the lower *Partzuf* exists together with you, and I rather represent it for you. Together we can latch onto the GE, to the part above, and thus be able to ascend.

The more we unite to include these desires into the AHP, the more I feel you, so that your desires go through me up to the Creator, the more effectively we will be able to act. This is the meaning of merging of all the groups in the world. We ought to create a huge, cumulative desire that will be equal to what we call MAN, a request to the upper Partzuf, which it cannot refuse. This is our goal.

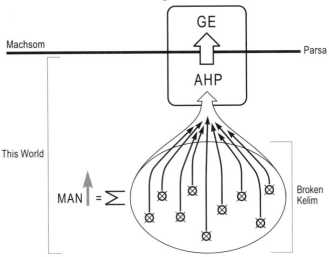

From this we see that there is absolutely no point to be attached to the people whose *GE* is not in the upper world; hence, we see how much we all must participate in the same process of connecting all of our desires into the one and only desire to the Creator.

We have said that man goes through a certain period in his spiritual development called "13 years". This is a period when the aspiration to the Creator has not yet awakened in him. It is then followed by the period of conscious spiritual development, when a person begins to feel a point in the heart, an aspiration to the Creator, and starts developing it deliberately. Now we are developing our point in the heart; therefore, our state is called "13 years" or "coming of age".

Why 13 years? While studying the *Partzufim* of the world of *Atzilut*, we discover that there are 13 corrections of the beard ("*Yud Gimel Tikunei Dikna*") of the upper *Partzuf*. There exists an upper *Partzuf Arich Anpin*

(AA), from whose head the light descends along the hair and the beard. Why "along the beard"? Because with regard to AA the beard constitutes the external *Partzuf*. AA is in the GAR, very powerful light. The light descends along its external *Partzuf* and then weakened so that the lower ones might accept and use it correctly for their growth, causing no harm to themselves.

Such a *Partzuf*, called *Se'arot*, is a part of AA. We receive the upper light through it, whereupon it is transformed in us, and helps us to grow. Therefore, the first 13 years of our development, the first 13 spiritual steps, are considered the years of unconscious development, as with children. Then we come of age and begin to grow consciously. The light that we receive is *Ohr Nefesh* of the world of Assiya. That is what Baal HaSulam writes about in paragraph 45.

> 45. *The aforementioned light of Nefesh is called the light of the still level of the world of Assiya. It is correspondingly aimed at purifying the still level of the will to receive in man's body* (it is said about our present condition). *It shines in the spiritual world much like the still category in the corporeal world, whose particles do not move independently ...*

Inanimate objects in our world do not move independently. They have no desire to move or change. Their only desire is to remain constantly in the same state and that is where their effort is directed. For example, the structure of a crystal is only aimed at preserving its particular state. Obviously, if external conditions exceed the forces of internal preservation of the material's properties, then they will destroy such a material, its inner connections.

Therefore, *there is a general movement that surrounds all the details equally*, like the movement of the planet Earth, and everything else in a galaxy, in the universe, in our world. *And so it is with the light of the Partzuf of Nefesh of the world of Assiya. Although there are 613 organs to it, 613 forms of receiving the bounty* (they are already in us, but they are undeveloped yet existing only in potential) *yet these changes are not apparent, but just a general light whose action surrounds them all equally, without distinction of details* (separate desires).

The light develops desires in one direction or another, like an embryo that is forming inside the mother's womb. Different parts of the embryo's body begin to develop at different times, the head, then the arms, then suddenly the torso, the legs, and so on. There is a specific time for development of every organ or body part. However, on the lowest level of *Nefesh de Nefesh*, there is only a general development with no manifestation of particular stages.

46. *Bear in mind, that although the Sefirot are divine...* (related to the Creator, and being in the state of similarity to Him. But do we already have them within ourselves? Believe it, we do. And if we have even the slightest desire, aspiration for the Creator, then we have already achieved some microscopic similarity to Him).

There is no distinction between the first Sefira Keter in the world of AK and the last Sefira Malchut in the world of Assiya... There is no difference in the structure of creation. It is either in the world of Infinity, or in our world. We are made of the same components, the same Ten *Sefirot*. The question is in the screen. How can the absence of the screen compress the Ten *Sefirot* into a point, while its presence develops the *Sefirot* to become a huge, infinite vessel? All 613 parts of our spiritual body are compressed into the point within us.

Physicists assert that the entire cosmos developed from a micro point that consisted of an infinitely compressed substance. All of a sudden, there was a bang, and so the universe was created. Some day we will discuss this act of conception and birth of the universe. In fact, the transition from the spiritual world to the material world happened in exactly this way.

The point, that emerged from the spiritual and became somewhat like the essence of matter, still possessed the same properties. It only changed its form, became material, and yet retained absolute similarity. Our universe, planet Earth, the solar system, and we ourselves, are all created in complete correspondence to the worlds of *Assiya*, *Yetzira*, *Beria*, etc. All the worlds are parallel to each other, and all their parts resemble each other, but each of the upper worlds is made of a more spiritual substance.

> *Bear in mind that although the Sefirot are divine, and there is no distinction between the first Sefira Keter in the highest world of AK and the last Sefira Malchut of the world of Assiya, there is still a great difference with regard to the receivers.* (even though the highest *Sefira* in the world of *AK* and the lowest *Sefira* in the world of *Assiya* are the same. Then what is the difference?). *For the Sefirot are composed of lights and vessels. And the light in the Sefirot is absolutely divine* (emanated by the Creator, the Creator's part inside the *Kli*). *But the vessels called KaHaBTuM in each of the lower worlds of Beria, Yetzira and Assiya are not divine. They are merely covers that conceal the light of Infinity within them and ration a certain amount of light to the receivers, that each will receive according to its degree of purity.*

Here Baal HaSulam wants to say that the universe is arranged in the following way: the world of Infinity, then the world of *AK* (*Adam Kadmon*), which is *Keter* (as regards the others) and all of its parts. It consists of five *Partzufim* called the *NaRaNHaY* (*Nefesh*, *Ruach*, *Neshama*, *Haya*, and *Yechida*) that emanate the light. Then follow *Atzilut*, *Beria*, *Yetzira*, *Assiya* and our world, as the last level of the world of *Assiya*.

All of these worlds consist of similar parts, and there is no difference between them. The only distinction is in the material from which they are created.

Baal HaSulam says that the worlds of *Beria*, *Yetzira*, and *Assiya* constitute three huge filters that weaken the light descending to us from the worlds of *AK* and *Atzilut*.

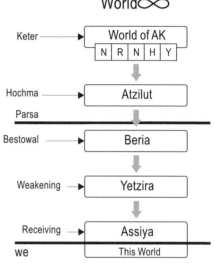

The world of *Atzilut* is *Hochma*, where all the light of Infinity is waiting for our later reception. *Beria* is *Bina*. But the world of *Beria* located below helps us to keep the *Kelim de Ashpa'a* (desires of bestowal) under the *Parsa* and be corrected with their help. *Beria* is *Bina*, the property of bestowal. *Bina* is specially isolated from the world of *Atzilut* to help us. The world of *Yetzira* is a weakening of the property of bestowal and the world of *Assiya* is reception. We are a part of the world of *Assiya*.

The difference between these parts of the universe stems from the fact that the *Sefirot* are divided into the *Kli* and the light. The light of the *Sefira* is divine, whereas the vessels in each of the worlds: *Beria*, *Yetzira*, *Assiya* are not divine. Why? The *Kelim* in the worlds of *BYA* are not divine because they are below the *Parsa*. They consist of the *Kelim* that were broken and corrupted. Now they need to be corrected and elevated to the world of *Atzilut*.

Although the light is one, we still name the lights in the Sefirot NaRaNHaY because the light is distinguished according to the attributes of the vessels. Malchut, which is the coarsest cover, hides all the light of the world of Infinity. The light that it does pass on to the receivers is only a small portion related to the purification of the still level in the body of man. It is called Nefesh.

If we imagine a person in this world and the world of Assiya above him, it means that the only light that will reach him through the world of Assiya will be Nefesh.

The vessel of Tifferet (Kli of the world of Yetzira) is finer than Malchut and the light it passes from the world of Infinity relates to the purification of the vegetative level of man's body, because there the light is more powerful than that of Nefesh. It is called Ruach.

One receives the light of Nefesh in the world of Assiya and corrects one's still level. Those who are in the world of Yetzira receive from Assiya the light of Ruach, which corrects the vegetative level of desire.

The vessel of Bina is finer still than Tifferet, and the world that corresponds to it is called Beria. Those who are in the world of Beria receive the light of Neshama that purifies the animate level of man's body, and it is called the light. The vessel of Hochma is the finest of all (this is the world of Atzilut). It passes the light of Haya, which purifies the human level in man and whose action is unlimited.

	World ∞	Torah →	Creator (Thought)
Keter	AK →	Yechida →	similarity to the Creator (Action)
Hochma	Atzilut →	Haya →	human
Bina	Beria →	Neshama →	animate
Tifferet	Yetzira →	Ruach →	vegetative
Malchut	Assiya →	Nefesh →	still

Why is it unlimited? The reason is that all the light that the Creator passes through the *Kli Keter* is here. The *Kli Keter* is AK, while *Yechida* is already completely similar to the Creator. Then follows *Olam Ein Sof*, the world of Infinity, where man reaches the combined light called the Torah, *NaRaNHaY*. In this case, he becomes similar to the Creator not in actions, but in his thoughts. We define *Keter* as "the Creator's actions with regard to creation". "The Creator's thought with regard to creation" that precedes action is above *Keter*.

47. *In the Partzuf Nefesh, which man has attained through observing the Torah and Commandments without intent, there already dresses a point from the light of Ruach.*

The *Partzuf Nefesh* is the smallest of all. We have already started acquiring it. We obtain the light of *NaRaNHaY de Nefesh* both in the world of AK and here in our world. This can be done by observing the *Torah* and Commandments without intent, i.e., by performing all kinds of actions that can correct us. Baal HaSulam describes them in his article "Free Will".

What is the meaning of an "action"? "Action" means working with the book during your studies in the group. This directs you toward the Creator, enables you to increase your desire for Him. If you accumulate all your powers, all your desires combined with the desires of your friends while aspiring to achieve the states described in the book, you will cling to the *AHP* of the superior spiritual *Partzuf* (the teacher) together with others, so that he will elevate you and attract the *Ohr Makif*.

To this end, you do not need to have special intentions for the sake of the Creator, for they cannot yet appear in you. They will appear because of the Upper Light's influence, but we can attract the light while still having egoistic intentions. In this case, the light that shines upon us is called not the *Ohr Pnimi* (it cannot enter us), but the *Ohr Makif*; and it will purify us all the same.

This way we acquire our first *Partzuf NaRaNHaY de Nefesh*. As soon as we complete it, its uppermost point will be the root of the next *Partzuf Ruach*. We will then begin building *Nefesh, Ruach, Neshama, Haya,* and *Yechida* of the *Partzuf Ruach*. Once we have finished it, the beginning of the next *Partzuf* will be in the point of Yechida: *Nefesh, Ruach, Neshama, Haya,* and *Yechida* of the *Partzuf Neshama*. When we are done with it, we will begin working on *Nefesh, Ruach, Neshama, Haya,* and *Yechida* of the *Partzuf Haya, etc.*

This "ladder" originates in the descent of the worlds. During this process the upper world brought forth the next one below, therefore the lowest point of the upper *Partzuf* is connected with the uppermost point of the lower *Partzuf*. Man can say that he passes from one level to another when he reaches the highest point of a given *Partzuf*. An aspiration for the next level automatically awakens in that *Partzuf* and prerequisites of the next level's *Kli* appear. Thus, man keeps ascending.

Yet the work we do in order to advance, i.e., the screens, the depth of self-knowledge, the attainment of the surrounding world and the contact with the Creator, is totally different each time. This resembles a newborn baby that is still unable to hear, see, or understand anything. It gradually develops and begins to participate in the world's doings: first through games and playthings, later through contact with playmates and finally through interaction with adults.

An individual's advancement along the levels occurs because of a diverse influence of the environment and the development of alternative senses, powers, and means. This is what happens in the spiritual world; hence, we observe the same in our world as well. What are the nuances of man's work on these levels? I seem to be surrounded by the same world, and my inner essence remains unchanged. I just interact with myself and with the surrounding world at different depths in order to compare myself with the Creator. More and more, I deeply penetrate my inner world and that which surrounds me, so that they begin to form one single *Kli*. All the levels of nature, still, vegetative, animal, and human, merge with the Creator. Here Baal *HaSulam* explains how and on what levels it takes place.

All that we can do is called commandments, or drawing the Upper light (the *Ohr Makif*) known as the Torah (from the word "Ohrah", "Ohr"). The Torah is the most general, all-inclusive Upper light. However, the light that reaches us in our state through all worlds, the *Ohr Makif*, is also called the Torah. This indivisible light is intended for all humankind in its final most exalted state. We receive the *Ohr Makif* that affects us even though we still have no intention for the sake of bestowal. If man does everything he can, he purifies and corrects his still level.

> When one strives to observe the Torah and Commandments with the desired intent, he purifies the vegetative part of his will to receive and rises to the next level. To that extent, he builds the point of Ruach into a Partzuf. Performing the 248 "Positive" Commandments with the right intent brings forth the formation of the 248 spiritual organs in this point. And the observance of the 365 "Negative" Commandments brings forth 365 additional spiritual organs.

Although the point of *Ruach* originated in the previous *Partzuf*, it already refers to the next one.

At the vegetative level man already begins to differentiate between good and evil, benefit and harm. Everything useful for the growth of the altruistic desire and intention is attracted and absorbed, while the opposite is repelled. So far, he does not possess the ability to move independently, and lacks the sensation of the past and the future. It still exists together with those similar to him, in the same states moving under the influence of the light. He still cannot work independently, and like a flower, withers at night and springs back to life at dawn.

Nonetheless, he already understands what he needs for his growth, hence he separates the 248 commandments-desires, which he aspires to work on, and correct from the 365 desires with which he has no right to work. Already at this level, his *Partzuf* is divided into GE and AHP, 248 and 365, in all 613 desires. In the state of *Nefesh*, he is yet unable to feel or distinguish these desires, let alone analyze them. This will happen at a later stage.

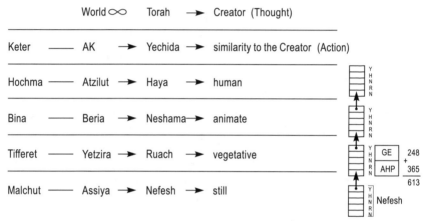

When the formation of all 613 organs of the Partzuf is completed, it rises and dresses the Sefira Tifferet of the world of Assiya, which conducts the more important light called Ruach from the World of Infinity. The light Ruach is meant for the correction of the vegetative part in the person's body. The world Assiya has the still, vegetative, and animal parts that belong to the level of the Sefira Tifferet. All of these parts help the Partzuf Ruach of a person to receive the complete light from the Sefira Tifferet, as it happened earlier with the light of Nefesh. Therefore, it is called "spiritual vegetation".

What does Baal HaSulam wish to say here? All that was corrected in the previous *Partzuf* now begins to help the following one on the level where it works. On the one hand, each *Partzuf* constitutes a prerequisite for mastering the next; on the other hand, mastering of the subsequent *Partzuf* helps the realization of the preceding one.

Suppose I acquired certain skills a few years ago. Today, I become familiar with some notions or theories. I begin to use the skills acquired in the past as a means for implementing the concepts of today. Now I understand better what I acquired previously, and begin to analyze the past and correlate it with the present.

By rising to the level of the *Partzuf Ruach*, I do not stop building my *Partzuf Nefesh*. On the contrary, with the development of *Ruach*, I continue realizing and using the *Partzuf Nefesh*. Nothing disappears and nothing sinks into oblivion of the past. At every level, I realize myself in accordance with my current position, so at the level of *Nefesh*, *Ruach*, or *Haya*, I realize all the previous *Partzufim* I built.

Consequently, I receive a much greater amount of light and the *Kelim*, which form my world of Infinity. It is formed from such multitude of my thoughts and abilities that there is absolutely everything there. All the opportunities are bound with concepts, forces, and intents, so as to prepare the complete realization, beginning with the first level and up to the very last.

The nature of this luminescence on the vegetative level of the material world is such that changes in movements are noticeable in every individual part. The spiritual light of the vegetative level is able to shine in a special way upon each of the 613 organs.

The descending light of *Ruach* singles out each of the particular 613 desires within my inner common desire. I already differentiate between them, see the character of each desire, and understand whether I can adapt it to the Creator or not. I see that it is necessary to modify or put aside some desire to establish contact with the Creator. The light tells me about my soul; hence, it is called *Ruach, Ruchaniut* – the spiritual light. It is with this *Ruach*, spirituality that my individual growth and the contact with the Creator begin.

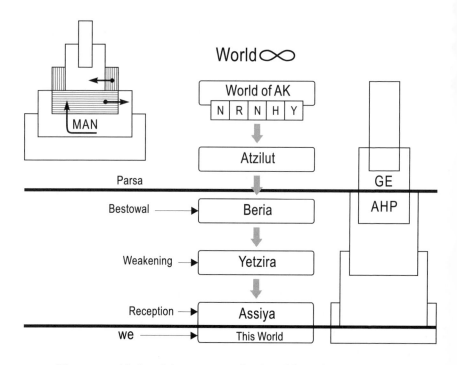

The spiritual light of the vegetative level is able to shine in a special way to each of the 613 organs of the Partzuf Ruach. Every organ expresses its special power of this act. When the Partzuf Ruach is born, it receives the point of a higher level that is the point of the Partzuf Neshama.

The same principle works in the worlds AK, Atzilut, Beria, Yetzira, and Assiya. Each world is at its own level of GE, its AHP always being at the level of the lower world. Their ends overlap, as in a telescopic antenna, while none of them exists by itself. It turns out that no Partzuf has an independent, free part. In any of them, we see that its entire top, GE, dresses onto the upper Partzuf, whereas its bottom, AHP, sits inside the lower Partzuf. In other words, all of our thoughts or desires are connected with either the upper or the lower level. Therefore, development is only possible thanks to this connection. I cannot possibly rise higher than my own level, unless I bond with the Upper level and receive desire, MAN, from the lower level.

Every one of us is just a link in a chain and can only rise if he connects with the upper *Partzuf* and pulls all the others up. It is impossible to advance alone, without being connected with the group.

> 48. *However, when a person attains the secrets of the Torah and the tastes of the commandments, he corrects the animal level of his will to receive. By doing this, he expands and builds the point of Neshama that dresses into the 248 and 365 organs of his body.*

We have studied how man advances in the worlds *Assiya* and *Yetzira*. In the world of *Yetzira*, he already has a different attitude to his duties and responsibilities. Unlike in *Assiya*, where he was not aware of what he was dealing with, in *Yetzira* he already distinguishes between the desires of bestowal and reception and acts accordingly. The next level of correction, the world of *Beria*, is where man studies the secrets of the Torah and the tastes of the commandments. In *Beria*, he begins to treat his desires (created in us by the Creator) and the light, the power that he receives from above, in a very different way.

What is his attitude to it? How does it feel to be between something that the Creator created in him and the power that He sends to him now? Man receives the *Kelim* and the light, and has to position himself correctly between these two sources of desire and pleasure. At the level of *Beria*, he continues advancing, while attaining the secrets of the Torah and the tastes of the commandments.

The Torah is the most general light that influences us. What is the meaning of "the general light's secrets" and "the tastes of the commandments"? Man already reaches a level where he feels the light of *Hochma* (wisdom), from which he attains the secrets, i.e., how the light created the creation, how it corrects it, adapts it to itself, and absorbs it. The secrets of the Torah are the inner processes that take place in our desires under the light's influence.

By attaining the most profound processes in the universe, man corrects the animal level of his desire (by comprehending the Creator's actions, he becomes similar to Him at the deepest levels of his desire) and extends the soul's point of *Neshama*, which develops in 248 and 365 of its organs.

Naturally, this part too consists of 248 and 365 sub-parts, albeit on a different level. If the world of *Assiya* is a general inanimate movement devoid of the intention for the Creator's sake, the world of *Yetzira* is a yet undefined general intention, and the world of *Beria* is an advancement by way of the Torah and commandments. The world of *Beria* may be characterized as the light and the *Kli*. This is a very high spiritual level of the secrets of the Torah and the tastes of the commandments.

In the picture you see the still (*Shoresh*, 0), the vegetative (*Aleph*, 1), the animal (*Bet*, 2) levels of desire. These are desires on the level of *Neshama*, i.e., of absolute bestowal, when man acquires the property of *Bina*.

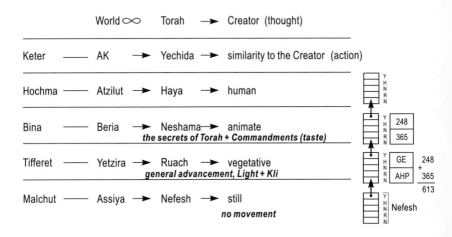

Every part, still, vegetative, and animal, in the world Assiya of the Sefira Bina helps the person's Partzuf Neshama to receive the complete light from the Sefira Bina. This is also called a "pure animal", because it is meant for the correction of the animal level of the person's body. The nature of its luminescence is the same as that in the animal level of the material world described above; it gives the individual a sense of life to each of the 613 organs of the Partzuf. Thus, they feel independent of the Partzuf to the degree that the 613 organs become the 613 Partzufim and each of them contains its special, individual light.

Man is isolated from others in our world. Unlike plants that turn towards the sun, he can move independently. In contrast to plants and animals that are born and die at a certain time (it is less pronounced in animals than in plants, although they mate at specific periods of the year), man is entirely free in his movements, in the sensation of the past and future, in his contact with the world, etc. The soul that reaches the level of *Neshama* is similarly individual.

When this completely individual Partzuf Neshama emerges, the superiority of this light over the light of Ruach in the spiritual world is equivalent to the difference between the animal, vegetative, and still levels of nature in the material world. In addition, a point of the light Haya is placed in the Partzuf Neshama. Further, man continues developing the level of Haya.

49. When a person merits receiving the great light called Neshama and the 613 organs of this Partzuf are each shining with its complete light aimed at him, each of them as a separate Partzuf, the person discovers an opportunity to observe every commandment with the true intent.

A special light of every commandment is shining upon every organ (desire) of the Partzuf Neshama (Baal HaSulam speaks of the previous *Partzuf Neshama* on the animal level). *The power of these lights corrects the "human" part in his desire to receive and turns it into the desire to give* (The light of the level of *Neshama* rises as well, and man corrects the level of *Haya*). *To this extent, a point of the Ohr Haya is built in him.*

When the Partzuf is complete, it rises and dresses the Sefira Hochma. This Kli is exceptionally transparent (the matter concerns the *Kli Haya* as it rises to *Atzilut*) *and, therefore, passes a huge light from the World of Infinity to man. This light is called Ohr Haya. All* (previously acquired) *parts of the world of Assiya, i.e., the still, vegetative, and animal that belong to the Sefira Hochma help the person to receive the complete light of the Sefira Hochma.*

This is called a "spiritual human". His essence is directed towards the correction of the "human" part in the person's body. The meaning of this light in the spiritual world corresponds to the meaning of the human level in the four levels (still, vegetative, animal, and human) of the material world. The greatness of this light exceeds that of the light of the still, vegetative, and animal levels in the spiritual world. This can be compared to the difference between humankind and the still, vegetative, and animal kinds in the material world. The light of Infinity "clothed" in this Partzuf is called the Ohr Yechida.

Yechida is already *Keter*, Infinity, but the Infinity relative to that particular person, that particular *Partzuf*, and not the whole light of the Torah in the world of Infinity. Moreover, this light (we will call it individual Infinity), the light of *Yechida*, is similar to the Creator in its "actions" and is individually infinite.

Here the 248 and 365 commandments are created, the corrected desires, from which we enter the world of *Yechida*. Baal HaSulam and the Zohar do not discuss the world *Yechida*, the world of *AK*; there is only a hint in those books about the world of *Atzilut*. That is because we mostly

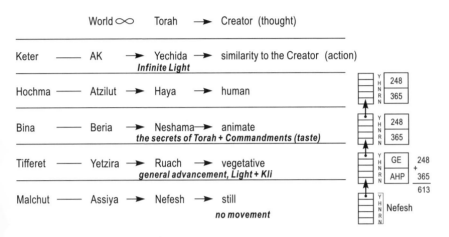

have to undergo correction on the levels of basic desires: still, vegetative, and animal, and then raise these desires of the worlds of *Assiya, Yetzira, and Beria* into the world of *Atzilut*. As was stated before, those worlds under the *Parsa* weaken the light and contain the yet uncorrected vessels within them. By correcting and raising them into the world of *Atzilut*, we complete our mission.

We spoke only about the world of *Assiya* and the five levels that a person passes through in it: *Nefesh, Ruach, Neshama, Haya, and Yechida* of the world *Assiya*. After that comes the world of *Beria*. All the levels that are shown here only described the five levels of the world *Assiya*.

So, what is the difference between ascending the levels of *Assiya, Yetzira, Beria, Atzilut, AK* in the world of *Assiya* and the ascent of the same worlds or levels, *Partzufim*, in the world of *Beria*?

50. *However, you need to know that all of these five lights of NaRaNHaY are merely NaRaNHaY of the light of Nefesh. They do not have anything from the light of Ruach because Ruach exists only in the world of Yetzira, Ohr Neshama is in the world of Beria, Ohr Haya is in the world of Atzilut, and Ohr Yechida is in the world of AK.*

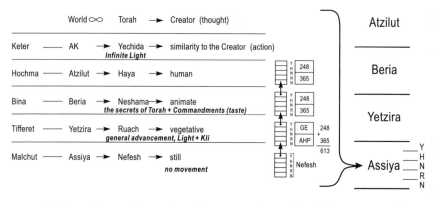

In fact, the work on the still, vegetative, animal, human, and general levels of our correction only refers to the still desire.

However, everything that exists in the general creation is also present in its every part, no matter how tiny it might be. Therefore, the world of Assiya has the five lights of NaRaNHaY, which refer to the light of Nefesh. Similarly, the world of Yetzira has the five lights of NaRaNHaY that refer to the light of Ruach. In the same way, the world of Beria has the five lights of NaRaNHaY that are only a part of the light of Neshama, and so on.

51. You should know that the desire to be spiritually elevated and purified is accepted by the Creator only if it is constant and if there is a certainty that man will never return to his folly. The Creator Himself testifies that man will never return to his previous state.

How can we merge with Him if we have no points of contact? How can we at least come near Him, let alone enter into Him if He is absolutely opposite to our natural property?

Baal HaSulam writes in this article that we cannot establish any contact with the Upper world. However, everyone in this world is given a prototype of the spiritual world in the form of a group and a teacher. Even though we are not immersed in constant desires of bestowal, by merely wishing to attain them, we, as it were, train ourselves, and can gradually develop a correct attitude to the spiritual realm. We cannot establish contact with the Upper world unless we can correctly get into touch with the upper *Partzuf*, meaning a group and a teacher.

If man has a constant desire for the spiritual, he can ascend higher. There can be no state in which man always rises and never falls. Moreover, what is a fall? This means not tumbling down from one's spiritual level, but rather acquiring an additional desire without balancing it with the necessary correction, and remaining on the same level of desire.

Suppose I am at the "zero" spiritual level. I am given an additional new desire, but I cannot yet balance it with the property of bestowal. At that, I still retain the level of my previous desire, and in no circumstances fall back into egoism.

The desires of bestowal are always constant in their direction. They can only grow, but never diminish. This is because the person that ascends spiritually is under constant influence of the light. It comes down from the world of Infinity through all worlds, constantly sustains him, and will never let him fall.

Man is never his own master because only the light can hold him on a certain level, as a magnet holds a piece of iron and does not let it fall.

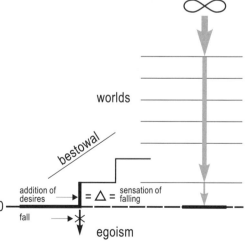

In the Introduction to "The Study of the Ten *Sefirot*," it is said that the Creator testifies to man's righteousness. How can a person know whether he is righteous or not? It is only possible to know if the Creator reveals Himself to him and does not let him slide back. Naturally, if the Creator concealed Himself and cut man from His light, he would immediately fall from this level. We are constantly "suspended in the air". Between our world and the world of Infinity, we always depend on the intensity of light, which descends from above and sustains us on this or that level.

However, as man enters the spiritual realm, he is always given a minimal level from which he begins to ascend. By correcting himself completely on a certain level, man turns it into his minimal spiritual platform, below which he will never fall and continues ascending. To the extent of man's similarity to Him, the Creator constantly guarantees that he will never fall from the achieved level.

We find that, as it has been said, were a person to correct the inanimate level of his will to receive, he would merit the attainment of the Partzuf Nefesh. He rises and "dresses" the Sefira Malchut of the world of Assiya, and of course, he merits the Final Correction of the still level. That is, he will not return to his past (under the Machsom, below the world of Assiya), *but will be able to rise to the spiritual world of Assiya because he is purified and absolutely equal to this world's properties.* According to this law, the transition from this world to the world of Assiya is only possible if man acquires a minimal constant spiritual property.

However, the other levels of the world of Assiya are Ruach, Neshama, Haya, and Yechida. To obtain their lights one needs to correct the vegetative, animal, and human levels in one's desire to receive. The correction does not have to be final "until the Creator Himself testifies that the person will never return to his folly" (meaning his previous state).

If I passed from this world into the world of Assiya, I continue developing, i.e., I build a *Partzuf* consisting of 613 commandments. Since it is impossible to differentiate between the affirmative and negative com mandments in the world of *Assiya*, I divide them into *Nefesh, Ruach, Neshama, Haya*, and *Yechida*.

Baal HaSulam says that man should constantly be in the world of *Assiya* in his sensations, whereas his presence on other levels may not necessarily be permanent. In fact, he will be unable to do that. It is possible only on the level of *Assiya de Assiya*, because the world of *Assiya* is characterized by just this level.

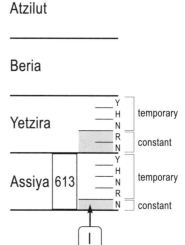

After that, when I ascend to the level of the world of *Yetzira*, it is important for me to make the levels *Assiya* and *Yetzira* in the world of *Yetzira* permanent. The levels *Neshama, Haya*, and *Yechida* may remain temporary, and so on.

Every time I reach a certain level, I need to correct it within me. All other levels complementing my *Partzuf* may be temporary. As, for example, an expert on metallurgy should know his field very thoroughly, while his knowledge in other spheres is necessary to him only as much as it can help him to be proficient in his own trade. The same applies to desires. If I work on my desires of the vegetative level, all other levels just assist me to distinguish it in them and work with it.

It is said, "Until the Creator Himself testifies to the impossibility of man's return to his previous state".

How does the Creator testify to that? He shines upon us with a certain light and according to this light's intensity; He keeps us on a certain spiritual level. If He shines more, we rise, if He shines less, we fall. In other words, only the intensity of the light determines our spiritual level, because our desire is constant and unchanging. Only the power of the light does serve as a counteraction to our desire, it elevates us or pulls us down.

If the light's power reaches a certain distance or level from the Creator, let us say, level two, and then I know exactly that I will not fall below it. This constant power of the light is the Creator's guarantee that I will stay on that level.

If man corrects the still level of his desire to receive and deserves to transform the point in his heart into the Partzuf Nefesh, then he ascends and "dresses" the Sefira Malchut of the world of Assiya.

It is clear that man will not return to his previous state. He ascends to the world of *Assiya* and reaches his constant level, because his correction on that level has been completed. However, the remaining levels of the world of *Assiya* – *Ruach, Neshama, Haya,* and *Yechida* are not finally corrected yet.

So in order to enter the world of *Assiya*, man should completely correct his still level to prevent deterioration. Why? It is because the entire world of *Assiya* corresponds to the still level. All the remaining levels – vegetative, animal, human, and Divine – may still be temporary.

			Y		•
			H		•
Ruach	= vegetative level	= Yetzira	N		•
			R	const	●
			N		•
			Y		•
			H		•
Nefesh	= still level	= Assiya	N		•
			R		•
			N	const	●

Parsa

Similarly, to rise to the level of *Yetzira*, I need to make my *Ruach* constant, because the entire level of *Yetzira* corresponds to *Ruach* (the vegetative level).

Thus, the level corresponding to the world in which I am and constituting its characteristic property should be completely corrected in me, while all the others can have various degrees of correction. So if *Yetzira* is *Ruach*, then *Ruach de Ruach* of the entire world of *Yetzira* should be constant and so forth. Baal HaSulam explains it very clearly and it is not difficult to understand it.

> However, the remaining levels of the world of Assiya – Ruach, Neshama, Haya, and Yechida do not necessarily have to be finally corrected in order to receive the light and correct the vegetative, animal and human levels of its desire to receive.
>
> It stems from the fact that the entire world of Assiya in each of its five Sefirot (Keter, Hochma, Bina, ZA and Malchut) is none other than Malchut, which has corrected its attitude to the still level (Assiya is Malchut, Yetzira is ZA, the same applies to Keter, Hochma, Bina, ZA and Malchut of the world of Yetzira). The five Sefirot are just the five parts of Malchut (the still level of the desire to receive).
>
> For example, the Sefira Tifferet of the world of Assiya receives the light from the world of Yetzira, which is Tifferet and the light of Ruach. The Sefira Bina of the world of Assiya receives the light from the world of Beria, which is Neshama. The Sefira Hochma of the world of Assiya receives the light from the world of Atzilut, which is Haya.

What is Baal HaSulam trying to tell us? If we take the world of Assiya, only *Nefesh* is its own level, while it receives *Ruach* from *Tifferet*. Then it receives *Neshama* from *Malchut* of the world of *Beria*, *Hochma* - from *Malchut* of the world of *Atzilut* and *Keter* - from *Malchut* of the world of *AK*.

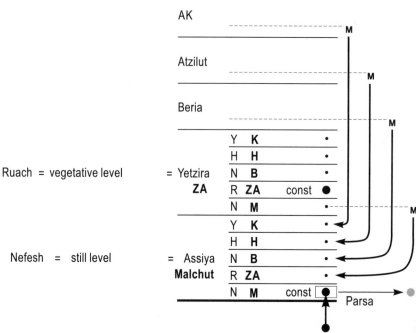

Consequently, since all of this constitutes *Malchut*, it receives each light (except for its own) from the corresponding world. Thus, since ZA here refers to *Malchut*, it receives the light of ZA from the *Malchut* of the world of *Yetzira*, which represents the general ZA. *Bina* that refers to *Malchut* receives the light from the *Malchut* of the world of *Beria*, because *Beria* is *Bina*.

That is, each part receives the light from the part that corresponds to it in the Upper world.

Sefira Tifferet of the world of Assiya receives the light from the world of Yetzira, which represents Tifferet and the light of Ruach. The Sefira Bina of the world of Assiya receives the light from the world of Beria, which is Neshama. The Sefira Hochma of the world of Assiya receives the light from the world of Atzilut, which is Haya. Consequently, regardless of the fact that man has not yet corrected any other level but his "still" one (the last one), if the three other parts of his desire to receive are partially corrected, he can still receive the lights Ruach, Neshama, Haya and Yechida from Tifferet, Bina and Hochma of the world of Assiya. This reception, however, is temporary, because as soon as one of the three parts of his desire awakens, he instantly loses these lights.

Baal HaSulam means that if man completely corrected himself on the still level and only partially on all the others, then he is in the world of Assiya. Make a note that even if his uncorrected parts fall, he still retains his constant level. This allows him to retain the level above the Machsom. Thus, it turns out that the person who has crossed the Machsom will never again fall below it.

52. After man finally corrects and purifies "the vegetative" part of his desire to receive, he permanently ascends to the world of Yetzira and attains the level of Ruach...

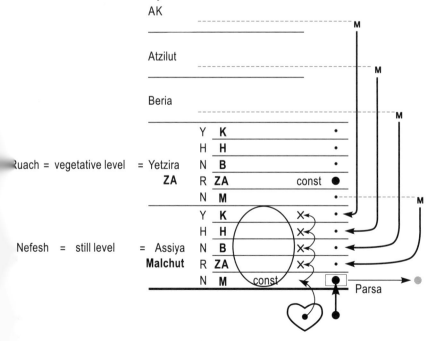

255

Now the constant is in the world of *Yetzira*. This means that man receives *Neshama, Haya,* and *Yechida* from the higher worlds. They fill him, but he does not have to correct them completely. The correction of the level of *Ruach* is quite sufficient. That is, *Nefesh* and *Ruach* should be totally corrected, while all the other higher levels may remain uncorrected. Therefore, if man reached the level of *Ruach* of the world of *Yetzira,* it means that he permanently corrected this state and will never fall below it.

Each level in each world should be completely corrected. This is the way that constant spiritual ascent takes place.

But what if man falls from these levels? When this occurs, it only helps him! Unless he fell, he would not be able to rise. He should fall from these levels in order to acquire the additional *Aviut*. By doing so, he ascends from the level of *Ruach* of the world of *Assiya* to the level of *Ruach* of the world of *Yetzira.*

The same happens to the other levels: the additional desires are acquired and man falls again. Therefore, the falls are essential. The rise entails the fall; the lower the fall, the higher the rise, but it refers only to the levels where man has not yet completely corrected himself. There is always some fixed (previous) level, whereupon man ascends to the higher level. Each consecutive state is more critical (both in minus and in plus) than the previous one.

52. *After man finally corrects and purifies "the vegetative" part of his desire to receive, he permanently ascends to the world of Yetzira and attains the level of Ruach...*

Now the constant is in the world of *Yetzira*. This means that man receives *Neshama, Haya,* and *Yechida* from the higher worlds. They fill him, but he does not have to correct them completely. The correction of the level of *Ruach* is quite sufficient. That is, *Nefesh* and *Ruach* should be totally corrected, while all the other higher levels may remain uncorrected. Therefore, if man reached the level of *Ruach* of the world of *Yetzira*, it means that he permanently corrected this state and will never fall below it.

Each level in each world should be completely corrected. This is the way that constant spiritual ascent takes place.

But what if man falls from these levels? When this occurs, it only helps him! Unless he fell, he would not be able to rise. He should fall from these levels in order to acquire the additional *Aviut*. By doing so he ascends from the level of *Ruach* of the world of *Assiya* to the level of *Ruach* of the world of *Yetzira*.

The same happens to the other levels: the additional desires are acquired and man falls again. So the falls are essential. The rise entails the fall; the lower the fall, the higher the rise, but it refers only to the levels where man has not yet completely corrected himself. There is always some fixed (previous) level, whereupon man ascends to the higher level. Modulo each consecutive state is more critical (both in minus and in plus) than the previous one.

53. *After correcting "the animal" part of his desire, man receives and transforms it into the desire to bestow, so much so that the Creator Himself testifies to the permanence of this condition. He achieves the similarity to the world of Beria, ascends, and receives the light of Neshama (in the world of Beria).*

That is, he ascends to the world of *Beria*, where the level of *Neshama* is completely corrected. Naturally, the levels *Ruach* and *Nefesh* are also fully corrected on the level of the world of *Beria*. At that, the levels *Haya* and *Yechida* remain uncorrected. This is necessary to ascend to the world of *Atzilut* while correcting the level of *Haya* and proceed to the world of *AK* while correcting the level of *Yechida*.

54. *When man deserves to correct "the human" part of his desire, he becomes similar to the world of Atzilut, ascends there and receives*

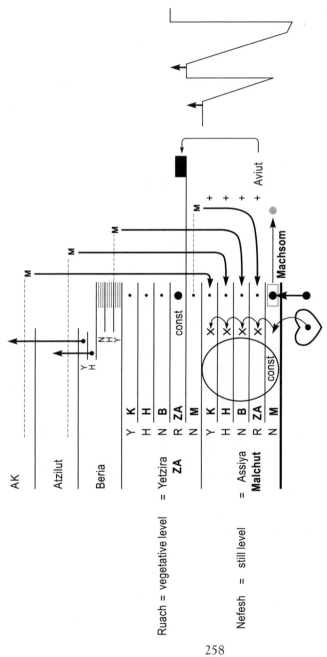

the light of Haya. When he deserves even more (i.e., Yechida), he attains the light of Infinity and Ohr Yechida "dresses" into Ohr Haya. There is nothing to be added to that.

55. *Thus we have found the answers to the previously asked questions: what is the purpose of all these Upper worlds (what is this special invention for)? We can see now that man is unable to bestow upon the Creator without the help of these worlds, because to the extent of correction of his desire to receive (his self-correction) he attains the lights, the levels of his soul, which is referred to as the NaRaNHaY.*

What does the phrase "all these worlds" mean? This is a calibration of my soul. The gradual correction of each of its parts generates in me a sensation of ascending to the Creator from the state when none of my *Kelim* were corrected (the lowest level) to the state when I completely correct all of my soul's vessels.

Rising from the lowest level inside my *Kli* to the highest one, I as it were pass through five parts called five worlds. Only the absolutely amorphous Upper light surrounds me. The sensations of concealment and revelation of my partial connection with the Creator – all this is felt within me and is determined by the inner part of me that I have corrected.

We shall see later that all the worlds are within us. How? We feel the general light called *Ohr haSovev* (the Surrounding light), which we can neither analyze nor feel inside. We term it "the Creator". The light, which enters and fills us to the extent of our correction, is referred to as *Ohr Pnimi* (the Inner light). This is a partial penetration of the same Surrounding Light that shines in us.

At the End of correction, all the light will enter into us leaving nothing outside. The infinite simple light will be both inside and outside of us.

In other words, we cease to be a closed shell with a minimal dose of the light inside it and achieve the state where the light transcends us. In our properties, we become absolutely similar to the light and stop being an obstacle in its way. This is what we call the complete merging with the light. Despite the fact that the desire remains opposite to the Creator, by neutralizing and correcting it with the help of our intention (to use it for the Creator's sake) we purify it so that it stops hampering the light.

> 56. One should know that all the aforementioned levels of the NaRa-NHaY are the five parts of which the entire creation consists. All that exists in the general creation is also present in its smallest part. For example, one can attain five parts of the NaRaNHaY even in the part of "the inanimate" level of the world of Assiya, because they sort with the five parts of the NaRaNHaY of the entire creation.

> It is impossible to attain even the light of "the inanimate" level of the world of Assiya without including four parts of man's Aviut.

Baal HaSulam wants to say that, however small a Kli we might take (our small desire), if we ascend to the minimal level, it will still consist of the 10 Sefirot: Keter, Hochma, Bina, ZA and Malchut, and also of five parts: Nefesh, Ruach, Neshama, Haya and Yechida that originate in the five worlds.

This way, he wishes to show us the structure of the entire universe: the world of Infinity, the world of AK where the light is separated into Nefesh, Ruach, Neshama, Haya and Yechida and descends to the other worlds. The same occurs in each of the worlds – there are Nefesh, Ruach, Neshama, Haya and Yechida.

Thus the light descends from the Upper world to the lower worlds, each time passing through the corresponding Kelim. For example, the light of Haya from Hochma of the world of AK will be bound to only enter into Hochma of the world of Atzilut, Hochma of the world of Beria, Hochma of the world of Yetzira and Hochma of the world of Assiya. It cannot be any other way, because no Kli can distinguish any other light in this particular one, only to what corresponds to its properties. Therefore

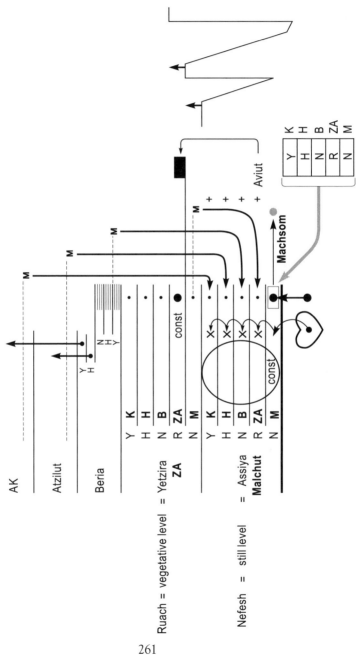

the *Kli Hochma* picks only the light of *Hochma* (*Ohr Haya*); the *Kli Malchut* picks only the light of *Nefesh*, and so forth.

What does it mean? If man entered the world of *Assiya* with his minimal *Kli*, which consists of five parts, he receives in them the light from all the five worlds. It passes through them, because in fact, the world of *AK* is a source of the light of *Yechida*; the world of *Atzilut* is a source of *Haya*; the world of *Beria* is a source of *Neshama*; the world of *Yetzira* is a source of *Ruach*, and the world of *Assiya* is a source of *Nefesh*.

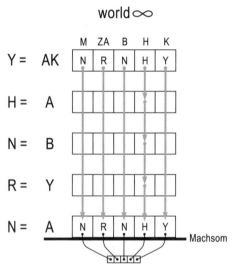

If I reach the minimal level of the world of *Assiya* and cross the *Machsom*, then already on this level I have the sensations of all the worlds, of the entire universe, because I already consist of the 10 *Sefirot* filled with the lights (albeit very small) from each world. That is on the one hand, my minimal level allows me to receive the lights from the other worlds. On the other hand, my work should also include all the worlds.

But how can I include all the worlds on such a low level? The next paragraph speaks about it.

> *It is impossible to even attain the light of "the inanimate" level of the world of Assiya without including the four parts into man's work. Hence everyone should be engaged in the Torah and the commandments* (i.e., use all the possible means of correction and purification) *in order to acquire the level of Ruach. Man should also study the secrets of the Torah to acquire the level of Neshama and the tastes of the commandments* (i.e., to start receiving the

Inner light, since the light of *Neshama* cannot fill the *Kli* without this work).

Baal HaSulam says that even if reaching the minimal level of the spiritual world requires the knowledge and attainment of the Upper light, then naturally, without the study of Kabbalah, the secrets of the Torah one cannot ascend even to the first spiritual level.

If somebody believes that by reading such "literature" as *the Talmud* and the *Halachot*, or by studying other parts of the Torah he can correct himself and enter the Upper world, he is absolutely wrong. This is because entering the spiritual world requires the correction (even though to a minimal extent) of all the five parts of his desire. As the Introduction to "The Book of Zohar" says, they can be corrected only through the study of Kabbalah. Otherwise man will not correct the level higher than the light of *Nefesh*.

57. *From the aforesaid we can understand the darkness and ignorance much more prevalent in our generation than before. Because all who study the Torah neglect the secrets of the Torah* (i.e., do not study Kabbalah).

Therefore the Rambam gives the following example: "If a thousand blind people drag themselves along the road and there is one person who is able to see at the head of that column, then all the blind can be sure they will not go astray. However, if they have no sighted guide among them, they will surely get lost".

The same refers to us. Imagine that there are people who study Kabbalah and attract the light of Infinity, lead the generation after them and the people follow them, and then all will be sure they will never err on their path. But if, instead of Kabbalah, people prefer to study other parts of the Torah (which do not correct the soul), *no wonder that the whole generation errs through their fault.* Consequently, the people (the Jewish people) do not fulfill its mission. *So deep is my grief that I am unable to continue speaking about it.*

In items 155 and 156 of the Introduction to The Study of the Ten Sefirot, Baal HaSulam explains that without the study of Kabbalah one cannot achieve even the minimal *NaRaNHaY.* Kabbalah has been neglected since the destruction of the Second Temple, i.e., for about 2000 years. The great Kabbalist begins his Introduction with the following words: "I have found a great need to break down the iron wall which separates us from the wisdom of Kabbalah. Unless we do that we will end up by falling into abyss. All our problems, all our sufferings are caused by our inability to attract the Upper light of correction with the help of Kabbalah".

Then he proceeds to explain the reason that led to neglect of Kabbalah.

58. *Indeed I have known the reason: that it is mainly because faith has generally diminished, especially faith in the holy men, the wise men of all generations. And the books of Kabbalah and the Zohar are full of corporeal parables.*

That is, the language of the Kabbalistic books is so confusing that man imagines that Kabbalah speaks about our world and not about the Upper worlds. The language uses the words of our world.

Therefore people are afraid lest they will fail by materializing (making idols) *and will lose more than they will gain* (from studying the books in this way).

That is people would think that the world is ruled not by the Creator, but some Supreme forces are in the objects of our world. The reader thinks that all the books of the Torah speak of this world.

And that is what prompted me to compose a thorough interpretation of the writings of the ARI and now to the holy Zohar (the HaSulam Commentary). *And I have removed completely that concern* (the fear of imagining our world instead of the spiritual one), *for I have proven the spiritual message behind everything, which is* abstract and devoid of all physical resemblance, above space and time as the readers shall see, in order to allow all to study Kabbalah and the Zohar and be warmed by its sacred light.

And I have named that commentary HaSulam (The Ladder), to show that the purpose of it is, as with every ladder - that if you have an attic full of goods, then all you need is a ladder to reach it, and then all the bounty of the world is in your hands. But the ladder is not a purpose in and of itself, for if you pause midway and not enter the attic, the purpose will not be fulfilled.

And so it is with my commentary to the Zohar. Because there has not yet been created the way to clarify these most profound of words. But nonetheless I have constructed a path and an entrance for all, that using it they can rise and scrutinize in depth "The Book of Zohar" itself (i.e., all that the Zohar reveals), for only then will my purpose of this commentary be completed.

The Commentary on "The Book of Zohar" is composed to elevate man to the peak called the Zohar.

In the chapter "Bereshit" we learned that the Zohar corresponds to the Partzuf Arich Anpin. It is Keter of the world of Atzilut, which includes the entire surrounding Upper world as well as the world of Infinity. With regard to us AA is the world of Infinity and it is called the Zohar (or Zihara Ila'a). The task of "The Book of Zohar" is to elevate us to that level.

59. All those who understand what is written in the Book of the Zohar, unanimously agree that it was composed by the Godly sage Rabbi Shimon Bar Yochai. Only those who are far from this wisdom doubt this origin and tend to say, relying on opponents' fabricated tales that its composer is Rabbi Moshe De Leon (who lived in a different time).

In principle, this is not so important for us. He just wants to point out that "The Book of Zohar" is more ancient and valuable than some tend to believe; hence, he wishes to make things clear regarding the authorship of the book.

Rabbi Moshe de Leon lived in the 11th century. He was an outstanding Kabbalist and wrote a number of books on Kabbalah. As I wrote in my foreword, "The Book of Zohar" was lost and later rediscovered by chance (naturally it was no chance). From the scraps of the book a small number of extracts and separate sheets were compiled into what we now call "The Book of Zohar".

Rabbi Moshe de Leon inherited it from his teacher, who in turn had received it from his teacher. The book was initially found by a merchant in the 7th century A.D. It was used for wrapping spices in the Jaffo market.

The merchant, who happened to be a Jew, had evidently known a little of Kabbalah, because he discovered some very special writings on the parchment folio that contained the purchased spices. He rushed to the market place and started rummaging through the garbage and finally found all these sheets. The entire collection was afterwards passed on to one of his pupils, who left it to his, and so finally the texts reached the Rabbi Moshe de Leon in the 11th century.

The Kabbalist rewrote the book, had it beautifully bound and kept it. He knew that it was too premature to publish the book, because the people were not ready for it yet.

His wife did not know about all that, so when the Rabbi had passed away, she sold the book in the hope of coping with her financial straits. Obviously it was bought by a good business man, for he had it rewritten and put on sale. The book was a success, because at that time there were no similar compositions, except for "The Book of Creation" ("*Sefer Yetzira*") authored by Abraham. However, "The Book of Creation" was far too difficult to be studied, since it contains just a number of vague hints. So "The Zohar" was really like radiant light, splendor at that time.

A great number of rewritten copies spread around instantly. Though it was known to be a part of the famous Rabbi de Leon's legacy, the real Kabbalists knew it had actually been written by the Rabbi Shimon Bar Yochai with the help of the Rabbi Aba in the 2nd or the 3rd century A.D.

Baal HaSulam writes about it, because he wants to elevate the book to the level much higher than that of the Rabbi Moshe de Leon. Judging from all the other compositions penned by the Rabbi de Leon, it becomes clear he was an outstanding Kabbalist, but not of the spiritual level of "The Zohar".

Therefore he says: *All those who understand what is written in the Book of the Zohar, unanimously agree that it was composed by the Godly sage Rabbi Shimon Bar Yochai. Only those who are far from this wisdom doubt this origin and tend to say that its composer is Rabbi Moshe De Leon.*

This book could not have been written by a man who lived 5 to 7 centuries after the great Rabbi Shimon, because, as we know, the generations have gradually descended from the highest level down to ours, when we start from zero. In general, there are no Kabbalists of that level among us. My Rabbi was the last one; the descent ended with him. We begin this ascent by ourselves.

60. Baal HaSulam tells us that during its long history "The Book of Zohar" was ascribed to many different Kabbalists. But only the person who penetrates the inner meaning of this book and understands from what high spiritual level it descended (from *Arich Anpin* of the world of *Atzilut*, i.e., it reaches the world of Infinity), can also realize that it could be written by none other than Rabbi Shimon Bar-Yochai.

We know that Kabbalah divides all history into the following periods: first man develops as an animal, then the soul descends into him (in the year 0 according to the Jewish calendar, i.e., 5764 years ago), and then the development of a point in his heart (soul) begins.

Let us have a look at a graph and see how the body was developing. The spiritual point descended into man's heart 5764 years ago and activated for the first time. The next manifestation of the spiritual desire took place in Abraham in around 1947 B.C. The point in the heart continued its development in parallel with egoism, whose growth led to the destruction of the Temple.

Both the first and the second Temples were ruined, i.e., all spiritual levels fell with regard to the point in heart. "The Book of Zohar" was written after the destruction of the second Temple. Its author Rabbi Shimon lived before and after the destruction of the Temple, but the book could not have been written prior to that event, because there had been no need for such a spiritual source to raise people from the level of a completely shattered screen.

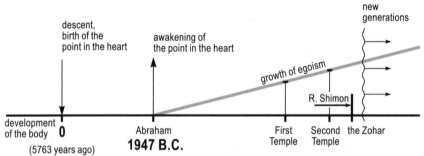

Rabbi Shimon was one of the disciples of the famous sage Rabbi Akiva who left us the entire spiritual legacy available today. This man's story is amazing. He was neither a Jew nor a believer until the age of 40. Then he began to study Kabbalah, and later became a great scholar and teacher. His life was full of unexpected turns, but finally he achieved the highest possible spiritual level.

Needless to say, being Rabbi Shimon's teacher, he was on a much higher level than his disciple. One of Rabbi Akiva's students wrote the

Babylonian Talmud, another – "The Book of Zohar". In other words, Rabbi Akiva was the embodiment of a vast amount of wisdom about the universe that filled many sacred books.

However, Rabbi Akiva could not write a composition like "The Book of Zohar" because before the destruction of the Temple such a great, exalted power was not necessary. There was still nothing to correct. When the Temple ceased to be, his last disciple Rabbi Shimon wrote "The Book of Zohar". Naturally, the book could not have been written by any other man born after the destruction of the Temple.

This happened in around the 2nd Century A.D., and there have been no such Kabbalists ever since. Only in the 16th Century did the Ari's special soul descend to our world and elevate Kabbalah to a new level. In the 20th Century the soul of Baal HaSulam appeared.

This is what the great Kabbalists writes:

From the very day that I merited the light of the Creator and saw what was written in the Book of Zohar, I have not had any need to research the facts about its authorship. This is due to the simple reason that the content of the book raised the prominence of Rabbi Shimon to the unattainable height above all other Kabbalists in my heart.

However, if I had found that the author of the book is someone else, for example, Rabbi Moses de Leon, the greatness of this Kabbalist would rise in me more than for all the rest, including Rabbi Shimon.

Honestly speaking, according to the depth of wisdom in this book, had I learned that its author was one of the 48 prophets (the Kabbalists who attained a high spiritual level called prophecy), *my heart would rather agree with this than with the fact that Rabbi Shimon Bar-Yochai wrote this book* (for R. Shimon was only a Tana, i.e., a Kabbalist who lived after the destruction of the Temple). *If*

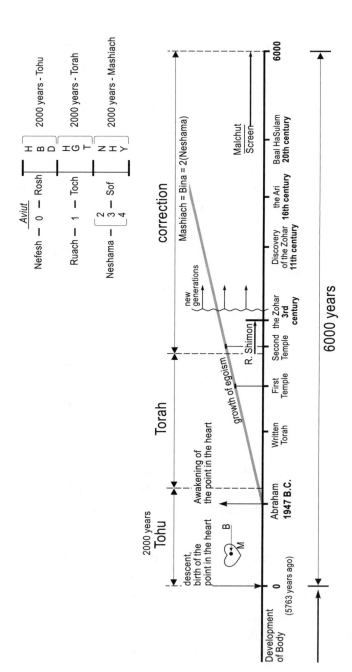

I had learned that Moses had received this book from the Creator Himself on Mount Sinai, I would rest assured. This is how great this book is.

Since I merited creating a commentary suited for anyone with a desire to understand what is written in the book itself, I believe I have fulfilled everything to keep from such work and research (regarding the authorship of "The Zohar"). *This is because, as anyone who understands "The Book of Zohar, I cannot be satisfied with the notion that the author of the Book of Zohar can be someone less holy than Rabbi Shimon* (i.e., born later than R. Shimon, because holiness diminishes with time).

61. We should ask at this point why "The Zohar" was not revealed to earlier generations, whose merit was undoubtedly greater than of the later ones, and who were more worthy of studying the book?

Since, as we see, "The Book of Zohar" was given for the correction of our egoism, a question arises: why could the first generations not receive it? If the Creator created us so opposite to Himself, why could He not at the same time hand us an instruction for correcting that state?

Why do we have to suffer during thousands of years, only to discover later that there is an opportunity to make such a correction? Why are babies and innocent adults living in such pain, why is there so much anguish in the world? This refers to the same question: why is "The Book of Zohar" revealed to us only now?

So I would like to repeat:

Why was "The Zohar" not revealed to earlier generations (that lived before the destruction of the Temple)?

Perhaps, it could have encouraged them to disseminate the wisdom of Kabbalah the world over, and humankind could have avoided such a lengthy period of suffering. We have no idea how much time people are destined to suffer before they accept this method of correction that will elevate them to the level of perfection and eternity.

Their merit was undoubtedly greater than of the later ones, and who were more worthy of studying the book.

On the one hand, their egoism was small, on the other – they had enormous inner resources unsuppressed by egoism, so they undoubtedly could study this book much more effectively. They were much closer to this material than we are with all our mercantile problems, modern technology, stupefying advertising, etc.

We can also ask why the commentary to "The Zohar" was not revealed together with the book to the Ari or to the earlier Kabbalists.

Why is there such a long prelude stretched along the axis of time – the Torah, the Ari (the 16th Century), and Baal HaSulam (the 20th Century) – before we in our time begin discovering "The Book of Zohar"?

The answer is that during the six thousand years of its evolution the world must go through a full period of correction.

We do not take into consideration the world that existed before a new spiritual point (of *Bina*) appeared in man's heart (*Malchut*). Until there is no interaction between the heart and the point in it, nothing else really matters, because it simply constitutes a development of the body, animal existence.

The world during the six thousand years of its existence is like one Partzuf (spiritual entity) that is divided into three parts: Rosh, Toch, and Sof, or HaBaD (Hochma, Bina, Da'at), HaGaT (Hesed, Gevura, Tifferet) and NHY (Netzah, Hod, Yesod). Alternatively, as our sages said: "The first two thousand years are called Tohu (lit. Unformed), the second two thousand years are called the Torah, and the last two thousand years are called the days of Mashiach (Messiah)".

In the first two millennia (Rosh or HaBaD), the lights were very small, and they were regarded as a head without a body. It only has the light of Nefesh, because there is an inverse relationship between lights and vessels. The rule is that the upper vessels grow first in each Partzuf, whereas, for the lights the opposite applies - the lights with a smaller Aviut dress first in the Partzuf. Thus, as long as there are only the upper parts of the vessels, i.e., the HaBaD vessels, only the lights of Nefesh can dress in the Partzuf, which are the lowest lights.

Hence, the first two thousand years are called the Tohu. In other words, there can still be no correct interaction between the Kelim (vessels) and Orot (lights).

During the second two thousand years (the Kelim of HaGaT) the light of Ruach (Aviut Aleph) descends to the world. It is also called the light of the Torah (Torah is something that gives life, Ruach already constitutes a movement). *Therefore, the second two millennia are called the Torah.*

The last two thousand years are the Kelim of NHY (the period of correction, or the Mashiach, the year 0 according to the Gregorian calendar), *therefore, at this time, the light of Neshama descends.*

The lights that descend are basically Neshama, Haya, and Yechida inside the light of Neshama. This is because it is impossible to correct the third and the fourth levels of desire before the Gmar Tikkun.

Only the levels zero, one, and two can be completely corrected. *Hence, the level of Neshama is called the days of the Mashiach.*

That is, this level is already a force that brings egoistic desires to correction. The Mashiach is a force of Bina, i.e., the second level of the screen, because when Malchut acquires the properties of Bina, it transforms its desires and makes them similar to the Creator's. In other words, it provides Malchut with the screen necessary for correction. The descent of the *Ohr Neshama* to our world corrects *Malchut*. The light of *Neshama* is alternatively called "*Mashiach*" (from the word *Limshoch* – to *pull*), meaning the light that pulls egoism up to the level of altruism.

This order applies to each particular Partzuf (each soul) as well as to the entire universe. Every soul, yours or mine, goes through all periods of its development. Long ago, we were in those periods when our body was developing, and then the point in heart appeared and gradually grew in all of us.

It does not matter in what souls or bodies it all happened, for everything is mixed at the soul's level. The division into nations and sexes is purely relative. All parts gradually and constantly intermix because after *Adam's* soul had broken, all souls were mixed. So, whatever corrections the different souls made, ultimately they become thoroughly interconnected.

The lights in the Kelim HaBaD and HaGaT to Chazeh of the Partzuf are concealed, so that the light of Hassadim does shine openly. This means that the luminescence of Hochma appears from Chazeh and below, i.e., in the Kelim of NHYM (Netzah, Hod, Yesod, Malchut). The reason for this lies in the fact that before the Kelim de NHYM began to manifest in the Partzuf of the world, meaning the last two thousand years, the wisdom of "The Zohar" in general, and of Kabbalah in particular, was concealed from the world.

What does Baal HaSulam mean? The problem is that the light of Hochma cannot shine in the *Kli* unless the light of *Hassadim* enters it previously.

A vessel is created as a desire to receive pleasure. Unless the vessel acquires a screen, which complements the *Ohr Yashar* with the *Ohr Hozer*, no light can enter into the *Kli*. We can explain it in a different way:

until the vessel (egoism) is lined inside with the altruistic intentions (of bestowal), the light of *Hochma* has no way of entering it.

But how can these altruistic intentions manifest? This can only happen during the last two millennia, when the light of *Neshama* descends to our world. Therefore, before this period (i.e., before the *Sof*), prior to the appearance and development of the *Kelim de NHY*, Kabbalah cannot be revealed in our world. In other words, the light of wisdom, the knowledge about the structure of the universe, cannot be revealed to the souls. They are still insufficiently egoistic to be corrected with the light of *Neshama* and to receive even a minimal amount of the *Ohr Hochma*.

We are now living in the year 2004, which corresponds to 5764 of the Jewish calendar. This means that we have less than 240 years left.

Baal HaSulam says that *"...before the Kelim de NHYM began to manifest in the Partzuf of the world, meaning the last two thousand years, the wisdom of "The Zohar" in general, and of Kabbalah in particular, was concealed from the world. Only during the time of the Ari, when the time for completion of the Kelim from Chazeh and below arrived, i.e., in each of the three periods: HaBaD, HaGaT, and NHY, the Kelim develop and are corrected, afterwards followed by the Orot (lights). Suppose that the Kelim of NHY were developing from the beginning of this period and onwards until the time of the Ari.*

Thanks to the holy soul of Rabbi Isaac Luria (the Ari for short) the radiance of the Supreme wisdom was revealed. The *Kelim de NHY* were sufficiently developed by his time, hence this special soul descended to our world.

Any descent of souls, including yours and mine, is predetermined by the previous general and individual development of the *Kelim de NHY*. In our time, they are called NHY, in the past they were called HaBaD and HaGaT. So in fact, the history of humankind is a development of

275

Partzuf from up down. This determines what souls descend to this world, how they dress into bodies, in what society, state or environment they find themselves, etc.

> *But since the soul of the Ari appeared after the development of all the vessels of NHY, he was able to reveal the greatness of "The Book of Zohar" and the wisdom of Kabbalah and by so doing overshadow all of his predecessors.*

That is, from the moment "The Book of Zohar" appeared, it concentrated in itself all the knowledge that had been received from the Kabbalists living before the destruction of the Temple. The book is considered so great, not because the *Kelim* of NHY were still undeveloped, but because its wisdom was received by very exalted souls that lived at that time.

Baal HaSulam says that he would have been glad to hear that "The Book of Zohar" was written by one of the 48 prophets or by Moses, for it contains all wisdom of the previous generations.

Only the Ari could be the next in line; only he could explain and elevate Kabbalah by expounding everything that is available to us today. Practically, the Ari introduced the method of correction to the world. Since the *Kelim de NHY* had completed their development, his soul could descend to our world and provide us with everything necessary for the correction of our souls (*Kelim*). His soul is a collective image of all the *Kelim* of HaBaD, HaGaT, and NHY. He, as it were, completed their development. After the *Kelim* manifested, but before the lights entered them, the Ari appeared at once. Therefore, the collection of his works (more than 20 volumes) constitutes a complete method of spiritual ascent, spiritual correction.

None of the Kabbalists before the Ari could understand exactly how the spiritual correction takes place. No one could reach his level of attainment because these *Kelim* were not sufficiently developed in the

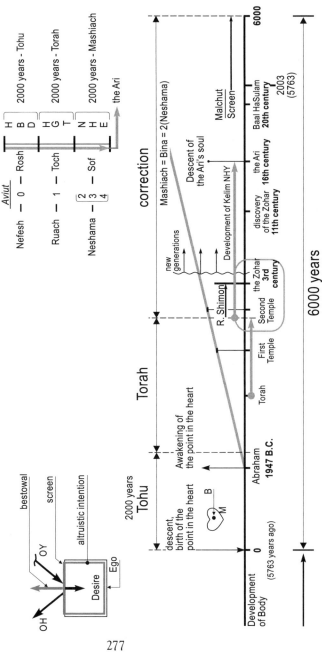

creation.

Before the Ari, all humankind existed at the stage of development of the *Kelim HaBaD, HaGaT,* and *NHY,* of all Ten *Sefirot.* Since his time and on the acquisition of a screen and reception of the light in these fully developed Kelim has begun. The entire universe was included in these *HaBaD, HaGaT,* and *NHY.* However, Baal HaSulam continues:

> *But these Kelim were not fully developed because the Ari did not have enough time to complete all the necessary corrections.*

We shall later discuss why the Ari failed. Naturally, it so happened because there were objective, profound reasons and not because he suddenly fell sick and died. Rather, he fell sick and died because there had been certain prerequisites in the development of these *Kelim.*

> *But these Kelim were not fully developed because the Ari, as we know, passed away in 1572 (5332 according to the Jewish calendar). The world was not yet ready for the Ari's revelations.*

He did not have enough time to pass to the world in action all that he wrote in his books.

> *His legacy, forbidden to be disclosed to the world, was used only by a chosen few.*

In one of his letters, Baal HaSulam tells this story. The Ari lived only 36 years. He never wrote any books by himself. During the last one and a half years of his life he had a disciple by the name of Chaim Vital (Marhu). Chaim was 28 at the time, while the Ari was 36. Think of how young these two men were!

During the time he spent beside the Ari, Chaim Vital learned everything that later allowed him to write more than 20 thick volumes. It seems incredible to us. While reading the Ari's compositions written down by Chaim Vital after his Teacher's death, it is impossible to imagine how this amount of information could be heard in a relatively short period, let alone be put down on paper.

Whatever H. Vital had learned from his great Teacher in only eighteen months, he described in a series of note-books, which were buried with him after his death. In his will he insisted that they be put in his grave in Safed (Tzefat, a town in North Galilee). The Ari and Chaim Vital used to live in this ancient town in the north of Galilee. My students and I often come to this place, and immerse ourselves in the same spring where the Ari used to have his ablutions. There is still a place above the old cemetery where the Ari's house used to stand.

Chaim Vital was unwilling to publish his writings, believing that neither he nor his generation was sufficiently mature for this knowledge. Only years later his son, grandson and great-grandsons began to publish the Ari's compositions. During three hundred years these books were gradually coming out, and today they are known to us as the collection of the Ari's works.

Some of them were revealed at the time of the Baal Shem Tov (Besht). This great Kabbalist lived in the 17th Century in the Ukraine. Like the Ari, the Baal Shem Tov never penned anything by himself.

A few books were written by some of his disciples. Baal HaSulam composed "The Study of the Ten *Sefirot*" and "The Sulam" as commentaries on the Ari's books and "The Book of Zohar".

With the help of these two books, we can complete our correction, because during the time period between the Ari and Baal HaSulam the *Kelim* of NHY completed their development and were filled with all principal lights. As this greatest Kabbalist of our time had predicted, starting from the end of the last century the spiritual ascent towards the End of correction began. With the help of his books all subsequent generations will follow our path.

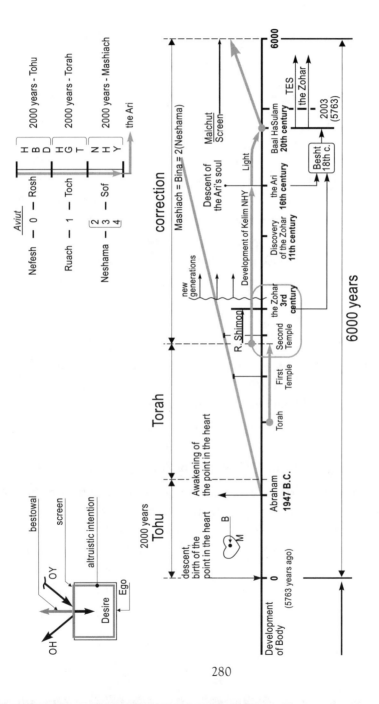

63. *Now we can clearly see that the souls of the earlier generations were immeasurably higher than those of the later generations. The rule for all Partzufim, both pertaining to worlds and to souls, is that the purest vessels are corrected first.*

Pure means having a small *Aviut*, small egoism, hence they are easier to correct

Thus, the Kelim of HaBaD (of Tohu) both of the world and the souls were introduced first to our world. Therefore, the souls of the first two millennia are incomparably higher than those that came after them.

The souls that descended during the first two thousand years of our world's existence were very sublime and pure. Man of that time needed very little. He was quite content with a shelter, a small amount of food, and security. His egoism did not push him towards any serious undertakings. Exalted souls are not necessarily those that have profound attainments. They can feel the spiritual worlds due to their purity.

Despite their tremendous elevation, they could not receive the full amount of light due to the lack of their own lower components, the Kelim of HaGaT and NHYM.

They lacked these two parts; therefore, the light in them was only *Nefesh*.

During the middle period, when the vessels of the worlds and of the souls that emerged were of the Kelim of HaGaT, the souls were still extremely pure.

They were pure because the *Kelim of HaGaT* are a replica of the *Kelim of HaBaD*, albeit on the corporeal level. We know that there are Ten *Sefirot*: *Keter, Hochma,* and *Bina,* then *Hesed, Gevura,* and *Tifferet,* then *Netzah, Hod, Yesod,* and *Malchut. Hesed* is similar to *Keter, Gevura* is like *Tifferet.* Baal HaSulam says that just because the *Kelim of HaGaT*

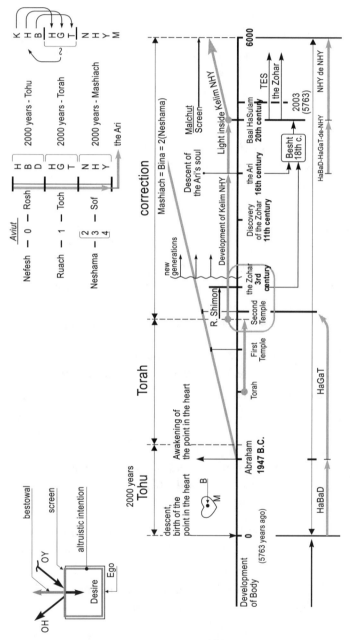

resemble the *Kelim* of *HaBaD* very pure souls descended to our world before the destruction of the Temple.

> *At the same time, the lights were still concealed in the worlds due to the lack of egoism in these Kelim.*

For the most part, egoism is in the Kelim of NHY. As soon as these vessels began developing, both the first and then the second Temples were destroyed. The spiritual collapse that took place as a result of a transition from *Bina* to the vessels of reception (*Kelim de Kabbalah*) through *Tifferet* echoed in our world as the physical destruction of the two Temples.

> *Accordingly, in our generation, in which the lowest souls in all creation that could not be corrected until now, they still complement the Kelim-Partzufim of the common soul. The work can only be completed with their help.*

Baal HaSulam says that although the *Kelim* of *NHY* are the worst and most egoistic, yet the completion of the work is impossible without them because they are exactly the vessels to be corrected. Their development starts after the destruction of the Temple, and then followed by the development of the lights in these *Kelim*.

The preliminary light entered into the *Kelim* of *NHY* thanks to the work of the Kabbalists who lived in the period between the Ari and Baal HaSulam. What does the name "preliminary light" mean? If we divide the *Kelim* of *NHY* into Ten *Sefirot*, we will come out with three periods, *HaBaD de NHY*, *HaGaT de NHY*, and *NHY de NHY*. From our time and on *NHY de NHY* constitute the most egoistic *Kelim*.

Therefore, all that is left for us to do is to realize this method of correction, i.e., to use the power that was given to us by Rabbi Shimon, the Ari, and Baal HaSulam. In our time this power is called *Mashiach*.

Hence, Baal HaSulam writes:

Now that the vessels of NHY are completed (as well as the lights in them) *and the vessels of Rosh, Toch, and Sof of the Partzuf* (all the Kelim in our world) *can draw on the full measure of the necessary lights in Rosh, Toch, and Sof, the complete lights of NaRaN* (Nefesh, Ruach, Neshama with Haya and Yechida inside them). *Therefore, only with the completion of preparation of these lowest souls could the highest lights be revealed, and not prior to this.*

Only thanks to us will the light enter into this world. We will attract it with our most evil, awful egoism because by this we complete the structure of the *Partzuf* of the entire creation.

64. This was a problem that pre-occupied the sages, and it was clear to them that the earlier generations were much more important than the later ones pertaining to their vessels, properties, and desires, which were considerably closer to the properties of the light.

Their vessels were very small, pure, and sublime in comparison with ours. They were much closer to the light, whereas we are completely opposite to it in our desires.

But the wisdom of Torah (all understanding, attainment and depth of sensations) *is manifested in the later generations a lot more, due to the increased general volume of the Kli.*

As is well known, the general volume of egoism is contained in the *Sof* of the *Partzuf*. So it turns out that the correction takes place with the help of the last generations.

65. This is because actions originate in the pure Kelim, whereas the secrets of Torah stem from the light of the Sefirot.

The revelation of light occurs inside the soul, in our Kelim, inside our consciousness. Since the Kelim and Orot are inversely related, the lower the Kelim of NHY are, the more the lights of Neshama, Haya, and

Yechida enter into them. Our generation is therefore able to draw tremendous light to this world.

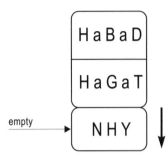

We are now in the *Kelim* of NHY, which approach their completion, but do not possess a screen. The *Kelim* that manifest now are empty. That is why our time is so tough, egoistic, cruel and barbaric in its essence. We are now standing at a threshold of reception of light in the empty *Kelim*.

If we acquire a screen, we shall instantly begin drawing the Upper light. It will pass through our souls to the rest of the world. We are now in a very critical state, when all the *Kelim* are ready, but devoid of light. In other words, our egoism, enormous and empty, is waiting to be filled with light.

A fearful state of dismay, disorientation, and confusion is growing steadily each day. Where is this world heading? Why does it exist? Why are we here? This is our condition today.

We are left with only one choice: to begin working with a screen, because only this way all our empty *Kelim* can be filled with light. If we take "The Book of Zohar", the works of the Ari with Baal HaSulam's commentaries provided specially for our souls, we will be able to attract the Upper Light. *HaBaD*, *HaGaT*, and *NHY* will begin to receive the light of *Neshama*. It is also called the light of *Mashiach* because this light of *Bina* corrects the properties of *Malchut*. All correction is based on this combination, merging of *Bina* and *Malchut*.

By feeling the influence of the light of *Bina* and the light of *Mashiach*, the creation will bond with the Creator. This will mark the complete and final deliverance from egoism, and entrance into eternity and perfection.

By knowing the roots of our past, we can graphically depict the history of our world. This graph can show all possible nuances and minute details. We can see in it the birth and predestination of any historical personality; understand the causes of historic events, catastrophes, and wars.

Everything is predetermined on this axis of human evolution, starting with the point from which our universe emerged, to the formation of the solar system, to the birth of the Earth and people on its surface, to the appearance of the spiritual point in man's heart, when he was sufficiently mature in his animal properties. Taking the point in the heart as a zero point, we begin our count up to the Final ultimate state, when the whole world will reach a state called "the End of Correction". After that, the world will continue its existence as it did before the zero point.

Previously, the bodies were developing, whereas by the end of the six-thousand-year period the souls will continue evolving, because the body will lose its significance. Our world, our universe, however, will not change in any way.

We can see many things on the axis of time. This is a part of the so-called historical Kabbalah or, rather, of the Kabbalistic history. We only need to receive from all this an answer to the age-old question about the meaning of our life.

Why should I know how this complex system is functioning outside me? Of course it is interesting information, but then what next?

Kabbalah is based on one single question: Why do I exist? By searching for the answer to this question, man attains the universe. He is first given the vessels, then is allowed to acquire a screen, and finally is filled with the light. Thus he finds the answer and reaches the Creator's level.

How does the correction take place beginning from 1995 and on according to what Baal HaSulam predicted? We are now living in 2004 or, according to the spiritual chronology, in 5764. How should we proceed?

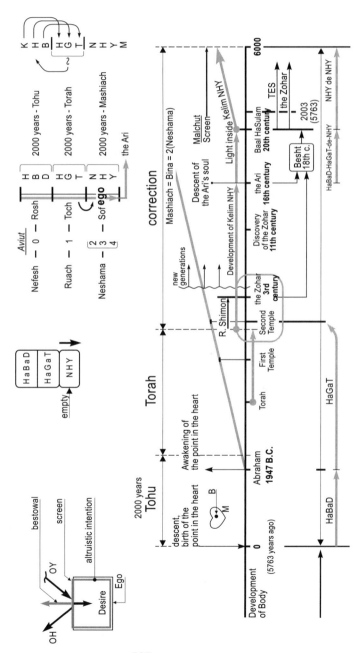

Baal HaSulam says; if we are destined to make corrections, naturally we should do it on ourselves. What does it mean? It should be done by people living in today's world; hence, each of us has his or her own mission, role, and a precise predestination.

66. Now you must know that everything has an inner aspect and an outer aspect.

The *Kelim HaBaD*, *HaGaT*, and *NHY* are further divided from up downwards into the inner and outer parts. Let us see what the difference between them is. They consist of Ten *Sefirot*, or, alternatively, of *Rosh*, *Toch*, and *Sof*.

Israel refers to the inner part of the world, whereas other nations are considered its outer part.

Please do not misinterpret these names; they do not concern nationalities, but speak of spiritual conformity. If we take this particular *Partzuf*, the *Kelim HaBaD* and *HaGaT* will be called Israel, and the *Kelim* of NHY will be called the nations of the world. In this case, we see that without engaging the nations of the world in this work Israel will be utterly unable to receive the Upper light.

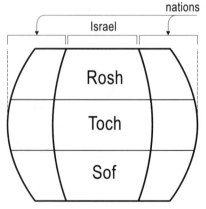

The nations will be left without the light unless Israel passes them Kabbalah, the method of spiritual correction. That is, the combination of Israel and the nations of the world are similar to the combination of *Galgalta Eynaim* and *AHP*.

Within Israel itself, there is an inner aspect that consists of those people who are committed to serve the Creator, and an outer aspect consisting of those who are not involved in spiritual work. Likewise, amongst the nations of the world there is an inner part called the righteous of the world and an outer part, which consists of those who are destructive and coarse.

In other words, there is a division into GE and AHP. Each of these parts has its own GE and AHP. GE and AHP in GE correspond to those who work for the Creator within Israel and those who are not. GE and AHP in the nations of the world are the righteous people and those who cause damage.

Even amongst those of Israel who work for the Creator, there is an in- ner part and an outer part. The inner part is comprised of those who are privileged to achieve spiritual attainment, and to grasp the secrets of the creation through attaining the Upper light. The outer part consists of people who only perform actions without comprehending their inner meaning.

Similarly every individual person has the inner part (GE, the point in heart) and the outer part referred to as the nations of the world, or the body.

Both the nations of the world and Israel are also divided into these parts. What is the essence of this division? It began from the time of Abra- ham who received the very first point in the heart and developed it.

When a man of Israel elevates his inner part over his outer part, meaning that he dedicates most of his time and effort to the enhance- ment of his innermost part as regards his outer part, the body, then by this he raises his spiritual aspect of the material one.

But if the opposite occurs, and a man of Israel elevates his outer material part over the inner, spiritual one, the outer part (the coarse and harmful elements in the nations of the world) accordingly rises over the inner part (the righteous among the nations of the world) and calamities and wars befall the world.

These actions raise the outer part of the nations of the world, prevail over the inner part, and consequently the destructive elements within the nations of the world prevail over Israel.

Thus, through suffering, everything facilitates the return to a state where *Galgalta Eynaim*, the souls of Israel, draw the Upper light to the world.

> 68. *Do not be surprised by the fact that even an individual person, through his or her deeds, can cause an elevation or degradation of the whole world. This is an unalterable law that the whole and its parts are as identical as two drops of water. Everything that occurs in the whole occurs in its parts as well, and vice versa. Furthermore, whatever happens in the parts happens in the whole, because the whole is only revealed through the manifestation of its individual parts, according to both their measure and quality.*

We are all dependent on one another. Until all of us have their vessels corrected, no one will be able to achieve full individual correction. The complete, truly absolute correction is when not only I am corrected through the world, but through me the whole world reaches the same state. We are all parts of one universe, one closed system, one soul called *Adam*, which emerged from the zero point.

Kabbalah correlates the notion of the zero point with the creation of *Adam*. What is *Adam*? *Adam* is the spiritual point in man's heart. We all originate from this point, from which all the *Kelim* of HaBaD, HaGaT, and NHY – *Tohu*, Torah, and *Mashiach* – began to emerge.

Baal HaSulam writes:

> So certainly, the influence of every soul, i.e., each one of us, may lower or elevate the whole system, all the Kelim of HaBaD, HaGaT, and NHY.

> This is how we can understand what is written in "The Zohar" that through the study of this book and the practice of the true wisdom,

we can put an end to our state of exile and achieve a complete redemption.

A question may arise: What could studying "The Zohar" have to do with redeeming Israel from among the nations of the world? How can it possibly help to redeem the nations of the world and Israel from their egoism?

69. From what we have read, it is clear that the Torah, like the world itself, has an inner and an outer aspect.

There are two levels in the Torah. If man concentrates his efforts on the inner part of the Torah, namely on Kabbalah, in the same degree he elevates the inner part in the world. Then, consequently, a redistribution of forces takes place, when Israel and the nations of the world begin to realize the importance of spirituality, see the greatness of the Creator, and aspire for Him.

Other coarser parts gradually subside, fall off, and lose contact with the nations' aspiration for spirituality.

But if those of Israel who must study Kabbalah and then pass it on to the nations of the world diminish the importance of the inner part of the Torah in comparison with the mechanical observance of the precepts, the outer part of Israel, all opponents of Kabbalah, prevail over Kabbalists. As a result, the outer part of the nations, the destructive elements, rises above the righteous person, which leads the world to wars, catastrophes, hostilities, and suffering.

Furthermore, this leads to strengthening of the outer part of the nations over their inner part, so that the worst and most destructive of them prevail over their inner part, the righteous ones. This brings destruction and death, such as our generation has been a witness to.

Therefore we can see that the redemption of Israel and the rest of the world, wholly depends on the learning of "The Book of Zohar" and

Kabbalah. The opposite is true also. All the afflictions that have befallen Israel and the world are due to their neglecting the study of Kabbalah (as compared to the external rituals) and treating it as something superfluous.

70. This is what "The Book of Zohar" says: "Come and wake up for the sake of spiritual ascent. Your heart is empty and you lack wisdom and the understanding of the Creator".

In other words, "The Zohar" states: whatever you may be doing should only be for the sake of achieving equivalence of form with the Him.

This way, we rise to the level of eternity and perfection. Only Kabbalah can guide and correct us, whereas all other teachings and even the outer part of the Torah increases egoism. The nations with a higher level of egoism are greedy, resourceful, craving for pleasures of this world. Why is this so?

It is because instead of elevating their soul, they focus more on the body. Naturally, since this is not what they are supposed to do, although successful in their undertakings, they push themselves and the whole world to a catastrophe.

It is said about this generation that the Upper spirit (light) disappears and never returns. This is the spirit of Mashiach which is necessary for redeeming all people from suffering. This spirit disappears and stops shining in the world. Woe to those people who cause the light of Mashiach to depart and leave the world by making the Torah dry and tasteless, without Upper understanding and knowledge. They confine themselves to the practical aspects of the Torah and make no effort to try and understand the wisdom of Kabbalah. They do not wish to contemplate the secrets of the Torah, grasp the meaning of man's actions and attain the Creator. Woe to them, who by their actions cause poverty, war, violence, pillage, killings and destructions in the world.

This is a quotation from "The Book of Zohar", not the words of Baal HaSulam or one of the modern Kabbalists.

Thus, all good and bad in the world is predetermined by the presence or absence of the Upper light in it proportionate to the *Kelim* that have already developed in the world – HaBaD, HaGaT, and NHY. It therefore turns out that Israel, whose mission is to bring the Kabbalistic method to the nations, is responsible for the state of the world, both good and bad.

71. These words, as we have explained, concern those people who study the outer part of Torah, treating its inner part as something unnecessary, and pay little or no attention to it.

This fault is typical all over the world. The outer part of Israel influences the inner part, meaning that common believers are openly hostile to Kabbalists and are convinced that they are engaged in something totally wrong. Accordingly, the outer part of the nations of the world prevails over the inner.

All destructive elements raise their heads and wish to destroy the world, and primarily the people of Israel. This is because they do not fulfill their mission. The general governance is designed in such a way that the inner part could influence the outer one, while the outer part would in turn exert pressure and adjust the inner part.

After our grave sins, we have born witness to the sufferings predicted by "The Zohar". The finest of us perished, for "the righteous are the first to suffer". Of all the most prominent Kabbalists who used to live in Russia, only a small number remained in this country.

Baal HaSulam says that 200-300 years ago there were many Kabbalists in Russia and the Ukraine (the Baal Shem Tov with his disciples, the famous cradle of Kabbalistic learning in Kotzk, Poland). All of them have disappeared because, as he states, if the generations fall, the best are first to perish.

It is now incumbent upon us, this tiny remnant, to right the wrong (i.e., the mechanical observance of precepts and the indifference to Kabbalah).

If every one of us takes upon himself with all his soul and mind to enhance the inner aspect of the Torah and to give it its rightful place, then each of us will strengthen the inner part within him and in the whole world.

Then our inner part and the inner part of the whole world, meaning the righteous of the nations of the world, those that aspire to the Creator (and wish to justify His actions) unite in such a joint effort that they will correct the world. A correct pyramid construction will be created in which the pure vessels will be at the top, and the coarse vessels will be at the bottom, so that we will draw on ourselves the Upper light.

In this way, the Upper light will be manifested in all the *Kelim* of *HaBaD*, *HaGaT*, and *NHY*, in all souls. Through us it will reach the rest of the world's vessels. Nature on all of its levels, the still, vegetative, animal, and naturally, human, will be good and prosperous. It will receive the spiritual fulfillment that it needs, rise to the level of the Creator, and we will achieve the Purpose of creation.

It depends on how quickly we will accomplish this task in the 236 years left until the end of the 6000-year period starting from where we are now. Instead of it being a path of development of the *Kelim*, it will turn into a path of compulsion by the absence of light, i.e., a path of horrific suffering. The Holocaust and the two world wars may be just a beginning.

Baal HaSulam speaks of the third and the fourth world wars. Already in 1934-1936 he was writing about a neutron bomb. One can find it in his manuscripts. He gives many things different names, but actually he writes about the destructive forces that will be in man's hands in the future. It is in our power to prevent all this; it depends

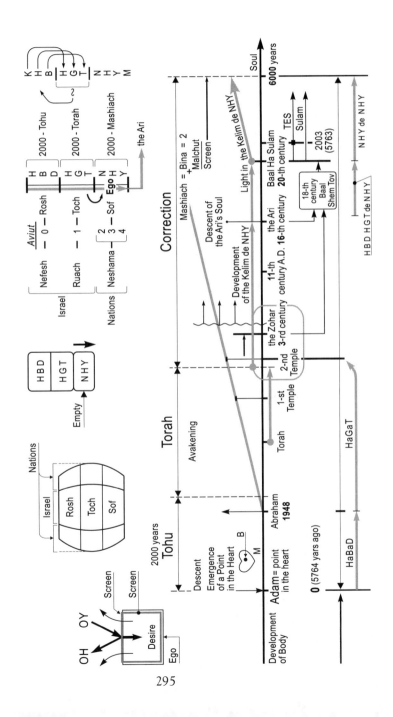

solely on us.

We know that the world consists of four stages of development according to the four phases of the descending light. Correspondingly, there are four destructions and four exiles. Our exile was the last. It has ended physically, and it must end spiritually. The two world wars may be complemented by two more, unless we change. We are not obliged to drink the cup of woe to the end; it is in our power to prevent these two world wars that are looming ahead of us.

So everything depends on us, on the first generation that begins its correction under the influence of the light. All the vessels are completed, we only need to acquire the *Masach* (screen) and start transferring the light to this world. Thanks to that, the world will painlessly achieve its predestination. We have to set it as our goal, for, as we know, the general and the particular are completely equal, so it turns out that each one of us determines the state of the whole world.

I hope that we will be worthy of our great teachers, and capable of bringing their legacy to the world. We have every opportunity to become the Creator's special messengers and fulfill our mission. We are already doing it, i.e., the Creator has already entitled us to accomplish this task. Now the question is whether we are ready to take it upon ourselves or not.

I believe that we will succeed in conducting the light to the world, as befitting the heirs of great Kabbalists. Imagine what spiritual reward is prepared for all of us who take part in this noble mission.

Baal HaSulam has written four introductions to "The Zohar": "The Introduction to the Book of Zohar", "The Preface to the Book of Zohar", "The Preamble to the Commentary of Sulam", and "The Preamble to the Wisdom of Kabbalah". They give us an adequate understanding of the book, so that by tuning ourselves to it, we can draw the Upper, Divine Light, the force, which ushers us into the spiritual realm.

We learn that the light is emanated from the Creator. This light is referred to as a "zero (or root) phase", which is afterwards called *Keter* pertaining to the *Sefirot*. The zero phase builds for itself a *Kli*, phase one, the will to receive, or *Hochma*. By acting inside the *Kli*, the light creates a sensation of its source in it, i.e., of the zero phase.

Therefore, first, the light creates a desire in the zero phase, and then gives it a sensation of itself. Since the desire wants to feel pleasure, enter into it, connect with it, it reveals the root, the source of this desire, namely the zero phase.

Thus, sub-phases emerge within phase one. A desire is created and feels pleasure. Consequently, by feeling pleasure, the desire longs to enter it, "cling" to it. While being "inside", it begins to feel the source of pleasure, and, naturally, this sensation creates in it a new desire to become similar to the source.

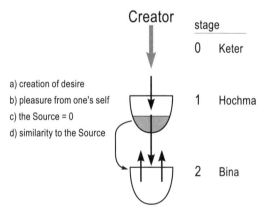

This similarity to the source of pleasure happens to be a transition from phase one to phase two. Phase two wishes to become similar to the source, but this decision is made at the end of phase one. Thus, it gives birth to a new desire – to bestow. This second phase is called *Bina*.

Bina in its turn consists of several sub-phases. In this way, the light's influence inside the desire creates in it a series of consecutive transformations.

Here I see fit to emphasize that the Upper Light affecting us is able to do with us absolutely everything: make us either similar or opposite to itself. We should only expose ourselves to its maximum influence, try to connect with it as closely as we possibly can. All of this can be achieved by studying "The Book of Zohar", provided we are correctly tuned to the ultimate purpose.

Therefore, all the aforementioned introductions are of great significance to us. Baal HaSulam wishes to expose us to the light that is emanated during the study of "The Zohar", to help us penetrate more deeply into this light with the intention of merging with its source. This depends on us.

While the descending development of the four phases of the light and of all the *Partzufim* in the worlds is a result of the Creator's actions, we must climb the spiritual ladder on our own by exposing ourselves to the influence of the *Ohr Makif*. Hence, we should study the introductions to "The Book of Zohar", which were specially written for this sole purpose.

OUR OTHER BOOKS

Guide to the Hidden Wisdom of Kabbalah with Ten Complete Kabbalah Lesson: provides the reader with a solid foundation for understanding the role of Kabbalah in our world. The content was designed to allow individuals all over the world to begin traversing the initial stages of spiritual ascent toward the apprehension of the upper realms.

Attaining the Worlds Beyond: is a first step toward discovering the ultimate fulfillment of spiritual ascent in our lifetime. This book reaches out to all those who are searching for answers, who are seeking a logical and reliable way to understand the world's phenomena. This magnificent introduction to the wisdom of Kabbalah provides a new kind of awareness that enlightens the mind, invigorates the heart, and moves the reader to the depths of their soul.

The Science of Kabbalah (Pticha): is the first in a series of texts that Rav Michael Laitman, Kabbalist and scientist, designed to introduce readers to the special language and terminology of the Kabbalah. Here, Rav Laitman reveals authentic Kabbalah in a manner that is both rational and mature. Readers are gradually led to an understanding of the logical design of the Universe and the life whose home it is.

The Science of Kabbalah, a revolutionary work that is unmatched in its clarity, depth, and appeal to the intellect, will enable readers to approach the more technical works of Baal HaSulam (Rav Yehuda Ashlag), such as "Talmud Eser Sefirot" and Zohar.

Although scientists and philosophers will delight in its illumination, laymen will also enjoy the satisfying answers to the riddles of life that only authentic Kabbalah provides. Now, travel through the pages and prepare for an astonishing journey into the Upper Worlds.

Kabbalah for Beginners: By reading this book you will be able to take your first step in understanding the roots of human behaviour and the laws of nature. The contents present the essential principals of the Kabbalistic approach and describe the wisdom of Kabbalah and the way it works. Kabbalah for beginners is intended for those searching for a sensible and reliable method of studying the phenomenon of this world for those seeking to understand the reason for suffering and pleasure, for those seeking answers to the major questions in life. Kabbalah is an accurate method to investigate and define man's position in the universe. The wisdom of Kabbalah tells us why man exists, why he is born, why he lives, what the purpose of his life is, where he comes from, and where he is going after he completes his life in this world.

Root of All Science: The process of examining our world with the help of the human mind and manmade tools is called science. All fields of science deal with what is perceived through our natural five senses, yet the Wisdom of Kabbalah deals with acquiring knowledge that exceeds their limitations.

In Root of All Science, Rav Michael Laitman presents the differences between Kabbalistic scientific method and the current method used by scientists. The distinction is in the ability of Kabbalah to incorporate human awareness in a verifiable analysis of reality. The enormous significance of this additional focus, to both the scientific researcher and the seeker of spirituality, is that it provides the leap in dimensions enabling the observer to penetrate the causal level of all aspects of existence and all events that occur in this world.

Wondrous Wisdom: Today interest in Kabbalah has exploded world-wide. Millions of people are seeking answers as to what this ancient wisdom really is, and where they can find authentic instruction. With so many conflicting ideas about Kabbalah on the internet, in books, and in the mass media; the time has finally arrived to answer humanity's need, and reveal the wisdom to all who truly desire to know. In Wondrous Wisdom you will receive the first steps, an initial course on Kabbalah, based solely on authentic teachings passed down from Kabbalist teacher to student over thousands of years. Offered within is a sequence of lessons revealing the nature of the wisdom and explaining the method of attaining it.

> *But if you listen with your heart to one famous question, I am sure that all your doubts as to whether you should study the Kabbalah will vanish without a trace. This question is a bitter and fair one, asked by all born on earth: "What is the meaning of my life?"*

Rav Yehuda Ashlag,
from "Introduction to
Talmud Eser Sefirot"

ABOUT BNEI BARUCH

Bnei Baruch is a non-profit group centered in Israel that is spreading the wisdom of Kabbalah to accelerate the spirituality of mankind. Kabbalist Michael Laitman PhD, who was the disciple and personal assistant to Kabbalist, Rabbi Baruch Ashlag, the son of Kabbalist Rabbi Yehuda Ashlag (author of the Sulam Commentary on the Zohar), follows in the footsteps of his mentor in guiding the group.

Rav Laitman's scientific method provides individuals of all faiths, religions and cultures the precise tools necessary for embarking on a highly efficient path of self-discovery and spiritual ascent. The focus is primarily on inner processes that individuals undergo at their own pace. Bnei Baruch welcomes people of all ages and lifestyles to engage in this rewarding process.

In recent years, an awakening of a massive worldwide quest for the answers to life's questions has been underway. Society has lost its ability to see reality for what it is and in its place easily formed viewpoints and opinions have appeared.

Bnei Baruch reaches out to all those who seek awareness beyond the standard view. It offers practical guidance and a reliable method for understanding the world's phenomena. The group's unique method not only helps overcome the trials and tribulations of everyday life, but initiates a process in which individuals extend themselves beyond the standard boundaries and limitations of today's world.

Kabbalist Rabbi Yehuda Ashlag left a study method for this generation, which essentially 'trains' individuals to behave as if they have already achieved the perfection of the Upper Worlds, here in our world.

In the words of Rabbi Yehuda Ashlag, "*This method is a practical way to apprehend the Upper World and the source of our existence while still living in this world. A Kabbalist is a researcher who studies his nature using this proven, time-tested and accurate method. Through this method, one attains perfection,* and takes control over one's life. In this way, one realizes one's true purpose in life. Just as a person cannot function properly in this world having no knowledge of it, so also one's soul cannot function properly in the Upper World having no knowledge of it. The wisdom of Kabbalah provides this knowledge."

The goal-orientated nature of these studies enables a person to apply this knowledge on both an individual and collective basis in order to enhance and promote the spirituality of humankind, and indeed the entire world.

HOW TO CONTACT BNEI BARUCH

Bnei Baruch
1057 Steeles Avenue West, Suite 532
Toronto, ON, M2R 3X1
Canada

E-mail address: info@kabbalah.info

Web site: www.kabbalah.info

Toll free in Canada and USA:
1-866-LAITMAN
Fax: 1-905 886 9697